This book may prove to be
one of the most disturbing books
you'll read in a long while,
but it may also be
one of the most critical.

ALIEN ENCOUNTERS

ENCOUNTERS

The Secret

Behind the UFO

Phenomenon

CHUCK MISSLER
MARK EASTMAN

KOINONIA HOUSE
Coeur d'Alene, Idaho 83816-0347

ALIEN ENCOUNTERS

Copyright © 1997 by Koinonia House
P.O. Box D
Coeur d'Alene, ID 83816-0347
Web Site: http://www.khouse.org

ISBN 1-57821-061-5

Design and production by Koechel Peterson & Associates,
Minneapolis, Minnesota.

Scripture quotations in this book are taken from the King James
Version of the Bible.

Printed in the United States of America.

CONTENTS

A FOREWORD REVISITED

"Every once in a while a book comes along
that has great impact on the world, its societies,
its belief systems, its people. The impact of
Voyage to the New World *will be measured*
in these terms. . . ."

DOUGLAS JAMES MAHR
VOYAGE TO THE NEW WORLD

The excerpt on the preceeding page, from the foreword of my 1985 book, *Voyage to the New World,* may have sounded flamboyant, but it proved astonishingly prophetic. That book did, indeed, lead the way to a new wave of publishing called New Age, according to *Publisher's Weekly.* And, the New Age publishing wave has had a profound impact, just as predicted.

It was an exciting voyage for me, an adventure inviting audiences of millions to watch and listen during nearly 100 television and radio interviews. And, as foretold, the book launched a complete paradigm shift of thought which now dominates the shelf space in virtually every book store . . . and the minds of more than 50 million people in the United States alone.

It also led to my becoming a friend, a colleague, advisor, mentor and pal to Shirley MacLaine, whose *Out on a Limb* would demolish the mini-series ratings records and officially launch the New Age, with my books riding the publicity. I was the guy who helped bring in the New Age in all of its birthday glory. I was, in practical terms, one of the "founders" of the New Age movement. I was caught up in its euphoria, and, yes, became part of its deceptions.

The most well-known channeled entity in the universe, Ramtha, recruited me to be his chief writer—his "Masterscribe," actually. Ramtha was the mysterious thing who introduced me to Shirley MacLaine. (Ramtha advised Shirley while she was writing *Out on a Limb.* Ramtha is the mysterious entity who has been studied, analyzed, and attacked for debunking without apparent success. Ramtha ostensibly orchestrated the popularization of the New Age, incidentally.) And the next question is, Why? (The answers are in this book you now have in your hands.)

As one who was very much caught up in this new wave of thought, I am in a unique position to evaluate this unusual book. I believe this book by Chuck Missler and Mark Eastman may well prove to be the most significant book of our times. It could also prove to be the most critical book you have ever read personally. The conclusions the authors carefully develop may alter your own entire world-view in ways that may significantly affect your personal destiny. The insights contained in this book have certainly altered my own!

It's all about the war. An invisible war. A cosmic contest which may, indeed, engulf the planet Earth in ways that very few have any capacity to anticipate. Anyone who has been watching the news, or has been profiling the entertainment media, realizes that our society is increasingly being confronted with the "invisible" world—and what was once the domain of science fiction and the lunatic fringe, has now become the preoccupation of serious scientific investigations and has also become a major centroid of policy within the classified government community.

Beyond the recent space discoveries, beyond the upheavals from the realm of quantum physics, beyond the bizarre reports from the paranormal, beyond the current conjectures about black holes, wormholes, and time warps, *Alien Encounters* addresses the new reality: what it is, what it's made of, who's in the driver's seat, where we're heading, and how to make the correct turns. There is a cosmic deception being orchestrated and you are one its targets. Prepare yourself for an amazing adventure, moving into a vast hyper-new view of thinking as you begin to explore unseen dimensions of deep space-time.

Let the adventure begin!

Douglas James Mahr

Author, *Voyage to the New World,* who has returned
as a wiser and deeply concerned watchman.

Big Bear Lake, California

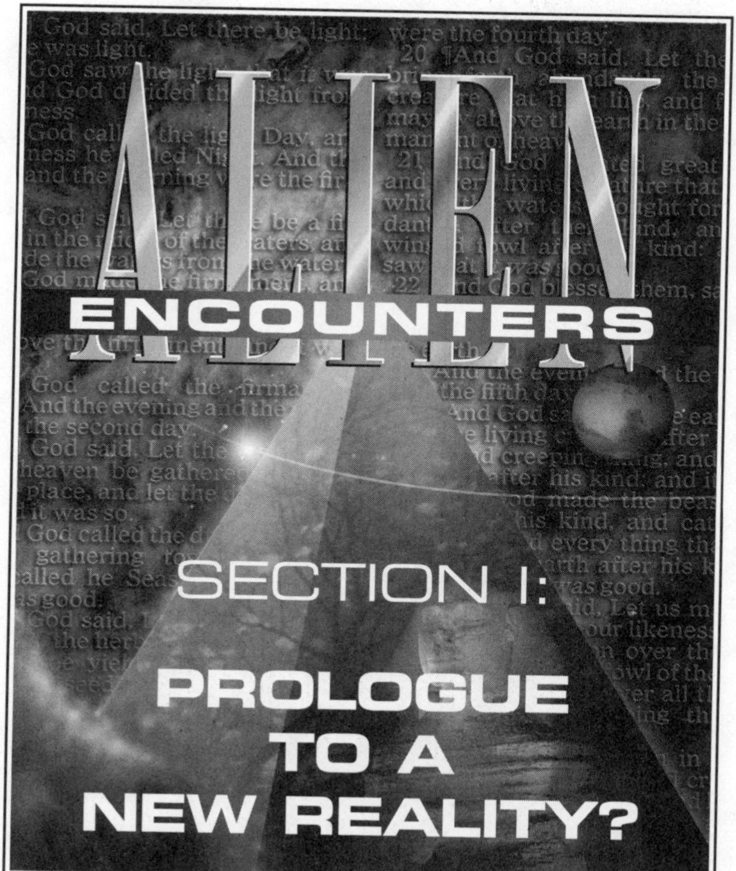
ALIEN
ENCOUNTERS
SECTION I:
PROLOGUE
TO A
NEW REALITY?

WHAT IN THE COSMOS IS GOING ON?

"A wave of unprecedented appearances of UFOs in the skies of Israel has stirred up UFO enthusiasts and several thousands of other people who have been witnesses to unforgettable sights. The mounting reports in recent weeks leave no room for doubt in the minds of many that UFOs have invaded Planet Earth!"

ISRAELI JOURNALIST IRIS ALMAGOR, MARCH 1997

In recent years, a number of astonishing events in our skies and in the corridors of power and influence have suggested to many that we are on the verge of open and global recognition of the reality of UFOs (unidentified flying objects) and extraterrestrial life.

To many, this great shift in our understanding of our place in the cosmic community will usher in a period of unparalleled peace, prosperity, and global unity. On the other hand, many, including top UFO researchers, believe that we may be headed for the most bizarre—and most far reaching—challenge ever seen on this planet. And your personal destiny—and that of your family—may depend upon how you deal with the strange events that may soon take place.

As we approach the dawn of the 21st century, life in outer space is now taken for granted by our educational and media establishments, and with this assumption comes the inevitable discussion of UFOs and alien life forms. Once relegated to the ostracized domain of the lunatic fringe or to science fiction writers, UFOs have now emerged as a socially acceptable topic for serious discussion. Previously regarded as the whacko delusions of the '40s and '50s, now they have become one of the hottest topics of our entertainment and news media of the '90s. One cannot even count the number of TV specials, documentaries (and pseudo-documentaries), and major movies that have been aired on this topic in recent years. Yet, in the last several years a number of staggering, although very well documented UFO events have occurred worldwide and have received no coverage by the mainstream U.S. media.

However, beginning in 1996, we have witnessed what some have called a "leak a week" strategy being orchestrated by agencies of the federal government and the scientific establishment. Many believe this is part of a global strategy toward open acknowledgment of "ET reality."

Are the UFOs real, or are they some form of delusion? Can anyone really take them seriously? What's *really* going on?

It may come as a surprise to learn that a recent Gallup poll revealed that 72 percent of Americans believe in extraterrestrial life; 48 percent believe in UFOs and 15 percent believe they have seen a UFO. According to other polls up to 2–3 percent believe that they have been *abducted* by a UFO![1]

It turns out to be a gargantuan task to even catalog the volumes of the UFO reports in recent history. A bibliography of just the *professional* articles—excluding newspapers, etc.—lists 6,000 publications in English, 2,200 in foreign journals, and 1,350 periodicals published on the subject.[2]

Wading through the mountains of reports of sightings, encounters, and even accounts of abductions, one is confronted with an unmanageable barrage of unconfirmable testimonies, hoaxes, frauds, and deliberate disinformation—even from the government. Yet, there remain behind it all too many serious cases which involve multiple reliable witnesses and even tangible physical evidences, enough to bury even the most ardent skeptic.

A SUDDEN CHANGE OF POLICY

On August 6, 1996, a dramatic shift in policy was apparently set in motion. A press release, personally endorsed by none other than the NASA administrator Daniel Goldin himself, startled the entire world:[3]

"NASA Scientists Find Evidence of Life on Mars."

The next day, President Clinton joined the elation with a press announcement on the South Lawn of the White House:

"This is the product of years of exploration and months of intensive study by some of the world's most distinguished scientists. Like all discoveries, this one will and should continue to be reviewed, examined and scrutinized. It must be confirmed by other scientists. But clearly, the fact that something of this magnitude is being explored is another vindication of America's space program and our continuing support for it, even in these tough financial times. I am determined that the American space program will put its full intellectual power and technological prowess behind the search for further evidence of life on Mars. . . .

"Today, rock 84001 speaks to us across all those billions of years and millions of miles. It speaks of the possibility of life. If this discovery is confirmed, it will surely be one of the most stunning insights into our universe that science has ever uncovered. Its implications are as far-reaching and awe-inspiring as can be imagined. Even as it promises answers to some of our oldest questions, it poses still others even more fundamental.

"We will continue to listen closely to what it has to say as we continue the search for answers and for knowledge that is as old as humanity itself but essential to our people's future."

Since the announcement, a number of investigative teams have expressed considerable doubt regarding the evidence presented by Goldin and the NASA team.[4,5] Nevertheless, the event marked a significant policy change for the administration. Life in space was now "in."

The cynics snickered that it was just a clever ploy by NASA to facilitate desperate funding. It may, however, be far more than that. In subsequent months the Mars announcement was followed by similar, less dramatic announcements by NASA touting the discovery of liquid water on Europa, one of Jupiter's moons:

"Jupiter's Europa Harbors Possible 'warm ice' or Liquid Water"

"Tantalizing new images of Jupiter's moon Europa from NASA's Galileo spacecraft indicate that 'warm ice' or even liquid water may have existed and perhaps still exists beneath Europa's cracked icy crust. Europa has long been considered by scientists and celebrated in science fiction as one of the handful of places in the solar system (along with Mars and Saturn's moon Titan) that could possess an environment where primitive life forms could possibly exist."[6]

A subsequent news release heralded the possibility of a mass of ice in the giant crater known as the Aitken Basin near the south pole of the moon.[7] More announcements of this kind are sure to follow.

Understandably, this fanfare has made life in space a hotter topic than ever. The euphoria is likely to be soon enhanced by the two current Mars missions, which will predictably supply more "evidence" to fan the interest. The Mars Global Surveyor should reach orbital insertion in March 1998 and will begin mapping for one Mars year (687 Earth days) until January 31, 2000. This is intended to be the first of a decade-long program of the robotic exploration of Mars, called the Mars Surveyor Program. An aggressive series of orbiters and landers are planned to be launched every 26 months, as Mars moves into alignment with Earth.

A second U.S. mission, the Pathfinder, is also on its way and is scheduled to land July 4, 1997. It is intended to land a small, 25 pound, six-wheeled robotic Rover ("Sojourner") for imaging and soil mechanics experiments.

In the meantime, while the U.S. press slept and the scientific community focused on the possibility of ancient microbes from Mars, a number of well-documented mass sightings of unidentified flying objects have continued around the globe which have convinced multitudes of the reality of UFOs.

THE DAY MEXICO CITY STOOD STILL

On January 1, 1993, at 2:00 P.M., Mexico City became host to the most astonishing and best documented UFO event in recorded history. According to numerous broadcasts[8] and published reports,[9] tens of thousands of people (including police, military personnel, and ordinary citizens) sighted a silvery craft performing aerial acrobatics over the central portion of Mexico City in broad daylight. Radio stations were inundated by phone calls while television stations preempted their regular schedules to broadcast the event. Videotapes of the event showed traffic backed up on Mexico City's main thoroughfare, Avenida Reforma, as drivers and passengers emerged from their automobiles to get a look at the strange metallic disks.[10] Later that day, at 3:51 and 5:21 P.M., two additional metallic, disk-shaped craft appeared and were also documented by local residents with camcorders.

On January 2, 1993, every major newspaper and news program covered the event which reportedly lasted five hours. One of Mexico City's major newspapers, *La Prensa*, carried the headline, "Astonishment! UFOs over the Capital." The event was also recorded by radar at the Mexico City International Airport.[11] Incredibly, there was no reporting of this event in the U.S. press.

This was not the first UFO event in the skies of Mexico in recent years. The Mexico UFO flap (a flap is a large number of sightings in a short time span) began on July 11, 1991, during the total eclipse of the sun that swept across the central part of Mexico. On that day, shortly after 1:00 P.M., 17 unrelated individuals, in four different cities, armed with cameras and camcorders, documented a metallic disk-shaped object hanging motionless below the eclipsed sun. This event became the first "mass-photographed" daylight disk in history. Interestingly, many of the witnesses didn't realize they had photographed the disk until subsequent viewing of their tapes.

Examination of the videotapes revealed a solid, metallic, "hockey puck-shaped" object with counterclockwise rotation. Since that time, researchers have collected more than 700 video tapes of metallic, disk-shaped UFOs observed in the skies over Mexico.[12] More than 100 of the videotapes are daylight shots. In addition, many of these have been videotaped by local residents while being simultaneously tracked on radar by nearby airports. On March 4, 1992, air traffic controllers in Mexico City recorded a group of UFOs on their radar screens. The blips stayed for 40 minutes.

UFO researcher Brit Elders discussed the radar tracking of UFOs over Mexico:

> ". . . Mexico has in place and operational a highly sophisticated radar system, the TDX 2000. This air traffic management system has tracked and recorded unidentified objects simultaneous to the eyewitness reports of OVNIs [the Spanish term for UFOs] both from the ground and from pilots."[13]

Commercial pilots and air traffic controllers have asked the Mexican government to investigate the problem due to a number of perceived "near misses." However, when officials of the Mexican government held a press conference—during which they acknowledged the sightings—they said the UFOs posed no significant danger to the public.

The UFO activity has even engendered the attention of Mexico's news magazine 60 Minutos (the Mexican counterpart of *60 Minutes*). The chief investigative reporter and editor of *60 Minutos*, Jaime Maussan, has directed extensive research on the Mexico UFO flap and reported his results on Mexican television on numerous occasions. In 1995 Maussan stated, "Thanks to the video camcorder, Mexico has become the site of the most documented UFO flap in history."[14]

Since 1991, sightings of UFOs have continued almost unabated in the skies over Mexico, especially over Mexico City. UFOs have been extensively sighted and videotaped by hundreds of ordinary citizens, commercial pilots, and Mexican governmental authorities. Although the sightings have been thoroughly covered in the Mexican press, according to researchers, the majority of the populace has become desensitized to their presence and have come to view the sightings as "routine." While opinions vary, many of the witnesses believe that the Mexico flap represents the fulfillment of ancient Mayan or Biblical prophesies.

ISRAEL: "THE BIG INVASION"

Starting in 1996, the borders of Israel became host to one of the most extraordinary UFO flaps in history. At 2:00 A.M. on Tuesday, September 17, 1996, traffic on High Road in the Ramat Aviv section of Tel Aviv, Israel, came to a standstill when astonished motorists emerged from their automobiles to watch a UFO hovering near the city. Tel Aviv police received dozens of calls about a lighted object doing aerial acrobatics over the northern end of the city that were considered impossible for any conventional flying plane or helicopter. According to a report in *Mai'ariv,* one of Israel's two largest daily newspapers, the event was witnessed by police along with hundreds of motorists at the scene.

Since the Israeli flap began, David Ronen, a reporter and editor for *Mai'ariv* newspaper has received hundreds of reports of

UFO sightings as well as accounts of alleged contact with aliens by Israeli citizens. In his column Ronen noted that the sightings, which were previously restricted to relatively deserted areas, have started to occur in the more heavily populated coastland and city regions of Israel. In a 1997 interview for the British Journal *UFO Reality,* Ronen summarized the goings-on in Israel:

> "All at once, UFOs have begun to appear in the centre of Israel and in other areas throughout the country, as well as simultaneously in Iran and Australia. At precisely the same time (August 1996) a tide of eyewitness reports came in, this time not from individual people, but involving a wave of mass reports, including an intervention by the police and the army. The succession of reports is so staggering that it is already impossible to keep track of the hundreds and thousands of eyewitness reports that pour in each day."[15]

One of the best documented sightings occurred on Sunday, August 4, 1996, around 2:30 A.M. in Eilat, Israel. According to some estimates, more than a thousand people saw a UFO traveling slowly over the perimeter of the city at a height of 200 meters above ground. The local police stations and emergency centers were deluged with dozens of reported sightings. An eyewitness to the event was the son of the deputy mayor of Eilat, Rafi Edri. Regarding the event, he stated:

> "At 2:30 A.M., a group of 50 people stood and watched a UFO, like a giant tent full of lights, light up the sky above two residential districts. The UFO passed just over our heads at a height of not more than 100–200 metres. The event lasted close to ten minutes. Suddenly, without any advance warning, it disappeared."[16]

Other residents who observed the UFO stated that at first it was semicircle-shaped; afterwards it split in two, then instantaneously disappeared. In a similar sighting in August 1996, the deputy editor of the local paper in Eilat reported an enormous red-and-purple boomerang-shaped UFO the size of "half a city" which split in two, then floated above the city of Aqaba and disappeared above Jordan.

According to published reports, in September 1996, in the village of Netanya, an estimated 5,000 people were terrified when a UFO descended between a group of nearby buildings. The event was witnessed by numerous local officials, including at least ten police patrol cars.[17]

On other occasions residents have reported disruption of electrical appliances, burn marks on the ground, burnt out street lamps, "crop circle" landing sites, cattle mutilations, close encounters with "giant alien entities," and yes, even alleged alien abductions.[18]

One of Israel's best known journalists, Barry Chamish, has extensively researched the recent events in the skies over Israel. Chamish, who is the chief editor of *Inside Israel,* an investigative news journal, stated that "Israel is recognized as an international UFO hot spot —with an unsurpassed quantity and quality of evidence."[19] Due to the enormity of the Israeli flap, Barry Chamish and many of his journalistic colleagues have dubbed the events as "The Big Invasion." In fact, the frequent sightings of UFOs and alleged contact with alien entities was even discussed—with no resolution—by the Knesset on February 12, 1997.[20]

According to those who have studied the events over Israel, there is a very puzzling aspect of this UFO flap. Researchers note that the sightings appear to be occurring almost exclusively over the tiny land mass of the Jewish state rather than throughout the Middle East. This peculiarity was also noted by Daniel Brynberg, a journalist for the *Jerusalem Report*:

> "Ufologists are at a loss to explain the lack of sightings in Israel's near neighbors—it is as if the aliens, unlike most Earthlings, are aware of Israel's borders."[21]

The "rationalists" in Israel, like those in the United States, prefer to deny the existence of the phenomenon, claiming the events are a simple case of mass hysteria. Many view the events as a sign from God. Still others believe that the events in Israel portend a sinister influence—a foreboding sign that something ominous is about to happen and that Israel will be its focus. Whatever the case may be, the events in Israel closely follow those that have comprised UFO folklore in the United States for more than 50 years.

PHOENIX RISING?

On the evening of Thursday, March 13, 1997 the state of Arizona became host of one of the most recent and best documented UFO sightings in history. The sighting began at 8:16 P.M. when a retired police officer in Paulden, about 60 miles north of Phoenix, reported "a cluster of five red lights headed south." Minutes later, calls from eyewitnesses in Prescott, Wickenburg, Glendale, Phoenix, Scottsdale and Tempe flooded telephone lines at nearby Luke Air Force Base and local police departments.

While some described the object as a globe or a sphere, the majority of the witnesses saw an *enormous* V-shaped object with six leading and one trailing light. Some of the witnesses described the object as a solid, massive triangular craft. Others said that it appeared to be somewhat transparent. Like "a gray distortion of the night sky."[22] Videotapes of the object confirmed its great size and the V-shaped leading edge composed of a bank of six bright lights.

The event, which lasted 106 minutes, apparently engendered the attention of nearby Luke Air Force Base. According to eyewitnesses as the object neared the base three F-16 interceptors were scrambled. However, when the jets approached the object it "shot straight up and disappeared like a blink of an eye."[23] Predictably, officials at Luke Air Force Base denied this claim stating that no aircraft were dispatched and they do not investigate UFOs.

Peter Davenport of the National UFO Reporting Center in Seattle, Washington received hundreds of calls on the sighting and said "the incident over Arizona was the most dramatic I've seen. . . .What we have here is the real thing. *They* are here."[24]

The object was also sighted by numerous local pilots and air traffic controllers. Bill Grava, a pilot and air traffic controller was on duty that night at Sky Harbor International Airport. Although he witnessed the event he disclosed that the object *did not* show up on radar. When asked about the sighting he stated, "I still don't know what to think, and I have no idea what it was. Something military, I guess."[25]

The event was big news in the Arizona press. Local television stations aired the video tapes taken by local residents and radio talk shows were inundated by calls about the events for several weeks. However, it was not until June 18, 1997, over three months after the event, that the sightings gained simultaneous national media attention when the network news programs on NBC, CNN, MSNBC and ABC covered the Arizona event with comprehensive prime-time stories. In the ensuing days the story was also aired by dozens of local television news affiliates.

Mike Fortsen, an eyewitnesses to the events of March 13, 1997, was interviewed on the *CBS This Morning* and asked to describe his sighting.

"It was 8:30 in the evening, I was going to bed, I was closing my bedroom window which faces to the west and as I closed the window my eyes immediately went to the north where I saw the three huge white bright lights...we watched this craft as it leveled off. We watched it from the north all the way to the south for approximately a minute and a half. It was a flat black triangle. It was approximately a mile in length. It was about 1,500 feet off the ground. It was totally quiet. It was a solid object, it was one vehicle and it was close to a mile in length."

When asked what he thought the object was Fortsen stated,

"I'm pretty well convinced that this was an alien visitation craft. I'm pretty sure that it was inter-dimensional instead of interplanetary and I'm quite sure that our federal govt. and our military knows exactly what it was."

The story was also covered by *USA Today* in a full page article on June 18, 1997. In the article investigative reporter Richard Price called the events "the most confounding UFO report in fifty years." According to Price the event, which was witnessed by thousands of Arizona residents, was described in remarkably consistent terms.

"Something happened in the skies over Arizona the night of March 13. No one is sure what it was, but thousands saw it, dozens videotaped it and people all over the state are still haunted by it. . . . Witnesses generally agree on three things. First, it was enormous. The most conservative estimate describes it as three football fields long. Computer analysis of the tapes puts it at *6,000 feet*, or more than a mile. Second it made no sound. Third, it moved slowly over Phoenix, cruising at 30 mph. Several times it hovered in place in the sky."[26]

In a scene that was reminiscent of the blockbuster movie *Independence Day*, dozens of night-time videotapes showed the outline of a massive object floating slowly near the downtown lights of Phoenix. Yet, despite the large number of witnesses, neither the Air Force nor the state and local governments were willing to officially investigate the incident. The origin of the enormous unidentified flying object will surely be the topic of much speculation and debate in the months and years to come.[27]

UFOS OVER KOREA

On November 23, 1996, the Associated Press (AP) in Seoul, South Korea, posted a story about a daylight sighting of a disk-shaped UFO that was witnessed by thousands of Koreans at 7:20 A.M., during rush-hour traffic. The story, entitled "UFO Footage Stirs Sensation in S. Korea," described the event and noted that it was videotaped and aired by a local television network.

The television pictures showed footage of a shining object floating motionless in the early morning sky, suspended in midair for about ten minutes before it suddenly disappeared. While skeptics attributed the event to conventional air traffic, according to AP, South Korean Air Force officials stated that there were no scheduled military or civilian aircraft flying in the area at the time when the object was allegedly sighted.

According to the published reports, South Korea had been overtaken by "UFO fever" in recent months as numerous sightings—documented by local photographers—have received widespread and prominent coverage in newspapers throughout the country.

Observers in South Korea said the flying pattern of the object was identical to another unidentified flying object sighted in 1995. The same day, at 7:30 P.M. PST, CNN *World Report* reported the "cigar shaped UFO" over Seoul. According to CNN, a number of witnesses recorded video footage of the UFO and this footage accompanied the CNN report. The incident was also reported in the United States by Reuters, making it one of the rare UFO events reported by the mainstream media.

PROJECT STARLIGHT

On April 9–10, 1997, an unprecedented congressional briefing occurred in Washington, D.C., to promote official and definitive disclosure regarding the reality of UFOs and extraterrestrial intelligence. The briefing was sponsored by the Center for the Study of Extraterrestrial Intelligence (CSETI) and represented the official start of CSETI's "Project Starlight" initiative.

The Project Starlight initiative was initiated in 1993 by Dr. Steven Greer, the director of CSETI, "to identify the best scientific evidence related to UFOs and Extraterrestrial Intelligence"[28] and for the open public release of this information. According to Dr. Greer, since 1993 CSETI has identified more than 100 "bona-fide military, intelligence, government contractor and other government agency employees with direct, firsthand knowledge of the UFO/ET subject."

Since 1993, Project Starlight team members have provided preliminary briefings of "best available evidence" for senior military leaders, senior United Nations leadership, White House staff, a sitting Director of the Central Intelligence Agency, international leaders, members of the Senate and House of Representatives, and leaders in foreign governments, among others. However, these briefings were simply a prelude to those of April, 1997. According to Dr. Greer, the congressional briefings were necessary because CSETI had learned that the UFO subject was being "managed in a way which kept the majority of our constitutional leadership uninformed on the subject."

During the April 1997 briefings, the CSETI Project Starlight team brought together nearly 20 firsthand government witnesses to UFO/ET events. According to CSETI, most of the witnesses formerly possessed top secret security clearances and testified to events that took place while they possessed those clearances. These UFO witnesses were active in the Air Force, Army, Navy, NASA, private industry, and intelligence operations from the early 1950s to the 1990s.

The closed, confidential briefings took place at the Westin Hotel in Washington, D.C., at the Pentagon, and at other locations in the Washington, D.C., area. They were attended by nearly 30 congressmen or their staff representatives, VIPs from the executive branch, representatives of the Dutch embassy staff, government scientists, and representatives from the National Academy of Sciences and two state governors' offices. Separate media briefings were attended by reporters from The *Washington Post, US News and World Report, The Boston Globe,* The British Broadcasting Corporation (BBC), WTNH-TV, United Press International, *USA Today,* and a producer from CBS' *"60 Minutes."* Briefing participants were provided with extensive photographic, written, and video documentation of "definitive and unambiguous" evidence for the existence of UFOs.[29]

In addition, 11 of the best witnesses were selected to testify before the assembled government leaders. The testimony included a statement from "a world-renowned astronomer who was present when an apparent extraterrestrial signal was received at the Harvard observatory (SETI) facility" in the late 1980s. In a subsequent interview several weeks later, Greer said that over three dozen signals of non-Earth-based origin have been received by the META (Million-channel ExtraTerrestrial Assay) System at Harvard University.[30] In our own research efforts we were indeed able to confirm Greer's statement.

The Million-channel ExtraTerrestrial Assay (META) at the Harvard/Smithsonian observatory is fed by a 26-meter, steerable Cassegrain radio telescope which became operational in 1985. After five years of scanning for narrow-band radio signals (near the 1420 MHz line of neutral hydrogen), the META hardware searched more than 60 trillion channels! During that time there were 37 candidate "events" that exceeded the average detection threshold.[31] These "events" were, in fact, electromagnetic signals of varying duration that were determined to be of non-Earth origin. However, they were published with no fanfare in the *Astrophysical Journal*.[32] When we inquired as to why the anomalous signals were not considered extremely significant, public relations officials at SETI in Palo Alto, California, stated that they were not repeatable events; that is, when the anomalous regions were re-scanned, the signals did not repeat.[33] No explanation for the signals was given other than they were "unidentified."

At the briefing, additional witnesses discussed firsthand knowledge of UFO artifacts; well-documented photographic evidence that was altered by NASA; as well as the testimony of a Naval employee who witnessed a major UFO encounter off the Eastern seaboard which was photographed, tracked on radar, and pursued by military aircraft in 1981.

The ultimate goal of the closed congressional briefing was to bring about open congressional hearings on the existence of UFOs and extraterrestrial life in a non-sensational, rational manner. However, if they are not forthcoming, CSETI plans to press for the disclosure of UFO/ET reality either through the United Nations or a public blue-ribbon panel of former and current military, NASA, intelligence, and government employees with direct, firsthand knowledge of the UFOs. Stay tuned!

THE TESTIMONY
OF THE ASTRONAUTS

For decades, purveyors of disinformation have carefully cultivated the notion that only wackos had sighted or believed in UFOs. This perception, widely promoted by the media and educational establishments, is one of the main reasons why the scientific establishment has not undertaken an open and thorough examination of the UFO phenomenon. However, in recent years this perception has began to crumble—perhaps by design—as numerous astronauts have spoken publicly about the reality of UFOs and their belief in the existence of intelligent extraterrestrial visitors.

GORDON COOPER

On May 15, 1963, Major Gordon Cooper, one of the original Mercury astronauts and the last American to fly alone in space, completed a 22-orbit journey around the world. During the final orbit, Cooper told the tracking station at Muchea (near Perth, Australia) that he had sighted a glowing, greenish object that was quickly approaching his capsule. The unidentified flying object was solid enough to be picked up by Muchea's tracking radar.

Cooper's sighting was reported by the National Broadcast Company; however, when Cooper landed, reporters were not allowed to question him about the UFO sighting. This was not the first sighting by Major Cooper. In 1951 Cooper had sighted numerous UFOs while piloting an F-86 Sabrejet over Western Germany. The UFOs, which were sighted over a two-day period, were described as metallic, saucer-shaped disks at considerable altitude that easily out-maneuvered the American fighter planes. Six years later, while supervising flight training at Edwards AFB, Cooper and his colleagues witnessed and photographed a "flying saucer" that landed near the base. The film was sent through the "normal channels" for processing and evaluation, yet he never received a report on the photographs. Due to security directives, Cooper kept these sightings to himself for many years.

However, on July 14, 1978, Gordon Cooper met with Secretary General of the United Nations Kurt Waldheim to discuss his personal knowledge of UFOs and to encourage international research. Also in attendance were Jacques Vallee, J. Allen Hynek, Calude Poher, David Saunders, and Prime Minister of Grenada Sir Eric Gairy. In a letter to the United Nation Security Council, Cooper wrote:

> "I believe that these extraterrestrial vehicles and their crews are visiting this planet from other planets and are obviously a little more advanced than we are here on Earth. . . . Most astronauts were reluctant to discuss UFOs. I feel that we need to have a top-level, coordinated program to scientifically collect and analyze data from all over the Earth concerning any type of encounter, and to determine how best to interface with these visitors in a friendly fashion. Also, I did have occasion in 1951 to have two days of observation of many flights of them [UFOs], of different sizes, flying in fighter formation, generally from east to west over Europe."[34]

On May 7, 1996, Cooper was interviewed on the nationally broadcast television program *Paranormal Borderline*. In the interview Cooper confirmed his personal encounters with UFOs in the 1950s and his belief that extraterrestrial life forms are visiting this planet.

During the interview Cooper expressed his belief that we are in an era of increasing revelation by the government and that he expects an announcement regarding the reality of UFOs and extraterrestrial life.

> "I think we'll see our government having a totally different approach really to the UFO situation, or extraterrestrials, whatever you want to call it. I think the pressure that comes to bear on the government from whatever reason they withhold information is certainly getting more and more and more, so I would like to think that they're going to release all the information."

In fact, in 1996, NASA announced Project Origins. Its goal is to search for inhabitable (inhabited?) planets orbiting nearby stars.

ED MITCHELL

At the highlight of his mission (January 31–February 9, 1971), Apollo 14 astronaut Ed Mitchell became the sixth man to walk on the moon and spent 33 hours roving the lunar hills of Fra Mauro with fellow astronaut Alan Shepard. At the age of 65, with the 25th anniversary of Apollo 14 coming up, Mitchell returned to Florida to shoot a segment for *Dateline NBC* about his experience.

In the episode, which aired in April 1996, Mitchell was asked about his beliefs regarding the existence of intelligent extraterrestrial life. He responded:

> "I have no firsthand experience, but I have had the opportunity to meet with people from three countries who in the course of their official duties claim to have had personal firsthand encounter experiences ... with extraterrestrials. ..." I'm convinced there's life throughout the universe. It's just a question of how developed. ..."

During the interview he also stated that he believes that the United States government covered up the evidence surrounding a case of an alleged UFO crash at Roswell, New Mexico, in 1947.

In a separate interview in January 1996, Mitchell was asked about the evidence for UFOs and extraterrestrial visitors. He said:

> "I am convinced there is a small body of valid [UFO] information and that there is a body of information, ten times as big, that is total disinformation put out by the source to confuse the whole issue. . . . The information is now held primarily by a body of semi- or quasi-private organizations that have kind of spun off from the military intelligence organizations of the past. . . . The dangerous part is, they're still operating under a black budget, which has been estimated at over $30 billion a year. And nobody knows what goes into black budgets. The prime requisite is security first and everything else second. Imagine an organization that has a black budget, an unquestioned source of funds, reports to no one, and has this exotic technology that they can keep to themselves and play with."[35]

In addition to these revelations by Ed Mitchell, he was one of the high-profile individuals who accompanied the CSETI team in April 1997 and revealed his knowledge of UFOs at the closed congressional briefing.

APOLLO 11

For many years, unconfirmed reports of UFO sightings by Apollo 11 astronauts Neil Armstrong and Edwin "Buzz" on July 21, 1969, were relegated to the world of science fiction and dismissed out of hand by NASA officials. However, according to Otto Binder, a former NASA employee, the agency has a longstanding policy of blocking sensitive transmissions through secret, non-public frequencies. According to Binder[36] an unnamed ham radio operator picked up the following transmission on a public bypass channel when Apollo 11 landed in the Sea of Tranquility:

> MISSION CONTROL: "What's there? . . . Mission control calling APOLLO 11."

> APOLLO 11: "These babies are huge, sir . . . enormous. . . . Oh, God, you wouldn't believe it! I'm telling you there are other spacecraft out there . . . lined up on the far side of the crater edge . . . they're on the moon watching us. . . ."

In 1979, Otto Binder's account was confirmed by the former chief of NASA communications, Maurice Chatelain. According to Chatelain, Armstrong had indeed reported seeing two UFOs on the outer rim of a lunar crater. Regarding the event he stated, "When Apollo 11 made the first landing on the Sea of Tranquility, and only moments before Armstrong stepped down the ladder to set foot on the moon, two UFOs hovered overhead." Regarding NASA's knowledge of the incident he stated, "The encounter was common knowledge in NASA, but nobody has talked about it until now."[37] Chatelain has also alleged that Apollo 11's radio transmissions were rerouted on numerous occasions to hide certain events from the public. To this day NASA officials and Neil Armstrong strongly deny that any UFOs were sighted.

Nevertheless, in his book, *Our Cosmic Ancestors,* Chatelain made a number of startling claims about UFO sightings during NASA missions.

> ". . . all Apollo and Gemini flights were followed, both at a distance and sometimes also quite closely,

by space vehicles of extraterrestrial origin—flying saucers, or UFOs, if you want to call them by that name. Every time it occurred, the astronauts informed Mission Control, who then ordered absolute silence."[38]

Regarding code names for UFOs used by astronauts, he stated:

"I think that Walter Schirra aboard Mercury 8 was the first of the astronauts to use the code name 'Santa Claus' to indicate the presence of flying saucers next to space capsules. However, his announcements were barely noticed by the general public. It was a little different when James Lovell on board the Apollo 8 command module came out from behind the moon and said for everybody to hear: 'PLEASE BE INFORMED THAT THERE IS A SANTA CLAUS.' Even though this happened on Christmas Day 1968, many people sensed a hidden meaning in those words."

Were it not for Chaletain's credentials it would be easy to dismiss his claims. As the chief of communications, Chatelain was in a very senior position at NASA and certainly in a position to know the truth. He was in the control room for many of the Mercury, Gemini, and Apollo flights during the 1960s and '70s. He established a very reputable career in the aerospace industry. As an engineer he secured 11 patents and held senior positions for Ryan Electronics and North American Aviation in the 1950s and '60s. In spite of that, NASA denies his claims.

DR. BRIAN O'LEARY

Another former scientist-astronaut, Dr. Brian O'Leary was being trained by NASA to go on a manned mission to Mars. He received his Ph.D. in astronomy at the University of California,

Berkeley, and he has served as a faculty member at UC Berkeley, Cornell University, California Institute of Technology, and Princeton University. On September 18, 1994, at the International Forum on New Science in Fort Collins, Colorado, Dr. O'Leary made a remarkable public statement regarding UFOs, extraterrestrial life and the government cover-up:

> "For nearly 50 years, the secrecy apparatus within the United States government has kept from the public UFO and alien contact information. . . . We have contact with alien cultures. . . . The suppression of UFO and other extraterrestrial intelligence information for at least 47 years is probably being orchestrated by an elite band of men in the CIA, NSA, DIA, and their like. This small group appears able to keep these already-hard-to-believe secrets very well. . . . Those who have investigated this hydra-headed beast believe that the Cosmic Watergate of UFO, alien, mind-control, genetic engineering, free energy, anti-gravity propulsion, and other secrets will make Watergate or Irangate appear to be kindergarten exercises."[39]

JOHN BLAHA

John Blaha is a veteran of five space shuttle missions, including a tour of duty aboard the Russian MIR space station. As commander of space shuttle Discovery, on March 24, 1989, Blaha was recorded on a secret NASA bypass channel by a ham radio operator as saying:

> "Houston, this is Discovery. We still have the alien spacecraft under observance."[40]

Not surprisingly, NASA denies that it was a reference to a UFO. Instead, they claim that Blaha was referring to the Russian space station.

With the credibility of our NASA astronauts being added to the public's awareness of the UFO mystery, we must ask the question, Why now? Although NASA is a civilian agency, many of its programs are funded by the defense budget and the astronauts are subject to military security regulations. For decades our astronauts were held to these "non-disclosure" oaths, so it is puzzling to see them confirming the existence of UFOs in such a public forum. Is the government turning a blind eye to these disclosures, or is this part of a gradual release of information to awaken the populace to the reality of UFOs? Is this a precursor to an announcement of UFO reality? We may soon find out.

WHAT IS GOING ON?

While the events discussed in this chapter may establish the existence of UFOs in the minds of many, they shed very little light on the question of their origin and agenda for mankind. Indeed, for more than five decades government and civilian researchers have attempted to unravel the mystery of the UFOs. Yet, there is nothing close to a consensus among those who have seriously examined the nature and history of the phenomenon.

To the skeptics the phenomenon is a product of mass hysteria or a shared visual hallucination. However, as Jim Marrs, author of *Alien Agenda* pointed out, with the advent of the camcorder hundreds of people have videotaped UFOs and "you can't tape a hallucination."[41] To others the UFO phenomenon is the harbinger of a New Age of spiritual awakening and evolution accomplished with the assistance of our highly advanced space brothers. Still others believe the UFO phenomenon represents the return of God's angels, who sometimes visit in "chariots of fire," who today are returning to herald the dawning of a new millennium and the arrival of the age of Apocalypse.

If these things are real, we believe that fact will lead to the biggest challenge ever faced by mankind. If these things are not real, they bear evidence of a gigantic delusion—one that is being orchestrated with a political end in sight. There are some who believe that we are all being "set up." These issues are no longer casual curiosities. There is increasing evidence that what lies behind these strange events will soon affect every living person on this planet.

Who are these extraterrestrials? Where are they from? What is their agenda? Whatever the case, one thing is clear: the appearance of unidentified flying objects is an ancient phenomenon which has perplexed—even harassed—mankind from the beginning of written history.

ANCIENT
VISITORS

"The copy of the Genesis Apocryphon discovered at

Qumran dates back to the second century B.C. . . .

When discovered in 1947, it had been much

mutilated from the ravages of time and humidity. . . .

When scholars finally made public its content,

the document confirmed that celestial beings from

the skies had landed on planet Earth. More than

that, it told how these beings had mated with

Earth-women and had begat giants."

I.D.E. THOMAS, THE OMEGA CONSPIRACY[42]

The appearance of unidentified flying objects in the skies of planet Earth is not a recent phenomenon. Indeed, flying chariots, celestial cars, winged disks, luminous cloudships, and glowing apparitions have profoundly impacted mankind since the beginning of recorded history.

According to Jacques Vallee, the world-renowned UFO researcher portrayed in the 1977 blockbuster movie *Close Encounters of the Third Kind,* the folklore of every culture throughout history is replete with sightings of extraordinary aerial phenomena akin to our modern UFO sightings. In 1969 Vallee wrote a fascinating book, *Passport to Magonia,* in which he catalogued the history of UFO sightings. Regarding such visitations, Vallee stated, ". . . The folklore of every culture, it turned out, had a rich reservoir of stories about humanoid beings that flew in the sky, used devices that seemed in advance of the technology of the time."[43]

UFO researchers John Weldon and Zola Levitt echoed this in their book, *UFOs: What on Earth Is Happening?:*

> "UFOs seem to have been around for a long time.
> We can find odd references to 'circles of fire in
> the sky' in many historical documents and even
> in cave paintings. While we seem to be experi-
> encing a great upsurge in reported sightings in
> our own day, every age seems to have had simi-
> lar stories."[44]

ANCIENT ASTRONAUTS?

It is widely believed that man's most ancient civilizations arose in the Middle East, near the Tigris and Euphrates rivers, in the region known as the Fertile Crescent. In fact, the most ancient written records we possess are from the Sumerians, who abruptly appeared in this area in the third millennium B.C.

The history of Sumer has primarily been reconstructed from thousands of clay tablets and cylinders written in cuneiform script. Recorded on those tablets are stories of the "gods which came down to Earth from the heavens." Popular authors— such as Erich von Daniken, Zecharia Sitchin, and others— have interpreted these texts as visitations by highly advanced "ancient astronauts" who flew to Earth in spaceships and were worshiped as "gods" by virtually every ancient culture. Proponents of this "ancient astronaut" theory believe that these extraterrestrials were responsible for the abrupt appearance of complex human societies and high technology that permitted ancient man to build the pyramids, Stonehenge, and many other artifacts that cannot be duplicated to this day. Many scholars disagree, arguing that the cuneiform texts are too cryptic to be interpreted as extraterrestrial visitations. Nevertheless, the Sumerian cuneiform texts do speak of beings from the heavens coming to Earth and interacting with mankind.

In support of the ancient astronaut theory, proponents point to a number of engravings that were carved on stone in ancient Sumer and Mesopotamia. These petroglyphs depict scenes which, according to the ancient astronaut theory, represent ancient flying ships piloted by humanoid extraterrestrials.

One of the most fascinating is a Sumerian engraving discovered on a clay cylinder which is suggestive of an ancient flying ship floating above the ground with wings or, as some have suggested, extended solar panels.

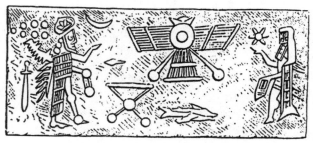

From the mythology of ancient Assyria we find the story of Ashur, the winged god of war. This ancient deity is typically represented as a humanoid form, bow in hand, adjacent to a winged disk.

According to many, Ashur was an adaptation of an earlier flying god, Ahura-Mazda, who was embraced by the prophet Zoroaster in the sixth century B.C.[45]

The ultimate origin of the myth of Ahura-Mazda, called "Lord of Wisdom," is not known. However, by the time this deity was embraced by Zoroaster, the legend of this flying god of wisdom had been in existence for at least a thousand years.

These winged humanoid deities are very reminiscent of those depicted in most ancient hieroglyphs of Egypt. In fact, the existence of flying humanoid "gods" who came to Earth, interacted with and even interbred with mankind, are found extensively in the literature of ancient Egypt, Greece, the Incas, Mayas, Hindus, Native Americans, and others.

THE WONDERS OF EGYPT

Egypt remains one of the most ancient and mysterious cultures in history. The stunning archaeological accomplishments of that region are unequaled in history. Two of the most mysterious monuments of Egypt are the Great Pyramid and the Sphinx of the Giza plateau. Their purpose unknown, they stand as architectural marvels.

The Great Pyramid of Giza, known as Khafre, is one of the Seven Wonders of the Ancient World and is believed to be the largest building ever erected on Earth. It has a volume that is 30 times that of the Empire State Building and weighs almost six million tons. Its base covers 13.6 acres. Its length is 755.75 feet (230.4 m) on each side, and its original height was 481.4 feet (147 m). It was constructed using over 2,300,000 limestone blocks, each with an average weight of 2.5 tons. Between the stones a gap of .02 inches was allowed for the placement of cement. Some of the stone blocks weigh almost a hundred tons. Yet, they are so carefully fashioned that a single piece of paper cannot be slipped between them. These specifications exceed the tolerances allowed for the tiles of the Space Shuttle! The pyramid was covered with an outer casing of 144,000 polished white limestone tiles, which could be seen from hundreds of miles away on a clear day.

Incredibly, the Great Pyramid is aligned to true north better than the Paris observatory. Its four sides are aligned to the four points of the compass with only a one-twelfth degree of variation. According to some experts this variance is due to the gradual movement of the Earth's axis rather than errors in design. The edges of the Great Pyramid are straight to less than half of an inch along its perimeter. And despite weighing millions of tons, the Great Pyramid has settled less than an inch. Tolerances such as these are unequaled in the modern era of architectural design and construction.

At the nearby Valley Temple of Khafre there are hundreds of stone blocks whose weight exceeds two hundred tons. According to Graham Hancock, "At present there are only two land-based cranes in the world that could lift weights of this magnitude. . . . In other words, modern builders with the advantages of high-tech engineering at their disposal can barely hoist weights of 200 tons. Was it not, therefore, somewhat surprising that the builders at Giza had hoisted such weights on an almost routine basis?"[46]

In recent decades, numerous international teams of structural engineers, architects, and scientists have attempted to decipher the methods used in constructing the Great Pyramid of Giza. Yet, even with current technology, our greatest minds still cannot duplicate the architectural achievements of ancient Egypt.

To date no one has found any records describing why, when, and how the pyramids and the Sphinx were constructed. Even more astonishing is the fact that recent archaeological studies indicate that the Great Pyramid and the Sphinx may have been built over 12,000 years ago.[47]

Throughout the mythology of ancient Egypt we find numerous stories of the flying "gods" who came down to instruct and guide the ancient Egyptians. According to some legends, these "gods" flew on "celestial disks" or "flying boats."

Because of their staggering technological achievements and the stories of the ancient flying "gods," many have speculated that the ancient Egyptians were given this advanced technology by an advanced race of extraterrestrials.[48]

THE "WINGED DISK" OF RA

According to Egyptian mythology the sun god, known as Ra, was lord of the universe and flew in a "celestial boat." He was usually depicted with a human body and the head of a hawk. Horus, a descendant of Ra and the son of Isis (the nature goddess), was the god of the sky, of light and goodness. Horus was usually depicted as a falcon or a falcon-headed man. Horus was one of the gods who, according to Egyptian mythology, flew on the "winged disk" of Ra, "which shined with many colors," a description which many believe is the most accurate description of a UFO in ancient history.

A description of the "winged disk" of Ra was inscribed in hieroglyphic text in the temple at Edfu, an ancient Egyptian city dedicated to Horus. The inscription deals with the activities of the gods long before the reign of the pharaohs.

> "So Horus, the Winged Measurer, flew up toward the horizon in the Winged Disk of Ra; it is therefore that he has been called from that day on Great God, Lord of the Skies. . . . Then Horus, the Winged Measurer, reappeared in the Winged Disk, which shined in many colors; and he came back to the boat of Ra, the Falcon of the Horizon. . . . And Thoth said: 'O Lord of the gods! The Winged Measurer has returned in the great Winged Disk, shining with many colors.' "[49]

In the Egyptian *Book of the Dead* a similar description is found in a story about the goddess Isis attempting to escape from the god Seth. In the story, Isis, the mother of Horus, is attempting to save the life of her son by escaping from Seth who is trying to kill him. With assistance from the god Thoth, Isis escapes from Seth in the Boat of the Celestial Disk.

> "Then Isis sent forth a cry to heaven and addressed her appeal to the Boat of Millions of Years. And the Celestial Disk stood still, and moved not from the place where it was. And Thoth came down, and he was provided with magical powers, and possessed the great power. . . . And he said: 'O Isis, thou goddess, thou glorious one . . . I have come this day in the Boat of the Celestial Disk from the place where it was yesterday . . . I have come from the skies to save the child for his mother.' "[50]

With these remarkable records of the gods of Egypt flying on a winged celestial disk and the flying boat of Ra, it is easy to see why UFO researchers have embraced these texts as proof of ancient visitations by a technologically advanced race of extraterrestrial beings. It is equally easy to understand why the ancient Egyptians worshiped them as gods. There are many other Egyptian texts which are equally suggestive of UFO activity in ancient times.

According to Weldon and Levitt, the sighting of UFO-like objects was again recorded by ancient Egyptians many centuries after the pyramids were built.

> ". . . The Egyptians, no mean scientists for those early times, also noted UFO phenomena. A papyrus record of the annals of Pharaoh Thutmos III (ca. 1600 B.C.) mentions 'circles of fire in the sky.' The circles were as bright as the sun, according to the record, very numerous and dominating the sky. A terrible stench, a factor

common to many modern reports, was associated with the appearance of these fiery disks."[51]

ANCIENT ROME

The appearance of unusual aerial phenomenon in the Middle East continued long after the events in ancient Egypt. During the period of the Greek and Roman empires from the fourth century B.C. to about 17 B.C., a number of unusual sightings were recorded. According to Weldon and Levitt,

> "The writings of certain Roman historians, when corroborated in other areas, record incidents of unidentified objects in the skies over Rome in the third and fourth centuries B.C.[52] Wilkins specifies that Pliny, Seneca, Tacitus, and Lycosthenes, among several other reliable chroniclers of the time, all make mention of this phenomenon. Titus Livius and Julius Obsequens list eight specific locations of sightings, extending from the Gulf of Venice in 213 B.C. to Umbria in 16 B.C. Pliny spoke of a "fiery shield" that swept across the sky, and the historian Livy used the words "phantom ships" when referring to celestial craft sighted in his time (60–17 B.C.)."[53]

Even the army of Alexander the Great is said to have been frightened by large, luminous aerial objects that "buzzed" the troops around 330 B.C.[54]

THE DARK AGES AND BEYOND

In the centuries that followed the rise and fall of the Roman Empire, the appearance of unusual aerial phenomenon continued unabated worldwide. The medieval times are replete with stories about "luminous cloudships," "shiny disks," "flying chariots," and the visitation of strange, but humanoid creatures.

> ". . . Cloudships and Luminous Strangers start popping up again in about the sixth century A.D. Glowing aerial objects become evident again in the literature of many countries. Jacques Bergier says that practically every year of the Dark Ages saw reports of 'luminous strangers' being made."[55]

In A.D. 583 Gregory of Tours, a French historian, saw numerous globes of fire that moved about in the sky.[56] One of the most intriguing incidents in history occurred during the reign of Charlemagne (A.D. 742–814). During this period Agobard, the Archbishop of Lyons, recorded an astonishing event in which four people were seen falling (floating?) from an "aerial ship." They were accused of sorcery, a capital crime, but were spared when the Archbishop intervened and said that the event never occurred.[57]

In the 13th century monastic records in Europe reported a number of unusual aerial phenomenon. According to Weldon and Levitt,

> ". . . In 1209 the monks of the Byland Abbey reported a large round silvery disk that flew slowly over them and caused great terror, interrupting an otherwise quiet routine. The brothers of the Cistercian Abbey of Begeland were favored with two such visitations that year. Monastic records often mention UFO phenomena reported by shaken clerics. The 13th century was rather a vintage period for UFOs in England. . . ."[58]

In the 15th century the most famous sighting was by no less a world traveler than Christopher Columbus. On October 11, 1492, only hours before land was sighted, Columbus saw a "glimmering light" moving up and down in the distant sky. The light appeared and disappeared numerous times during the night.[59]

JAPANESE SIGHTINGS

The historical records of medieval Japan are peppered with unusual aerial events which profoundly influenced those who viewed them. According to Vallee, "Ancient Japanese inform us that on October 27, 1180, an unusual luminous object described as an 'Earthen vessel' flew from a mountain in Kii Province beyond the northeast mountain of Fukuhara at midnight. After a while, the object changed its course and was lost to sight at the northern horizon, leaving a luminous trail."[60]

Early in the morning of September 24, 1235, Japanese General Yoritsume, while camping with his army, sighted a number of unusual aerial objects doing loops in the southwest sky. According to Vallee, this triggered the first "scientific investigation" of a UFO, and the results were predictable. The general's consultants determined that the entire phenomenon was "natural." They determined that the lights observed were the stars being swayed by the excessive winds![61]

Regarding the impact of these events, Vallee has stated that unusual "celestial phenomenon" over Japanese skies were so common in the Middle Ages that they "influenced human events in a direct way. Panic, riots, and disruptive social movements were often linked to celestial apparitions." The following is a partial list.[62]

•On August 3, 989, during a period of great social unrest, three round objects of unusual brilliance were observed. Later they joined together.

•In 1361, a flying object described as being "shaped like a drum, about 20 feet in diameter," emerged from the inland sea off western Japan.

•On January 2, 1458, a bright object resembling the full moon was seen in the sky, and this apparition was followed by "curious signs" in the heavens and on Earth.

• Two months later, on March 17, 1458, five stars appeared, circling the moon. They changed color three times and suddenly vanished.

• Ten years later, on March 8, 1468, a dark object, which made a "sound like a wheel," flew from Mt. Kasuga toward the west at midnight.

• On January 3, 1569, in the evening, a flaming star appeared to float in the sky. It was regarded as an omen of serious changes, announcing the fall of the Chu Dynasty.

• In May, 1606, fireballs were continuously reported over Kyoto, and one night a whirling ball of fire resembling a red wheel hovered near the Nijo Castle and was observed by many of the samurai.

• Chaos spread all over Japan on January 2, 1749, when three round objects "like the moon" appeared and were seen for four days. Such a state of social unrest developed and seemed so clearly linked with the mysterious "celestial objects" that the government decided to act. Riot participants were executed, but confusion became total when people observed three "moons" aligned in the sky and, several days later, two "suns."

THE "STAR PEOPLE"

Legends of ancient extraterrestrial visitations from "star beings" or "gods" from outer space is not limited to the Middle East, Europe, and Asia. Indeed, some of the most ancient and detailed traditions of such beings are found in the oral traditions of Native Americans. Some of the traditions are closely guarded secrets available only to those in the inner circles of tribal authority. Others are well-known by outsiders.

In June 1996 at the Yankton Sioux Reservation, South Dakota, a landmark conference called the "Star Knowledge

Conference" was convened by Lakota medicine man Standing Elk to share secret tribal traditions about the "Star People" (Extraterrestrials) with a prestigious group of prominent UFO researchers.[63] The information shared at this conference had never before been released to those outside tribal circles.

During this conference various tribal leaders of indigenous peoples from New Zealand, the Americas, and Lapland from above the Arctic Circle, shared numerous traditions about ancient and ongoing contacts with the extraterrestrial entities of the "Star Nations."

Among the many traditions shared by the participants was the belief in ancient "extraterrestrial craft" piloted by the "Star People," to whom the native peoples owe their origin. Legends of flying disks, flying arrows, and luminous cloudships, it was revealed, are abundant in the folklore of indigenous tribal nations of both hemispheres.

Chet Snow of the Hopi tribe shared his belief that modern day "Crop Circles," which started showing up in the late 1980s, are messages from the Star Nations and that the same "glyphs" are found in ancient Hopi hieroglyphs.

The conference climaxed with the prediction that the "Star Peoples" from seven different galaxies will return to Earth in the late 1990s. Before that happens we will experience severe Earth changes such as Earthquakes, fires, floods, drought, famine, and pestilence. Then the White Buffalo Calf Woman, an Extra-terrestrial who birthed the native peoples, will return to Earth and a new age of peace and harmony will emerge! Time will tell.

A curious aspect to the conference was the fact that the Native American conference participants who have allegedly been contacted by Star People did so by parapsychological means such as telepathy, channeling, out-of-body and near-death experiences.

ETS FROM THE PLEIADES?

Several of the Star Knowledge conference participants revealed a Native American tradition, widely held, that their ancestors were descendants of extraterrestrials from the star system Pleiades. According to UFO folklore, the Pleiadians are a "Nordic type" of extraterrestrial and are almost indistinguishable from modern man. Throughout history, legend has it, the Pleiadians have had emissaries among us who have assisted in our "spiritual development." Standing Elk, the Star Knowledge Conference organizer, spoke of a Sioux medicine man who allegedly has regular visitations by Star People from the Pleiades.

The legends of Pleiadian contact are not limited to North American Natives. In the legends of the Incas, Aztecs, and Mayas of Central and South America, there are also references to contact with "Star Beings" from the Pleiades. In an article, "ETs from the Pleiades," Robert Stanley notes:

> "Religious legends of pre-Inca people state that the universe was inhabited by 'gods' and celestial beings who arrived on Earth from the Pleiades. In Bolivia, near Lake Titicaca, are the ruins of the megalithic city of Tiahuanacu. Many of the city walls were constructed from blocks that weigh 60 tons which were further reinforced by metal clamps. Legends relate how it was built in one

night by mysterious bearded white men who were giants from Taurus, the constellation of the Pleiades. They are also believed to have descended from the clouds and to have had sexual intercourse with Incan women."[64]

In the city of Teotihuacan, a Mexican archaeological site about 25 miles northeast of Mexico City, are the remains of the earliest city in the western hemisphere. Its monuments include the Pyramid of the Sun, the Pyramid of the Moon, and the Avenue of the Dead, a broad passageway flanked by ruins of temples. The exact period of its construction is unknown. The majority of scholars believe that it flourished around 200 B.C. Others disagree, asserting that the city and its fantastic pyramids were built as early as 4000 B.C., prior to the eruption of a local volcano, Xitli.[65]

When the Aztecs arrived in this area in the 12th century A.D., the city of Teotihuacan was already in ruins. The identity of the builders of this city, the largest in the pre-Columbian era, is a complete mystery. However, there is a fascinating legend, passed down from the murky past of the pre-Christian era, which asserts that the city and its massive pyramids were also built by giants![66]

UFOS IN HINDU MYTHOLOGY?

While the mythology of the Middle East speaks of winged disks, circles of fire, and flying gods, the legends of the ancient Hindus speak of visitations by heavenly beings on aerial "lightning-cars." The primary sacred literature of the Hindu religion are known as the Vedas. Tradition holds that they were composed by the gods themselves in a previous age. One of the main divisions of the Veda, the Rig-Veda, was composed between 1300 and 1000 B.C. In the Rig-Veda we find a reference to these aerial cars flown by the gods.

> "The valiant god his car ascends, swept by his fer-
> vid bounding speeds, athwart the sky the hero
> speeds. The Marut-hosts his escort form, impetu-
> ous spirits of the storm. On flashing lightning-cars
> they ride, and gleam in warlike pomp and pride. . . .
> Like lions' roar their voice of doom; With iron force
> their teeth consume. The hills, the Earth itself, they
> shake; All creatures at their coming quake."[67]

According to some scholars in the ancient Hindu texts—the
Bhagavata-Purana, Mahabharata, and Ramayana—additional
descriptions of flying machines called vimanas can be found.
Some of the texts, which date back to as far back as 3000 B.C.,
discuss aerial cars which are described as bright, radiant, and
metallic in color. In the Vedas the mythic god of the atmosphere, storms, and rain, named Indra, had an aerial car that
was "swifter that thought." The car had lights on its side and
emitted a reddish hue.[68] In the Mahabharata there is a story of
the arrival of the gods for a wedding feast in their aerial cars.

> "The gods in cloud-borne chariots, came into
> view the scene so fair . . . bright celestial cars in
> concourse sailed upon the cloudless sky."[69]

ANCIENT RENDERINGS

Throughout the world a number of ancient carvings and paintings have been discovered which convince some researchers that
ancient peoples were visited by sophisticated flying machines and
creatures which fit modern descriptions of extraterrestrial entities.

According to Weldon and Levitt there are numerous cave
paintings and carvings that suggest the visitation by unusual
humanoid creatures and flying disks, cylinders, and ovals:

> "Granite carvings in a mountain cave in China's
> Hunan Province show figures with large torsos
> standing upon cylinder-shaped objects in the sky.

> Below them, pictured on the ground in the carvings, are other similar figures (the artists?). . . . Some 72 caves throughout France and Spain show drawings dating from around 13,000 B.C. of a variety of oval and disk-shaped objects resembling at least the shapes of today's UFOs."[70]

According to Hopi Indian Chief Dan Katchongva,

> "A petroglyph near Mishongnovi on Second Mesa shows flying saucers and travel through space. The arrow on which the dome-shaped object rests, stands for travel through space. The Hopi maiden on the dome shape represents purity. Those Hopi who survive Purification Day will be taken to other planets. We, the faithful Hopi, have seen the ships and know they are true. We have watched nearly all our brethren lose faith in the original teachings and go off on their own course. Near Oraibi was closely shown the Plan of Life, and we are gathered here to await our True White Brother."[71]

In the central Kimberly district of Australia a rock painting was discovered which depicts the mythical mouthless gods of creation, Vonjinda, the object of worship by ancient natives of that region. With their large oval heads and oversized eyes, the resemblance to modern extraterrestrials called "Grays," the aliens depicted in Steven Speilberg's blockbuster movie, *Close Encounters of the Third Kind,* is striking.

THE MINGLING OF MEN AND "GODS"

Throughout the world's religious texts we find a number of common threads regarding ancient visitations of beings from the heavens. In the mythology of the Greek and Roman empires we read of the Titans, the giants who were the off-spring of the "gods" and their human wives. According to mythology they also assisted in the building of the magnificent monuments of Greece. In the Bible, in the sixth chapter of Genesis, we read that giants were born when the "sons of God" (widely interpreted in modern UFO literature as a race of extraterrestrials) came to the "daughters of men," an obvious reference to human females. The Bible describes these hybrids as the "mighty men which were of old, men of renown." According to numerous authors, these "mighty men" of the golden age were the "third party" who assisted mankind in the building of the monuments of Egypt, Stonehenge, the Americas, and the Far East.

> "The records of ancient Sumeria tell of gods descending from the stars and fertilizing their ancestors. Like the gods of ancient Greece, the 'sons of God' in the sixth chapter of Genesis, and the Pleiadians of pre-Inca mythology, the flying gods of India begat children with women of Earth. These offspring possessed the supernatural skills and attributes of their extraterrestrial fathers."

> "According to the legends of South Sea Islanders, one of the 'gods of heaven' visited them in an enormous gleaming egg and fertilized human females, producing Earth's first offspring. A similar story is found in the Epic of Gilgamesh and the *Book of Enoch,* where the 'Watchers,' a group of supernatural beings, lusted after human females and begat giants. An ancient Persian

myth alleges that demons had corrupted Earth and allied themselves with women!"[72]

While the stories differ in detail, in each case we have the intermingling of extraterrestrial entities with women of the Earth with the production of supernatural offspring! The prevalence of such legends is echoed by Jim Marrs:

"As the similarities of widely spread cultures continue to be appreciated, a pattern of common worldwide connections is emerging. Egyptian legends tell of Tep Zepi, or the First Time, an age when sky gods came down to Earth, raised the land up from under mud and water, flew through the air in flying 'boats,' and gave man laws and wisdom through a royal line of pharaohs. It is intriguing to note that these ancient gods displayed very human attributes. They required food and clothing. They liked to imbibe wine and were not above consorting with comely young ladies. Likewise, South American legends tell of the white, bearded 'Viracochas' who lifted indigenous natives out of ignorance and taught them civilization, producing intricate highways and other wonders. They too lived among the native peoples for a time, eating, bathing, and conducting themselves in a very human way."[73]

The notion of extraterrestrial or angelic/supernatural beings consorting with mankind is a disturbing one indeed. Yet, as we have seen, even a casual perusal of the ancient texts of the people of every major continent reveals that this is a prevalent theme. For centuries scholars have either had to take the texts as allegorical myth or as representing some measure of historical fact. In this century the anti-supernatural bias has caused many scholars to favor the former. Yet, studies of ancient mythology have often shown that at their core there is usually a nugget of truth to the myths and legends of old. Moreover, archaeological studies have consistently proven the Bible to be incredibly accurate regarding its historical events. This is confirmed by author Zecharia Sitchen, an expert in Semitic languages who stated,

> "Archeological finds and the deciphering of Sumerian, Babylonian, Assyrian, Hittite, Canaanite and other ancient texts and epic tales increasingly confirm the accuracy of the Biblical references to the kingdoms, cities, rulers, places, temples, trade routes, artifacts, tools, and customs of antiquity."[74]

ANCIENT VISITORS, BUT FROM WHERE?

While the evidence examined in this chapter seems to confirm the antiquity of unusual aerial phenomenon and visitations by unusual humanoid entities, their origin remains a topic of great controversy, even among experienced UFO investigators. The common view is that they are extraterrestrial visitors from another star system. However, the extraterrestrial hypothesis (ETH), has been seriously challenged in recent years by a number of prominent UFO researchers. Well-documented accounts of UFOs that change shape, dematerialize, and defy the laws of physics have challenged the extraterrestrial hypothesis and caused many researchers to speculate that UFOs and their occupants may not be extraterrestrial, but extradimensional beings from beyond the four dimensions of our space-time domain!

Even more important than the question of their origin is that of their purpose for these visitations and their agenda for mankind.

As we will see, an examination of the nature of their contact with mankind and their messages given to human contactees has caused many to suspect that their agenda is indeed sinister and that mankind is being programmed and conditioned for a great deception.

INTERDIMENSIONAL VISITORS

"If UFOs are indeed somebody else's nuts and

bolts hardware, then we must still explain how

such tangible hardware can change shape before

our eyes, vanish in a Cheshire cat manner . . .

seemingly melt away in front of us, or apparently

'materialize' mysteriously before us without

apparent detection by persons nearby or in

neighboring towns. We must wonder, too,

where UFOs are 'hiding' when not manifesting

themselves to human eyes."

J. ALLEN HYNEK, EDGE OF REALITY

THE FIRST WAVE

On June 24, 1947, a 32-year-old businessman and pilot, Kenneth Arnold, was flying his single-engine plane at an altitude of approximately 5,000 feet near the Cascade Mountain Range in Washington State when he saw a blue-white flash in the sky and a chain of nine peculiar aircraft flying at incredible speed. He estimated the speed of the craft to be approximately 1,600 miles per hour, nearly three times faster than any plane in existence at that time. When he landed in Pendleton, Oregon, he was interviewed by a group of reporters about what he had seen. One reporter, Bill Bequette, recorded Arnold's words, "they flew like a saucer would if you skipped it across the water."

The next day the *Seattle Post Intelligencer* newspaper ran the headline, "Mystery Disks Hurdling Across the Sky." *The New York Times* picked up the story and suggested that Arnold had seen nothing more than atoms escaping from an overwrought bomb. Others suggested that he had seen experimental aircraft from the U.S. Government. Arnold's treatment by the media was less than favorable. He was ridiculed for years and eventually he stated that he wouldn't report a "flying ten story building."

THE ROSWELL INCIDENT

Sometime during the first week of July 1947, a local New Mexico rancher, Mac Brazel, while riding out in the morning to check his sheep after a night of intense thunderstorms, discovered a considerable amount of unusual debris.[75] Something had created a shallow gouge several hundred feet long, and debris was scattered over a large area. Some of the debris seemed to have strange physical properties. After taking a few pieces to show his neighbors, Floyd and Loretta Proctor, Brazel drove into Roswell and contacted the sheriff, George Wilcox. Sheriff Wilcox notified authorities at Roswell Army Air Field and with the assistance of his deputies, proceeded to investigate the matter. Shortly after becoming involved, however, the military sealed off the area for a number of days and retrieved all the wreckage. Whatever was found was initially taken to Roswell Army Air Field and eventually flown by B-29 and C-54 aircraft to Wright Field (now Wright Patterson Air Force Base) in Dayton, Ohio.

Roswell Army Air Field was the home of the elite 509th Bomb Group (at the time the only atomic bomb group in the world). On the morning of July 8, 1947, Colonel William Blanchard, Commander of the 509th Bomb Group, issued an official press release stating that the wreckage of a "crashed disk" had been recovered. The press release was transmitted over the wire services in time to make headlines in over 30 U.S. afternoon newspapers that same day.

Within hours, a second press release was issued from the office of General Roger Ramey, Commander of the Eighth Air Force at Fort Worth Army Air Field in Texas, 400 miles from the crash site. This second press release rescinded the first one and, in effect, claimed that Colonel Blanchard and the officers of the 509th Bomb Group at Roswell had made an unbelievably foolish mistake and somehow incorrectly identified "a weather balloon and its radar reflector" as the wreckage of a "crashed disk." With what appears to be a hastily contrived cover story, an extensive cover-up seems to have begun. These events at Roswell, and whatever followed, have been veiled in government secrecy ever since.

The man who issued the first press release, Colonel William Blanchard, would not seem to be someone prone to making mistakes, much less monumental blunders. (He would go on to achieve one of the highest peacetime ranks attainable in the U.S. military, a four-star general and Vice Chief of Staff of the United States Air Force.)

Credible witnesses, including two brigadier generals, have subsequently testified that the original press release issued by Blanchard was correct and that the Roswell wreckage appeared to be a flying disk.

While these events tend to evoke a response of immediate dismissal, the preponderance of subsequent evidence seems to indicate that some very significant event did occur. But what? And why 50 years of government cover-up?

On January 12, 1994, United States Congressman Steven Schiff of Albuquerque, New Mexico, stated to the press that he had been stonewalled by the Defense Department when requesting information regarding the 1947 Roswell event on behalf of constituents and witnesses. Indicating he was seeking further investigation into the matter, Congressman Schiff called the Defense Department's lack of response "astounding" and concluded it was apparently "another government cover-up."

Agencies in which something might be known, including the CIA, have refused to cooperate with investigators. When seeking Roswell or UFO-related documents through the Freedom of Information Act, researchers have been repeatedly stonewalled. Claims are made that documents don't exist or can't be released for national security reasons. (Events of 50 years ago?) The few documents that have been released have often been so blacked out that they are rendered meaningless. On the one hand, numerous government agencies continue to declare that UFOs don't exist, and yet they continue to hide behind "national security" to skirt the Freedom of Information Act and other inquiries. High-level inquiries have revealed that UFOs appear to involve the highest categories of security classifications available.[76] Why?

In October 1969, while Governor of Georgia, Jimmy Carter had reported a UFO sighting. Later, in 1976 as a presidential candidate, he pledged: "If I become president, I'll make every piece of information this country has about UFOs available to the public and the scientists." Yet after Jimmy Carter was elected President, he never said one more word about it publicly after taking office. If he found there was no information to release, why did he not announce it? Doing so would have been a natural and easy way to honor his commitment.

Yet, the detailed public information on the recovery of the wreckage at Roswell and of related events is quite extensive. A number of books, television documentaries, and movies have been made. Some years ago investigators were able to obtain a copy of the 1947 Roswell Army Air Field yearbook, which has enabled them to locate witnesses throughout the country.

The first witness located by investigators who was willing to testify and allow his name to be used was retired Lieutenant Colonel Jesse Marcel, the intelligence officer of the 509th Bomb Group at Roswell. He was one of the first two military officers at the actual crash site. It is hard to believe that someone with his qualifications and experience—the intelligence officer of one of the most elite units in the world—would have mistaken the remains of a weather balloon and its radar reflector for that of a craft that, in his words, was "not of this Earth."

When returning to the base, he stopped by his house with a few pieces of the unusual wreckage to show his wife and 11-year-old son. (His son, Dr. Jesse Marcel, Jr., now a practicing medical doctor, a qualified National Guard helicopter pilot, and a flight surgeon, remembers the incident well.) During his career, Jesse Marcel, Sr., went on to other important assignments, including the preparation of the report on the first Soviet nuclear detonation which went directly to President Truman.

The late General Thomas DuBose was a colonel and General Ramey's chief of staff at Eighth Air Force Headquarters at Fort

Worth, Texas, in 1947. Before his death in 1992, General DuBose testified that he had personally taken the telephone call from General Clements McMullen at Andrews Army Air Field in Washington, D.C., ordering the cover-up. The instructions were for General Ramey to concoct a cover story.

Retired General Arthur E. Exon was stationed at Wright Field in Dayton, Ohio, as a lieutenant colonel in July of 1947 during the time the wreckage from Roswell was brought in. In a 1990 interview, General Exon said of the testing that was done, "The overall consensus was that the pieces were from (outer) space."

According to members of Sheriff Wilcox's family, he was told by the military, in the presence of his wife, that he and his entire family would be killed if he ever spoke about what he had seen. The rancher who originally discovered the wreckage, Mac Brazel, was sequestered by the military for almost a week and sworn to secrecy. He never spoke about the incident again, even to his family. In the months following the incident, his son, Bill Brazel, found and collected a few scraps of material, which he kept in a cigar box. The material was eventually confiscated by the military. (Why, if it was just a weather balloon?)

What really occurred at Roswell remains a mystery. The predictable prejudice against an extraterrestrial incident, along with the fear of ridicule, has been further compounded by frauds, disinformation, and hoaxes.[77] For 50 years, the quiet tensions behind the intimidations, ostensible cover-ups, and ridicule has continued. Wading through the countless documentaries, interviews, etc., and allowing for emotions, exploitations, disinformation—much of it deliberate by the U.S. Government—one can clearly conclude there was, indeed, a cover-up of some kind. But why?

UNCLE SAM TO THE RESCUE?

By the end of 1947, more than 850 sightings of alleged unidentified flying objects had been reported to the U.S. Government. On September 23, 1947, the U.S. Government opened its first official investigation into the UFO phenomenon called "Project Sign." After several months of investigation, officials involved with Project Sign produced a top-secret document called the "Estimate of the Situation." To the dismay of many government officials, the document gave a startling endorsement for the "extraterrestrial hypothesis" for the origin of UFOs. General Hoyt S. Vandenberg, the commanding General of the U.S. Air Force, disagreed with the conclusions of Project Sign and had all copies of the "Estimate of the Situation" destroyed.

On February 11, 1949 Project Sign was replaced by Project Grudge. After examining 244 UFO reports in Europe and in the United States, they prepared a 600-page report which admitted that 56 sightings, or 23 percent of the cases examined, defied explanation. Project Grudge made no conclusions as to the origin of UFO sightings but did acknowledge that visitations by an advanced race of extraterrestrial life forms visiting our planet was a possible explanation. In the opinion of many UFO researchers, Project Grudge was more of a UFO debunking operation than a true investigative body.

In the late 1940s, much to the dismay of government officials, UFO sightings continued unabated with a wave of daytime sightings by military and commercial airline pilots. To pacify the public craving for "official inquiry" into the UFO phenomenon, the government revamped its investigative team into a new undertaking called "Project Bluebook."

Project Bluebook was commanded by Captain Edward J. Ruppelt and was supposed to be a serious attempt at analyzing the UFO phenomenon. Orders were given to every Air

Force group in the world to report local sightings of UFOs. Project Bluebook ended in 1969 after examining over 12,000 reports of UFO sightings worldwide. Investigators of Project Bluebook explained away more than 94 percent of the sightings as natural or man-made phenomena. Weather balloons, aircraft, the planet Venus, plasma discharges, and swamp gas are among the many explanations. However, more than 700 of the sightings investigated by Project Bluebook were never explained and officially categorized as unidentified flying objects. Civilian UFO researchers have arrived at similar numbers.[78] Before they were released to the public in 1969, the files of Project Blue book were "cleaned up," with the more sensitive material removed and sent to other agencies. Thus, in the minds of private researchers they are of limited value in apprehending the true nature of the UFO phenomenon.

THE MEDIA INVASION

In the 1950s public polls revealed that more than 90 percent of the population had heard of flying saucers. While the government remained officially silent on the 700 remaining UFO reports, the public was inundated by opinions in the popular press. UFO magazines, books, and movies promoted the notion that the remaining sightings represented either a secret technology of the United States or the Soviet Union, mass hallucinations, or visitors from another planet.

In the ensuing decades, sightings of metallic craft accelerated into the tens of thousands. The notion of unidentified flying objects and highly advanced extraterrestrial visitors became a media and social phenomenon. The media frenzy was characterized by hundreds of UFO publications and grade-B movies in the 1950s and 1960s.

The TV series *Star Trek* has captivated the world and popularized the notion of alien beings and interstellar travel. Movies such as *Star Wars, Close Encounters of the Third Kind, E.T.,* and most recently *Independence Day* and *First Contact,* have bolstered the notion of alien beings on distant planets and their Earthly visitation in fantastic ships as a reality in the minds of hundreds of millions of people worldwide.

As of this writing, three of the top five movies in history are based on the theme of extraterrestrials and UFOs. Every month there are dozens of television programs based on the UFO theme.

Movie	Released	Gross Receipts
1 *Star Wars*	1977	$610,500,135*
2 *E.T.*	1982	$414,305,221
3 *Jurassic Park*	1993	$244,345,630
4 *Return of the Jedi*	1983	$264,793,817
5 *Home Alone*	1990	$215,428,152

*INCLUDES 1997 RE-RELEASE FIGURES

The news media, museums, toy manufacturers, fast-food restaurants, and even children's textbooks promote the notion of extraterrestrial life and UFO visitations. Even though they haven't landed on the White House lawn, we are truly in the midst of a cultural alien invasion.

THE SECOND WAVE

In the early 1950s a second wave of UFOs began to sweep across the United States. On May 11, 1950, Paul Trent, a farmer in McNinnville, Oregon, saw a spectacular metallic disk floating silently over his farmland. Trent grabbed his camera and took two grainy black-and-white photographs of the object described as a flying saucer. These were the first photographs ever taken of an object described as a "flying saucer."

They were published in newspapers around the world. These pictures have been scrutinized in detail and have never been dismissed as fraudulent by Air Force officials. In the minds of many, the reality of UFOs had finally been established with this pair of grainy photographs.

In March 1950, Navy Commander R. McLaughlin published an article in *True Magazine* describing how scientists had tracked a silvery saucer-like object traveling at an overhead speed of 25,200 miles per hour near the White Sands Missile Range in New Mexico. This was a startling report because no physical object could travel at such speeds without burning up in the atmosphere.

"TAKE US TO YOUR LEADER"

The most startling UFO event of the 1950s occurred over the air space of Washington, D.C., in 1952. On July 19 at 11:40 P.M., seven UFOs were picked up on the long-range radar at the Air Route Traffic Control (ARTC) used for all air traffic around Washington D.C., as well as the short-range radar at the Washington National Airport. The encounter was fully documented by Edward J. Ruppelt, the director of Project Bluebook.[79]

According to Ruppelt's account, the UFOs were only a few miles southeast of Andrews Air Force Base and were initially traveling at a speed of 100 to 130 miles per hour. The UFOs were examined on the radarscope by four controllers including the senior air traffic controller on duty that night. Shortly after detection, two of the objects streaked away at approximately 7,000 miles per hour! The senior controller immediately called the main control tower at the Washington National Airport as well as controllers at Andrews Air Force Base. Air traffic controllers at both sites confirmed not only the existence of the UFOs, but their rapid disappearance as well.

Several times throughout the night commercial pilots confirmed the targets as "unusual lights." Shortly after midnight, the pilot of a Capital Airlines flight reported a fast-streaking UFO off the right side of the plane. It too was detected on radar. Over a period of 14 minutes the pilot reported six additional sightings. At one point the pilot reported that they were following him at "eight o'clock level."

The following weekend, on July 26 at 10:30 P.M. controllers at the Washington National Airport detected slow-moving unidentified targets traveling in an arc from Herndon, Virginia, toward Andrews Air Force Base. Controllers at ARTC detected the UFOs on their short-range scopes as well.

One hour later, at 11:30 P.M., officials at nearby New Castle County Air Force Base in Delaware dispatched two F-94 jet interceptors. Civilian air traffic was told to clear the area. When the jets began their intercept of the UFOs the targets disappeared from radar. The jet pilots never made visual contact with the UFOs and returned to base. However, visual contact was made by numerous witnesses on the ground who began to call nearby Langley Air Force Base to report the mysterious light that was "rotating and giving off strange colors." Moments later, controllers at Langley tower sighted the object and called the Air Defense Command, who scrambled another F-94 interceptor. This time the pilot made visual contact. However, when the pilot approached the object, it vanished!

Additional F-94 interceptors were directed toward another set of UFOs, and the pilots made visual contact. Each time the pilots approached the objects, they sped away. Eventually one of the UFOs did remain stationary. However, when one of the pilots approached the object, he found himself surrounded by the UFOs. Then while the pilot radioed to ask whether he should open fire on the unidentified flying objects, the UFOs instantaneously disappeared from sight and radar.

During his analysis, Rupelt researched the question of whether or not the radar signals could have been due to weather anomalies such as a temperature inversion. While such anomalies can cause a radar blip, the controllers at Langley, Washington National, and Andrews were convinced that the objects they detected showed a distinct radar pattern of solid, metallic objects. In addition, there were visual confirmations on the ground by civilian and military personnel.

Confirming reports from hundreds of witnesses tied up phone lines at the Pentagon and Project Bluebook for days. The story also generated newspaper headlines around the country.

Three days later, on July 29, the Pentagon held a press conference with Major General John A. Samford, the chief of Air Force intelligence, presiding. In the 80-minute briefing before a full room of reporters, the General stated that he believed UFOs did not pose a threat to the security to the United States and that the Air Force had nothing in its arsenal capable of the unlimited speed and massless behavior that UFOs often exhibit. Much of the news conference was spent trying to explain away the Washington, D.C., fly-overs as a weather anomaly.

However, neither Major Dewey Fournet, the Pentagon's liaison, nor the Navy radar specialist who were in the control room when the events occurred were at the Pentagon briefing. Both of these men rejected the weather anomaly hypothesis. These men were convinced that what they had tracked were metallic craft which traveled at speeds impossible for any man-made object at that time, objects which vanished instantaneously while under close observation.

In a fascinating postscript to this story, Jacques Vallee points out that "when the abnormal [radar] returns showed up on the screens an officer ordered two men to go out and with a camera to take pictures of the source. They soon came back, the photos were developed on the spot and they were immediately confiscated. All men in the room were told to remain silent and never to mention the photographs, which showed perfectly clear luminous objects."[80]

UFO REALITY

The physical effects of UFOs have been well-documented by government and civilian investigators. In many cases, alleged landing sites have revealed deep depressions and scorch marks on the ground. Plant material is often killed in direct proportion to the distance from the center of the landing site. Increased radioactivity at alleged landing sites has also been observed in numerous cases.[81]

The effects of UFO landings are confirmed by Weldon and Levitt:

> ". . . That UFOs occasionally land on the ground is lent credence by the indentations that have been found at possible land sites. A strange residue may be left on the ground, later to vanish. In rare instances, cows and smaller animals have been found at these places—mutilated or cut completely in two."[82]

During the time of an actual UFO encounter, a number of unusual physical phenomena have also been recorded. In a number of cases electronic appliances have been disrupted and gasoline engines shut down. Interference with radio and television reception and detection of pulsed electromagnetic discharges have also occurred. Surges of microwave and ultraviolet radiation have been recorded, and witnesses who have experienced close encounters have even been burned by intense ultraviolet radiation emitted by lights aboard a UFO. And, a curious aspect of the UFO phenomenon is that radar often detects UFOs on every other pulse.

Among the thousands of cases of UFOs reported in the last 50 years, more than 700 of the cases have been reported by experienced airline and military pilots. The reliability of such witnesses and the physical evidence left at landing sites are powerful indicators to many investigators that the phenomena are real.

One of the preeminent researchers of the UFO phenomenon was the late Dr. J. Allen Hynek, Chairman of the Northwestern University Department of Astronomy. Hynek was a skeptic regarding the existence of UFOs when he was commissioned by the U.S. Government to be the chief scientific advisor to Project Bluebook in 1952. During his time with this investigative body, Hynek examined thousands of cases of UFOs and alleged human contact with extraterrestrial beings. He amassed a library of such reports which has yet to be surpassed.

In his 1972 book, *The UFO Experience: A Scientific Inquiry,* Dr. Hynek chronicled his experience in UFO research and the data that he had collected. Regarding his attitude towards UFOs he stated:

> "When I first got involved in this field I was particularly skeptical of people who had said that they had seen UFOs on several occasions and totally incredulous about those who said they had been taken aboard one but I have had to change my mind."[83]

Like Hynek, many scientists, once skeptical regarding the existence of UFOs, have changed their minds when they thoroughly examined the evidence.

PROJECT DELTA

In 1994 a report was published by Richard F. Haines, a former NASA research scientist specializing in optics and vision, which documented UFO sightings involving two or more objects seen at the same time.[84] The report, called "Project Delta," relied on well-documented UFO sightings which included multiple objects seen by multiple witnesses. Many of the contemporary sightings were documented by radar contacts and/or photographs.

The study included 473 cases spanning the period from 1504 B.C. to A.D. 1993. This study, done with impressive care and professional skill, clearly indicated that the features of these multiple aerial phenomena have not changed significantly over the years. The report concluded that UFOs are aerospace vehicles of non-terrestrial origin being operated under highly intelligent flight control.

THE SUPERPHYSICS OF UFOS

It is important to point out that the UFO phenomenon is a multifaceted issue. Of the 12,000-plus UFO reports examined by Project Bluebook since the modern era began in 1947, the vast majority were identified as natural or man-made phenomena. In addition, many reports have certainly represented top-secret aircraft, both foreign and domestic. In our examination of the UFO phenomenon, we wish to focus on the truly unidentified accounts for which there is no apparent Earthly explanation.

The evidence examined to this point seems to confirm that UFOs are physical objects. However, additional data suggests that under certain circumstances this may not be the case. For example, UFOs have been tracked on radar traveling at over 25,000 miles per hour within our atmosphere. Yet, unlike physical objects, they do not cause sonic booms and they do not burn up. They have been known to make right-angle turns at over 15,000 miles per hour, something no physical object could endure. And despite visual confirmation, UFOs often fail to show up on photographic film or radar devices.

The bizarre physics of UFOs is further illustrated by the fact that many apparently reliable witnesses, including civilian and military pilots, have seen UFOs materialize and dematerialize instantaneously. This phenomenon was witnessed in the Mexico, Israel, and Arizona sightings in recent months. Furthermore, some have even reported metallic craft that change shape ("morph"), break into multiple objects, or merge into one UFO from multiple—all of this while in flight and on the ground![85]

Anomalies such as these suggest a paradox. While sitting on the ground UFOs betray the evidence of physical objects. Yet, when they are in flight they behave as though they are massless apparitions—in effect, a supernatural phenomenon!

This paradox was noted by engineer James Campbell:

> "Evidence left at landing sights leaves little room that UFOs are heavy, ponderous objects when addressed, yet in flight their startling departures, sudden stops, and right-angle turns at high speed require them to be virtually massless."[86]

In recent decades a number of well-documented, and startling encounters with UFOs have further illustrated the paraphysical nature of UFOs.

THE MYSTERY BALL

On December 17, 1996, scientists from the Atmospheric Sciences Department at Creighton University in Nebraska released video footage of a mysterious spherical object traveling at one one-hundredth the speed of light (1,860 miles per second) about 80 kilometers above the ground in western Kansas.[87] The videotape footage, taken on August 22, 1996, showed the object for about .003 second. In the six-frame sequence, the object can clearly been seen crossing upward and left across the field of view while retaining its shape and intense glow.

The incredible speed and angular momentum of the object was, according to researchers, impossible for a physical object! The object's fantastic flight pattern led Morris B. Pongratz, a scientist at Los Alamos National Laboratory, to state that "it is clearly something that does not have any mass, the angular speed is too fast to be anything at orbital velocity."[88]

After only six video frames, the object disappeared from view and was officially categorized as unidentified. Regarding the footage, Dr. Dean A. Morss, assistant professor of atmospheric sciences at Creighton University, stated, "It's the first and only event of this kind photographed to my knowledge."[89] Morss and his colleagues maintain that the ball's tremendous speed and apparent lack of mass eliminate any of the commonly offered explanations for unknown objects sighted in the atmosphere.

RENDLESHAM FOREST INCIDENT

A well-documented and fascinating UFO encounter occurred on the evenings of December 26 and 27, 1980, at Rendlesham Forest next to the USAF base at Royal Air Force (RAF) Woodbridge in Suffolk, England. According to military eyewitnesses a large, very bright "meteor" fell over the North Sea to the east of Woodbridge at 2:50 A.M. on December 26. Radar operators at RAF Watton in Norfolk registered an "unknown" flying object that moved toward the coast over the North Sea then disappeared in the vicinity of Rendlesham Forest.

Security police at the eastern ("back'") gate of the USAF activity on RAF Woodbridge saw light coming down from the sky into the trees. While approaching, their radios failed. The object would later be described in an official detailed letter by the Deputy Base Commander, Lt Col Charles I. Halt, as "metallic in appearance."[90] It "illuminated the entire forest with a white light" and "had a pulsing red light on top and a bank of blue lights underneath. The object was hovering or on legs." The object maneuvered through the trees and disappeared. It "was briefly sighted approximately an hour later near the back gate."

The next night the UFO was seen again. Lt. Col. Halt was called from a formal dinner and took a team to investigate. Halt tape-recorded his own comments as he and the others watched strange lights darting about. Two elliptical objects joined in the north, another in the south, illuminating the flight line by shining beams down to the ground. They all disappeared before 4:00 A.M. Some days later, USAF intelligence agents arrived at RAF Walton and confiscated the radar tapes.

There are numerous stories, conflicting and unverified, that have come from this incident. One of the more provocative ones involves one of the security policeman. He apparently was one of many in a convoy of both American and British military assembled that night at Rendlesham Forest. The assemblage included gas-powered "light-alls" (trailer-mounted lights used for illuminating large areas), large movie cameras, and helicopters overhead. He described the object at the center of attention as taking the appearance of a transparent aspirin tablet, hovering about one foot off the ground, approximately 50 feet in diameter, with a bright, pulsating, yellow mist inside. He and some others were about ten feet away. He heard a field radio announcement, "Here it comes." A red light appeared and hovered about 20 feet over the aspirin-shaped object and then broke up into a shower of particles. Suddenly, in place of the red light and the aspirin-shaped object, another vehicle appeared. He said it was a domed disk, bright white in color, with an intricately detailed surface.

> "As he and the other men walked around the object they noticed a strange effect. Their own shadows were cast onto the object, apparently from the 'light-alls' in the field. Not only did their

shadows bend upwards at the head, but as they walked and then stopped, the shadows would appear to advance one pace more and then stop. Stunned and disbelieving of this effect, he and the others walked and stopped several times, each time noticing the effect repeat itself. The third time they tried this a light came over the head of a shadow and moved from one head to another."[91]

Later, he and the others would be checked for radiation, debriefed, and cautioned to maintain extreme security. He maintains that versions of the story leaked to British media were deliberately contrived to mislead the public. False evidence was intended to be discovered to discredit and thus preserve secrecy.

THE BELGIAN WAVE

One of the best-documented and most mysterious UFO waves occurred over the skies of Belgium between November 1989 and March 1990. During this period more than 26,000 sightings of triangular-shaped UFOs were noted by civilians, policemen, military personnel, and NATO fighter pilots. During the four-month period a large amount of data was gathered by military police, Air Force officials, and civilian scientists from the Belgian Society for the Study of Space Phenomena, known as (SOBEPS). What is unusual about this wave of UFOs is that for the first time in history government officials, led by the Belgian Minister of Defense, Guy Coeme, authorized government personnel and Air Force officials to fully cooperate with civilian UFO researchers.

According to SOBEPS files, the first sightings occurred on the night of November 7, 1989, when two military policemen from Esneux observed a giant craft hovering silently with two powerful lights directed downward at the ground. On November 15, 1989, police officer Frances Michalczyk saw another large triangular craft floating silently over the village of Ans. On November 29, 1989, 41 eyewitnesses, including six military police officials, observed a huge triangular craft hovering over the village of Upen, Verviers, and numerous other locations in Wallonia near the German border.

The Belgian wave climaxed on the night of March 30 and 31 of 1990, when numerous unidentified flying objects were tracked by two NATO radar installations at Glons located southeast of Brussels and a second at Semmerzake west of Brussels. A report of the incident, prepared by Air Force Major P. Lambrechts of the Air Force General's Staff in Brussels, contains startling details of the nature of these triangular UFOs in flight. The report entitled "Concerning the Observation of UFOs During the Night of March 30–31, 1990" included a detailed chronology of events as well as numerous eyewitness descriptions from several military police and maps of where the various sightings took place.[92]

At 2250 hours controllers at the Glons radar installation received a phone call from military policemen who reported three unusual lights which formed an equilateral triangle near his house in Ramillies. Over the next two and one-half hours, numerous military police and other witnesses continued to observe triangular objects performing strange maneuvers at the outskirts of Brussels.

At 2349 hours the radar screens as Semmerzake confirmed the targets, and an order was given to scramble two F-16 fighter aircraft at 2356 hours. According to official Air Force records released to the public, the aircraft had brief radar contact on several occasions with the unidentified craft. During the first radar lock on at 0013 hours the speed of the target changed from 150 to 970 nautical miles per hour (a nautical mile is 6,080.2 feet) in only a few seconds. The craft also descended from an altitude of 9,000 to 5,000 feet in a matter of seconds.

At one point the objects were tracked on radar changing from 280 kilometers per hour to 1,800 kilometers per hour while descending from 3,000 to 1,000 meters altitude in one second. This represents an acceleration equivalent to 40 Gs. A human being can stand only 8 Gs in a G suit without blacking out. (A "G" is unit of acceleration equivalent to the gravitational pull of the Earth, 9.81 meters per second per second.) This behavior ruled out any human pilot on board the UFO. At one point, radar tracking equipment indicated that the UFO dipped below ground level and re-emerged above ground only a few seconds later, an accomplishment which is obviously impossible for a physical ship!

The F-16s were unable to engage the object because of a flying limitation of 1,300 kilometers per hour at 1,000 meters altitude. For over an hour the F-16 interceptors successfully locked on radar contact. However, each time they subsequently lost radar contact with the UFOs. Furthermore, despite flying significantly faster than the speed of sound the UFO craft never generated a sonic boom. During the radar tracking the UFO was seen to break into four separate parts and disappear in four different directions!

During the Belgium wave, a number of astonishing observations were made. Numerous witnesses reported seeing the triangular craft change shape before their very eyes. Others reported seeing the craft materialize and dematerialize in the presence of numerous witnesses.

The event was summarized by August Meessen, professor of physics at the Catholic University at Louvain:

> "There are too many independent eyewitness reports to ignore, too many of the reports describe coherent physical effects, and there is an agreement among the accounts concerning what

was observed. If all of the witnesses are lying, then it is a mental disease of such novelty and proportions that it must be studied."[93]

FROM THE FILES OF BLUEBOOK

During almost two decades of research, Project Bluebook examined more than 700 cases of UFOs that could not be explained. Among them were a number of UFO cases during which the "craft" exhibited the kind of superphysics we have just examined. The following is a partial list of the unexplained encounters:

•October 15, 1950, Oak Ridge, Tennessee, 3:20 P.M. Atomic Energy Commission troopers Rymer, J. Moneymaker, and Capt. Zarzecki observed two shiny silver objects shaped like a bullet or bladder. After observing them for several minutes, the objects dove with a smoke trail and one of the craft vanished before their eyes. The other hovered at five to six feet above ground, about 50 feet away, turned left, and returned several times during the encounter.

•February 27, 1953, Shreveport, Louisiana, 11:58 A.M. A United States Air Force airman/private pilot (name withheld by Bluebook) observed five yellow disks making circular turns in the sky. Under observance, three of the objects dematerialized and vanished, the other two flew erratically making right-angle turns for a total of 4 minutes, then flew away.

•November 26, 1957, Robins AFB, Georgia, 10:07 AM. Three control tower operators at Robins Air Force Base, one weather observer, and four other military personnel observed a single silvery metallic cigar-shaped object hovering near the base. After observing the object for eight about minutes, it suddenly dematerialized and vanished from sight.

•June 27, 1952, Topeka, Kansas, 6:50 P.M. On this evening a United States Air Force pilot Second Lt. K. P. Kelly and his wife saw a single spherical, pulsating red object floating stationary. Then it changed shape from spherical to a vertical oval. The sighting lasted for about five minutes.

THE CHRONICLES OF VALLEE

Sightings of metallic flying craft that dematerialize, change shape, and perform aerial feats impossible for a physical craft are abundant in the chronicles of civilian researchers as well. One of the largest collections of such encounters belongs to Jacques Vallee. Vallee is one of the few researchers who has had uncensored access to the files of Project Bluebook and is frequently sought to investigate unusual UFO encounters. In addition, in the 1960s and 1970s Vallee worked closely with the late Dr. J. Allen Hynek and had open access to his voluminous database.

During over four decades of UFO research he has personally interviewed thousands of eyewitnesses.[94] Because of their long history of unparalleled access to UFO and alleged abductee material, Hynek and Vallee are considered by many to be the "fathers" of the field of ufology. In the files of Vallee and Hynek are some of the best-documented cases of UFOs which defy conventional physical explanations.

CASE 1: THE VALENSOLE FARMER[95]

On July 1, 1965, in the city of Valensole, France, a farmer named Maurice Masse heard an unusual noise when he arrived in his field at 6:00 A.M. When he walked toward the noise, he saw a machine that had landed in his field. His initial impression was that it was some sort of prototype or experimental aircraft. However, when he approached the machine, at a distance of approximately 20 feet, he saw an egg-shaped craft no bigger than a car. In front were two pilots dressed in gray-greenish suits. They were humanoid in form, with very large heads, about four feet tall, and having only a very small slit with no lips for a mouth. They wore no helmets and seemed to breathe our air without difficulty.

When the "pilots" saw Masse, they took a small tube from its container and pointed it at him. He immediately found himself on the ground unable to move. A few moments later the creatures went into their craft. The craft rose above the ground and accelerated away rapidly. When the ship was about 60 yards away, Masse stated, it vanished. Questioned closely by investigators on this point, Masse made it quite clear. The craft did not streak away: "One moment, the thing was there, and the next moment, it was not there anymore." Masse remained alone in his field, paralyzed for about 20 minutes. For several weeks his relatives and friends reported that he was extremely drowsy, finding it very difficult to stay awake for over four hours.

The significance of this story is that it is representative of hundreds of cases in the files of experienced UFO investigators. Masse was not an eccentric. He was a well-respected pillar of his community and a former resistance fighter in the war. And yet, he encountered something that can only be described as impossible.

Encounters such as these are usually single-witness cases and draw considerable skepticism by authorities and the general public. However, similar cases have been witnessed by numerous unrelated witnesses.

CASE 2: JALAPA, MEXICO

In the sleepy town of Jalapa, Mexico, early in the month of September 1965, numerous witnesses saw a luminous, hovering oval object with slits along its entire circumference. Near the craft they saw an unusual "black clad being," holding a shining metal rod, with eyes that gleamed like a cat's eyes.

While under observation by a local reporter, two taxi drivers, and a bullfighter, the craft suddenly vanished.[96]

As discussed in the first chapter, since the Mexico UFO wave started in 1991 a number of UFOs have been observed to instantaneously materialize and dematerialize. According to Brit Elders, researchers in Mexico have utilized sophisticated equipment to analyze more than a thousand videotapes of UFOs seen over Mexico since July, 1991. On numerous occasions they have documented that UFOs have materialized and dematerialized in one-30th of a second, or one frame of videotape!

> ". . . Utilizing an Inovian PTS3, which was specifically designed to analyze raw video data and is used for such by the Department of Defense, we have been able to determine that the objects have the ability to materialize or dematerialize in one frame of video, which is one-30th of a second. We have also learned that they appear to be solid objects, highly reflective, which are some distance from the camera lens. The objects that were analyzed do not exhibit the normal flight behavior of aircraft or balloons. In short, they defy physics as we understand the term."[97]

Regarding the superphysics of such sightings, Jacques Vallee stated:

> "Consider what these sightings have in common. In each case the so-called spacecraft did not disappear by moving away, even at high speed. It simply vanished on the spot, or it slowly faded away like the Cheshire cat, sometimes leaving behind a whitish cloud, sometimes also producing the sound of an explosion. In other cases, UFOs have been reported to enter the ground. I hardly

need to point out that this behavior is contrary to what physical objects do and quite impossible to duplicate with our current spacecraft technology."[98]

The notion that UFOs are metallic, manufactured craft has also been challenged by their ability to change shape while in flight or on the ground. After two decades of examining hundreds of such accounts, in 1975 J. Allen Hynek also mused about the peculiar physics of UFOs:

> "If UFOs are indeed somebody else's nuts and bolts hardware, then we must still explain how such tangible hardware can change shape before our eyes, vanish in a Cheshire cat manner . . . seemingly melt away in front of us, or apparently 'materialize' mysteriously before us without apparent detection by persons nearby or in neighboring towns. We must wonder, too, where UFOs are 'hiding' when not manifesting themselves to human eyes."[99]

In 1976 Hynek added to the discussion the remarkable ability of UFOs to merge into a single object.

> ". . . Another peculiarity is the alleged ability of certain UFOs to dematerialize. . . . There are quite a few reported instances where two distinctly different UFOs hovering in a clear sky will converge and eventually merge into one object. . . ."[100]

John Keel has also been impressed by the super-physics of UFOs. He has examined thousands of UFO sightings and has amassed a large library of accounts where UFOs perform aerial acrobatics impossible for a physical object, as well as their ability to materialize, dematerialize, and instantaneously change into a myriad of shapes. In his book *Operation Trojan Horse,* he offers an answer to Hynek's question about the nature of UFOs.

"The statistical data which I have extricated indicate that flying saucers are not stable machines requiring fuel, maintenance, or logistical support. They are, in all probability, transmogrifications of energy and do not exist in the same way that this book exists. They are not permanent construction of matter"[101]

By "transmogrifications of energy" Keel means that they are concentrations of energy that have the ability to change shape. This is, of course, beyond the capability of a metallic, physical entity and suggests that UFOs are "paraphysical." Put another way, UFOs behave as both natural and supernatural phenomenon!

In an article in the international UFO journal, *Flying Saucer Review*, Physicist Jacques Lematre suggests that UFOs may not travel by conventional means in our space-time domain:

"We can consequently conclude that it is impossible to interpret the UFO phenomenon in terms of material spaceships as we conceive of the latter, i.e. in terms of manufactured, self propelled machines retaining their material nature and their mechanical structure to travel from one solar system to another by traversing the distance separating these systems in the Einsteinian Continuum."[102]

THE INTERDIMENSIONAL THEORY

While the vast majority (more than 90 percent) of UFO sightings can be explained by natural and man-made phenomena, the chronicles of Bluebook, Vallee, Hynek, and dozens of international civilian UFO research teams are replete with sightings, such as those just examined, which defy any physical or "natural" explanation.

The ability of UFOs to dematerialize, travel at speeds which cause ordinary matter to disintegrate, and their extraordinary capacity to perform right-angle turns at unimaginable speeds strongly suggests that UFOs and their humanoid "pilots" are not simply physical entities confined to our three dimensions of space-time.

However, if they are not "permanent constructions of matter," if they are not "manufactured, self-propelled" "nuts-and-bolts" ships which travel by conventional means through our universe's "Einsteinian continuum," then what are they and how do they travel from one solar system to another? What framework can we employ to understand the UFO phenomenon?

As we approach the end of the 20th century, radical new theories about the nature of our universe and the behavior of UFOs have suggested to many researchers that UFOs and their humanoid counterparts emerge from a dimensional reality beyond our space-time domain. With such a framework, UFOs can be viewed as an interdimensional phenomenon that can materialize and interact with us within our space-time domain. Then, with equal facility these entities simply vanish into unseen and unrecognized dimensions beyond our three-dimensional space-time domain.

After rejecting the extraterrestrial hypothesis as too simplistic, Jacques Vallee offers an alternative explanation:

> "If they are not space craft, what else could UFOs be? What research framework can account for the physical effects, for the impact on society, for the appearance of the occupants, and for the seemingly absurd, dreamlike elements of their behavior? How can we explain that the phenomenon makes itself obvious to rural populations but avoids overt contact, choosing instead to

deliver its message in bizarre abductions, in highly strange incidents? The theory that suggests itself, as we analyze and re-analyze the forces at play, goes beyond the notion that these are simply technological vehicles produced by an advanced race on another planet. Instead I believe that the UFO phenomenon represents evidence for other dimensions beyond space-time; the UFOs may not come from ordinary space but from a multiverse which is all around us, and of which we have stubbornly refused to consider the disturbing reality in spite of the evidence available to us for centuries. Such a theory is required in order to explain both the modern cases and the chronicles of Magonia—the abductions and the psychic component. I believe that there is a system around us that transcends time and it transcends space. Other researchers have reached the same conclusion."[103]

It is this multiverse that we examine next.

CHAPTER FOUR

REALITY'S TWILIGHT ZONE

"Anyone who is not shocked by quantum theory does not understand it."

NIELS BOHR

INTERGALACTIC VISITORS?

The commonly held assumption that the "aliens" inhabiting the UFOs are visitors from another galaxy, routinely traveling millions of miles for brief, spasmodic, encounters, has increasingly been doubted by the most serious investigators. Their typical objections to the "intergalactic traveler" theories derive from applying basic astrophysical assumptions. Traveling at a million miles per day from even our nearest star, Alpha Centari, would entail a trip that would take 70,000 years to accomplish. Furthermore, where are they in the meantime, between encounters? And, why don't we observe them en route?

The problems facing conventional conceptions of space travel include the limitations deriving from the velocity of light as well as the enormous supply of energy required. However, the objections advanced to interstellar travel may also prove to be naive. Two provocative alternatives have been suggested.

"WORMHOLES" AS SHORTCUTS

Mathematical subtleties in theoretical physics have suggested the possibility of exploiting deformations in the four-dimensional space-time which are known as transversible wormholes. A traversible wormhole could be a shortcut through both space and time.[104]

When Charles L. Dodgson, while teaching mathematics at Oxford, but writing as "Lewis Carroll," had Alice go through the looking glass, or fall down a rabbit hole, he was exploiting the wormhole concepts he had gleaned from Georg Riemann's advanced geometry. (We'll explore this shortly.)

There are some who believe that—theoretically—even time travel could be possible. In 1988, Kip Thorne and Michael Morris of the California Institute of Technology and Ulvi Yurtsever at the University of Michigan suggested that since these wormholes could connect regions that exist in different time periods, perhaps some form of time travel might eventually prove possible. (Not to change the past, but perhaps to fulfill the past. We'll explore this in chapter 14.)

DARK MATTER AS A FUEL SOURCE

It may come as a surprise to learn that most matter in the universe seems to be missing. More than 90 percent of the matter in our universe is known as "dark matter." Its gravitational effects are discernable, but it has yet to be directly observed by conventional methods employing photons of electromagnetic radiation—hence its name. Dark matter has been the subject of many conjectures and associated searches, but no one has resolved this elusive mystery. Dark matter has yet to be observed, and so its properties remain unknown.

Some mathematical conjectures about exotic forms of dark matter suggest that it could have properties that might be exploited in some form of highly advanced propulsion system. If dark matter could be exploited, it would be very fortuitous since it is so prevalent throughout the universe.

None of these speculative possibilities have any experimental confirmations and thus constitute major controversies among theoretical physicists, astrophysicists, and cosmologists. There is little credibility among serious researchers that these exotic conjectures hold the key to the UFO phenomena.

INTERDIMENSIONAL?

It has been suggested by some of the most knowledgeable observers that the apparent ability of the UFOs to materialize and dematerialize seems to suggest that they are "hyperdimensional" or from some other domain, able to enter and leave our space-time at will. While this sounds like a contrivance of some science fiction novel, this could be surprisingly consistent with current discoveries from the field of quantum physics.

You and I have come to understand that we live in three spatial dimensions—length, width, and height—along with a strange fourth temporal dimension we call time. Particle physicists have now discovered that we apparently live in a universe of ten dimensions.[105] It may well be that an understanding of spaces beyond the three dimensions with which we are familiar may hold the key to understanding the strange phenomena being observed with UFOs.

HYPERSPACE

Spaces with more than three spatial dimensions are called "hyperspaces." (For purposes of the following discussion, we are going to set aside time as our "fourth" dimension and confine our discussion to only spatial dimensions.)

It is extremely difficult for the average person to visualize a space of more than three dimensions, since that is the only spatial geometry with which we have had any personal experience. There are only two kinds of people that seem to be able to deal with hyperspaces: mathematicians with special training and small children. We are quite likely to miss entirely the implications and significance of higher dimensions when trying to translate them into our own three-dimensional terms. One approach to better understand some of the implications of our own dimensionality is to direct our attention "downward" rather than "upward." Let's explore the plight of a two-dimensional being living in a two-dimensional world.

FLATLAND

Imagine a universe of only two dimensions: a flat plane. This imaginary universe is inhabited only by two-dimensional beings—we'll call them Mr. and Mrs. Flat. They can only conceive of two dimensions since that is all they are capable of experiencing directly.[106]

Suppose a three-dimensional being comes along and pokes his finger into their two-dimensional space. What would Mr. and Mrs. Flat see?

The intersection of the three-dimensional finger into the plane of their existence would appear to them as a circle. That is *all* that would appear to them in the limitations of their two-dimensional world. The finger would seem to emerge from nowhere and would not be understood. And while intruding into their two-dimensional space, it could interfere with their freedoms and perceptions.

This three-dimensional "super being," possessing simply an additional dimension beyond Mr. and Mrs. Flat's, would enjoy remarkable advantages. The being, for instance, could easily enjoy a proximity with them independent of their own geographic placement within their known universe. The being could also remove or relocate either of them beyond the rules of their own geometry. Such a being would have capabilities totally beyond their comprehension.

Imagine a sphere of three dimensions passing through their two-dimensional universe. It would also seem to appear out of nowhere and then disappear in the same manner.

Perhaps even more puzzling to Mr. and Mrs. Flat would be a more complex geometrical object passing through their two-dimensional universe. The object would also continually change shape as it entered or withdrew from their universe.

Attempts to communicate the existence of a three-dimensional object to Mr. and Mrs. Flat would prove extremely difficult. One approach would be to "unravel" a template of the cube into a two-dimensional representation:

Even this would require visualization on their part beyond any of their experience or conceptual skills. It is just as difficult for us to visualize a four-dimensional object within our three-dimensional space. An example of such an object is a hypercube, a "cube" in four (mutually orthogonal) dimensions. It takes very special skills to deal with such an object. However, just

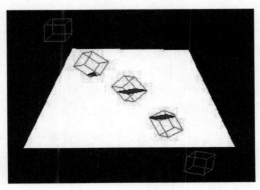

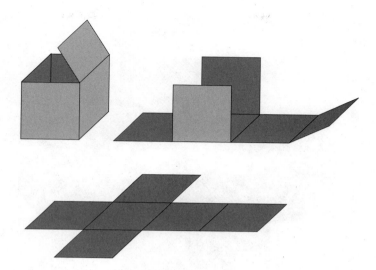

as a three-dimensional cube can be rendered into an "unfolded" version on flat two-dimensional surface, the four-dimensional hypercube can likewise be represented in three dimensions. These "unraveled" hypercubes are called Hinton cubes, or tesseracts.

Salvador Dali's unusual rendering of the crucifixion, "Christus Hypercubus," employs a tesseract to convey a four-dimensional aspect for this unique event.

Our recent advances in modern physics depend heavily upon the realization of even more complex hyperspaces. Scientists universally believe that the universe must eventually wind down and ultimately suffer a "heat death." It has been even suggested that the only hope for intelligent life to escape the final collapse will be by fleeing into hyperspace. (It may be that this could happen sooner than they realize!)

MATRICULATION TO
HIGHER DIMENSIONS

How many total degrees are there among the three angles in a triangle? The anticipated answer is 180 degrees.

Suppose a couple of us go out to a very large field and lay out an unusually large triangle. When we survey it, we discover that the angles total 200 degrees. What would you conclude? That we *erred* might be the anticipated answer!

Not necessarily. We may simply have encountered the curvature of the Earth. The 180-degree rule we all learned in school applies only to a universe of two dimensions: plane trigonometry. If you take a course in navigation, you will encounter spherical trigonometry. In three dimensions, such as on a sphere, one can encounter triangles with more than 180 degrees. The ostensible violation of our traditional rule is a hint of an additional dimension at work.[107]

This was the type of insight that came to Dr. Albert Einstein as he grappled with the problems of space and time and ultimately recognized that we live in more than three dimensions. The realization that time is an additional physical dimension led to his famed theory of relativity. (Incidentally, this theory was confirmed to 14 decimal places in 1993.[108])

However, the mathematical ability to deal with a hyperspace of more than three dimensions had been established 60 years earlier.

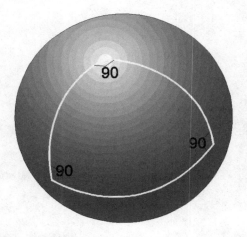

BEYOND EUCLID

After the Bible, Euclid's *Elements* was probably the most influential book of all time. For over 2,000 years, the keenest minds of Western civilization have marveled at the elegance of its basic geometry. We all have wrestled with Euclid's theorems, the value of and its relationship with a circle, the degrees in a triangle, etc.

On June 10, 1854, the most important lecture in the history of mathematics was given at the University of Göttingen, Germany. Georg Bernhard Riemann was the son of a Lutheran pastor, an intense Bible student, and had been mentored by Carl Friedrich Gauss, the "prince of mathematics." In one masterful stroke Riemann uncovered the mathematical foundation of geometries of higher dimensional space and thus opened the door to modern physics. Riemann recognized that "forces" were a consequence of a distortion of geometry and presented his metric tensors as a technique of dealing with them.

THE SEARCH FOR PHYSICAL REALITY

Progress in our physical understanding of the universe has been dramatic in many respects, but has remained segmented into fragments which have eluded being synthesized into a composite whole. There are four basic forces in nature, and they account for all the dynamics observed throughout our physical universe. They are gravity, the electromagnetic force, and the "strong" and "weak" nuclear forces.

Gravity causes an apple to fall to the ground, keeps our feet on the floor, and binds our solar system together. It keeps Earth and the planets in their orbits, prevents the stars from exploding, and guides the galaxies in their motions.

The electromagnetic force holds the atom together and determines the structure of the orbits of the electrons. Thus it governs the laws of chemistry and molecular formations. Its various forms include x-rays, radio waves, and light. The electromagnetic force can also overcome gravity on Earth and reduce the other forces to about the size of the nucleus of the atom. That's where two other forces take over.

The "strong" nuclear force binds together the protons and neutrons in the nucleus of the atom. The balance between the strong force and electromagnetic force limit a nucleus to about 100 protons. The energy released by the strong nuclear force is substantially greater than the electromagnetic (chemical) force. The explosion from atoms being split apart is substantially greater than one from chemical explosives. Thus the strong force causes the stars to shine and the sun to warm our Earth; it, too, is essential for life.

The "weak" nuclear force governs atomic instability and radioactivity. This is the force that causes the disintegration of heavier nuclei. This force can create heat, such as the decay of radioactive elements in Earth's core and in a nuclear power plant.

Michael Faraday introduced electrical and magnetic fields, and James Clerk Maxwell established their classic equations in the 1860s. In 1915 Einstein discovered the field equations for gravity. Finally, in the 1970s, relying on the earlier work of C. N. Yang and R. L. Mills, the field equations for subatomic forces were established (now called Yang-Mills fields).

Within six decades of Riemann's pivotal lecture, Einstein would use four-dimensional Riemannian geometry for his famed theory of relativity. Within seven decades, Theodr Kaluza at the University of Königsberg, Germany, would use five-dimensional Riemannian geometry to integrate both gravity and light. Light is now viewed as a vibration in the fifth dimension. Oskar Klein made several improvements, including the calculation of the size of the fifth dimension—the Planck length, 10^{-33} centimeters—much too small to detect experimentally. 130 years after Riemann's famous lecture, physicists would extend the Kaluza-Klein constructs to develop ten-dimensional geometry in their attempt to unite all the laws of the physical universe.[109]

Restricted to three or four dimensions and trapped by common sense, the field equations of these various forces eluded unification into a single view. We since have discovered that Einstein's gravity fields, Maxwell's fields, and the Yang-Mills fields can all be unified in hyperspaces. We have also discovered that the laws of nature become simpler and more elegant when expressed in higher dimensions.

SUPERSTRINGS

In 1984 Michael Green of Queen Mary's College in London and John Schwarz of the California Institute of Technology developed a more advanced version of the Kaluza-Klein theory. This advanced version was called "superstrings," in which all matter consists of tiny vibrating strings. "Strings" are one-dimensional line elements that vibrate or resonate in multiple spatial dimensions. All matter is composed of nothing but the harmonies created by a vibrating string. Each mode of vibration represents a distinct resonance or particle. The smallest vibration of the closed string is the graviton, the quantum of gravity.

Our universe is now viewed as being made up of ten dimensions.[110] Four of the dimensions are directly measurable, but six of them are "curled" into the Planck length, less than 10^{-33} cm., and thus are discernable only by indirect means.[111]

OBJECTS OR "WINDOWS"?

The reports that some of the UFO encounters involved their apparent materializing and dematerializing within our three-dimensional space has suggested to some sophisticated observers that they might be from another universe that is parallel—or more precisely, *orthogonal*—to our own.

Jacques Vallee, regarded by most as one of the most knowledgeable of the UFO researchers, summarizes his own speculations as follows:

> "Are we dealing instead with a parallel universe, where there are human races living, and where we may go at our expense, never to return to the present? . . . From that mysterious universe, have objects that can materialize and 'dematerialize' at will been projected? Are the UFOs 'windows'

rather than 'objects'? There is nothing to support these assumptions, and yet, in view of the historical continuity of the phenomenon, alternatives are hard to find, unless we deny the reality of all the facts, as our peace of mind would indeed prefer."[112]

The more one traffics in the current literature of advanced physics, the less strange the reported behavior of the UFOs appear. In fact, they may prove to be the very empirical verification that has been lacking. Even as this book goes to press, recent experiments with advanced colliders are apparently still overturning previous presumptions about the "Standard Model" of physical reality.[113]

So, despite their apparent ability to materialize and dematerialize, UFOs seem difficult to dismiss. They show up on multiple, simultaneous radars; leave physical traces, radiation, burns, etc.; and yet they often seem to change shape and then disappear without a trace. (An example of one recorded visitor who actually demonstrated his unusual hyperdimensional abilities will be discussed in chapter 14.)

Despite the many spurious or doubtful reports, hoaxes, disinformation, etc., there are too many competent, professionally trained observers on record to dismiss. What is really going on? Are there really sentient beings interacting with our space-time? If so, what is their agenda? Are they hostile, friendly, or manipulative? Or, is this all some kind of delusion? If so, it appears to be orchestrated to some end. Why, and to what end? Is it possible that we as a culture are being set up? If so, why?

There is increasing evidence that there *are* sentient beings interacting with our space-time and that they *do* have an agenda! We appear to be the subjects of a major cosmic deception. Let's examine our entire predicament more carefully. Our individual personal destinies may depend upon our diligence.

ALIEN CONTACT?

"The folklore of every culture, it turned out,

had a rich reservoir of stories about humanoid

beings that flew in the sky, used devices that seemed

in advance of the technology of the time, and said

strangely beautiful, although absurd, things to

those with whom they came in contact. These

beings abducted humans, and their victims

uniformly reported an alteration of the sense of

time when they were in the beings' company."

JACQUES VALLEE, *PASSPORT TO MAGONIA*, VII

To most of us the notion of extraterrestrial entities abducting human beings against their will is unfathomable. Verification of such occurrences would be a shattering blow to our prevailing notions of reality. Yet, when we examine the record of history and the contemporary UFO phenomenon, we find an abundance of such accounts.

In his book *Passport to Magonia,* Jacques Vallee examines the ancient folklore of mankind and finds that throughout history, in nearly every culture, mankind recorded stories of beings who flew in the sky, abducted, and even interbred with human beings! For most of us there is a tendency to dismiss such folklore, yet the stories of ancient times closely parallel the alleged encounters that have accelerated in the last half of the 20th century.

In previous chapters we have examined evidence which points to an interdimensional solution to the UFO phenomenon. The alleged abduction of human beings by alien entities is but another piece of the puzzle of this phenomenon.

M.I.T. CONFERENCE

In the 1950s the first modern accounts of alleged alien abductions were reported publicly and immediately dismissed as public-relations stunts or the ravings of lunatics. In the 1960s and 1970s the reports continued but were dismissed by the media, scientific, and academic communities. However, in the 1980s, bolstered by the success of movies such as *Close Encounters of the Third Kind, E.T.,* and others, the abduction phenomenon took center stage. The public and the media began to take a closer look at the question of alien abductions. Books such as *Communion* by Whitley Strieber and *Intruders* by Budd Hopkins made *The New York Times* bestseller list with grizzly details of alien encounters.

In June 1992, research into the alien abduction phenomenon gained a measure of respect when a scientific conference
was held at the prestigious Massachusetts Institute of
Technology (M.I.T.). The purpose of the conference was to
examine the veracity and nature of the UFO and alien abduction phenomena. The prestige of the conference was boosted
by the location and by the credentials of the cochairmen—Dr.
John Mack, M.D., a cum laude graduate of Harvard Medical
School and M.I.T physicist David E. Pritchard. Mack was the
head of the department of psychiatry at Cambridge Hospital,
Harvard University, and the author or coauthor of over 150
peer-reviewed scientific papers which have appeared in academic journals and textbooks. Dr. Mack also won the 1977
Pulitzer Prize for his biography, *A Prince of Our Disorder: The Life
of T. E. Lawrence*. Pritchard is a well-respected researcher in the
field of atomic and molecular physics.

In addition to Mack and Pritchard, the conference was
attended by a number of well-known abduction researchers
including Budd Hopkins, John Carpenter, and Temple
University historian David Jacobs. According to C.D.B. Bryan,
author of *Close Encounters of the Fourth Kind*, the conference
was also attended by:

> ". . . hundreds of individuals who, uncontami-
> nated by exposure to any previous unidentified
> flying object lore or to each other, have so hesi-
> tatingly, reluctantly, timidly, come forward with
> their utterly incredible accounts of having been
> abducted and examined in UFOs not by 'little
> green men' but rather, for the most part, by
> spindly limbed 3 to 4 1/2 foot-tall telepathic gray
> creatures with outsized foreheads dominated by
> huge, compelling, tear shaped black eyes."[114]

Throughout the conference these abductees shared stories of their contact with what they believed were extraterrestrial alien entities. While individual accounts varied, the similarities of their stories and the consistency of their details were astonishing. A conference such as this might have been rejected out of hand if it were not for the prestigious cochairmen and setting. Due to its high profile location the conference was well attended by scientific investigators, abductees, and the media alike.

Many have wondered why John Mack, a prestigious psychiatrist, would risk his career on such a controversial topic. In his own words Mack expressed his thoughts about the importance and impact of alien abductions on society:

> "The idea that men, women, and children can be taken against their wills, from their homes, cars, and school yards by strange humanoid beings, lifted onto space craft, and subjected to intrusive and threatening procedures is so terrifying and yet so shattering to our notions of what is possible in our universe, that the actuality of the phenomenon has been largely rejected out of hand or bizarrely distorted in most media accounts. This is altogether understandable, given the disturbing nature of UFO abductions and our prevailing notions of reality. The fact remains, however, that for 30 years, and possibly longer, thousands of individuals who seem to be sincere and of sound mind and are seeking no personal benefit from their stories have been providing to those who will listen consistent reports of precisely such events."[115]

We take a very skeptical view on the question of alien abductions. Despite population surveys which indicate that as many as 1–3 percent of the population may have had an abduction experience, the hard evidence for such accounts is lacking. Nevertheless, we do believe that to appreciate the nature of the UFO phenomenon, an examination of the history and nature of these alleged abductions is very important.

CLOSE ENCOUNTERS?

After the UFO waves of the 1940s and early 1950s, the phenomenon took an unexpected turn as people around the world began to report close encounters with the alleged occupants of UFOs. The Air Force's attempt to debunk UFOs was aided by a series of outrageous reports of human contact with extraterrestrials as well as reports of alleged abductions in the early 1950s.

Beginning with George Adamski, a parade of people in the 1950s claimed that they had experienced close encounters with extraterrestrials from places such as Mars, Venus, Jupiter, and a number of fictitious planets. They boasted of long discussions with extraterrestrials as well as trips to their planets.

Many of these contactees gained widespread press attention. Thousands of people were drawn into this web of charlatanism. At the same time, a small number of more reputable witnesses were reporting unusual small beings associated with UFO landings. These reports were, of course, dismissed. Ridicule of contactees became the rule in the media. To make matters worse, the government's refusal to aggressively research UFOs led to a number of public UFO organizations, staffed primarily by nonscientific personnel whose investigative techniques were marginal at best. UFO debunkers had a field day with the alleged contactee movement and poorly researched publications.

It was in this era of skepticism that the modern era of alleged alien abductions began.

VILLAS-BOAS INCIDENT

On the evening of October 14, 1957, at 10:00 P.M., a young Brazilian farmer named Antonio Villas-Boas saw a bright light at the northern end of his field. Each time he approached the light, it moved away. After numerous attempts to approach the light, it vanished. The next evening, Antonio claimed, he saw a luminous, egg-shaped craft flying near his field at terrific speed. The object landed directly in front of him and short-circuited his tractor. Then he was dragged aboard the UFO by four small humanoids wearing suits, helmets, and goggles. He claimed he was taken aboard the craft and stripped, covered with a oily liquid, and given a medical examination.[116]

After the examination, he was left alone with an unusual female humanoid alien entity, who initiated an episode of alien-human intercourse. After his release he was alarmed to find numerous wounds on various parts of his body. Antonio's case was examined by Dr. Olavo Fontes of the National School of Medicine in Rio de Janeiro. Dr. Fontes confirmed what he believed to be radiation poisoning, a common malady suffered by alleged contactees with UFOs.

Villas-Boas kept his alien encounter a secret for eight years. In late 1965 he told his story, which was eventually published in the book *Flying Saucer Occupants*. This encounter was the first modern abduction report given serious consideration by UFO researchers.

THE INTERRUPTED JOURNEY

The first abduction to gain significant press notoriety was the case of Betty and Barney Hill. Betty and Barney Hill claimed that while driving through the White Mountains of New Hampshire on the evening of September 19, 1961, they saw an enormous disk-shaped object with two rows of windows descending from the sky. At first they assumed that it was some sort of experimental craft or a satellite. Barney Hill, who was driving at the time, stopped and made a sudden turn off the road toward the object. From this position they claimed they were able to see six humanoid entities through the windows of the craft. They got back on the road and tried to evade the object, but shortly afterward their car began vibrating and they heard an unusual beeping sound. They claimed that a haze seemed to fall over them.

When they arrived home, they felt uneasy. When they were able to confirm their arrival time, they realized they were unaccountably missing two hours of time. After the incident Barney Hill began having problems with an ulcer, and Betty Hill began having severe nightmares. Several months later they sought the help of a Boston psychiatrist, Dr. Benjamin Simon. Dr. Simon began four months of independent regressive hypnosis of the Hills. He encouraged them not to discuss their sessions with each other. In the sessions the events recounted by the Hills were remarkably consistent.

They claimed that while they were on the road they had been abducted by humanoid beings, taken aboard the ship, and given humiliating medical examinations by the alien crew. They described the aliens as hairless entities with large heads, large eyes, and grayish skin. Betty claimed that while on board, a large needle-like object was inserted in her abdomen and she was surgically examined and given a pregnancy test.

Barney Hill's description of the encounter paralleled his wife's quite closely. However, it was not until many years after the encounter that Barney Hill eventually revealed that while on board the alien craft, he had been subjected to a sperm retrieval procedure. The story was published in a best-selling book by John Fuller entitled *The Interrupted Journey*, which was the basis of television docu-drama *The UFO Incident*.

While the veracity of this incident remains unconfirmed, it does parallel the thousands of incidents of alleged abductions that would be reported over the next 30 years.

INTRUDERS

In 1987 Budd Hopkins published a book entitled *Intruders,* which chronicles the alleged abduction accounts of Kathy Davis and her family members. Hopkins, who wrote the book *Missing Time,* has researched alleged the claims of alien abductions for more than 20 years. He admits that when he began studying UFOs and abduction phenomena, he was quite skeptical about such accounts. However, he eventually became convinced, against his better judgment, that the phenomenon was real and represented a significant potential threat to the human population.

According to Hopkins, Kathy Davis (an alias), who was born in 1959, began having strange encounters in the winter of 1966. On a family trip she encountered a strange object in a field, which she described as a white, windowless house. In it she met a group of strange-looking humanoid entities who performed a physical examination and removed a piece of skin from her lower leg. According to her account, the entities had the ability to change shape into gray-skinned, small humanoid figures with large heads and large eyes. After the incident she returned to her friend's house having no recollection of the events.

Between July 1975 and October 1983, Kathy claimed that she was repeatedly abducted, taken aboard alien space-craft and subjected to in-depth gynecological examinations, harvesting of ovum, genetic experimentation, and finally presented with the fruit of the these experiments—a small child which looked like an alien-human hybrid! Confirmation that this hybrid child was her "daughter," she claimed, came by telepathic communications from the aliens. The only evidence for the alleged abductions of Kathy Davis are the accounts themselves, obtained under hypnotic regression.

The veracity of such encounters based on evidence obtained under hypnotic regression is impossible to confirm, and for most of us accounts such as these are impossible to believe. Skeptics often argue that these accounts are more akin to fantasy or a delusional state than to actual events. Hopkins himself admits the incredible nature of the stories and the unbelievability of what the abductees report. Yet, the abduction events reported by Kathy Davis fit into a clear and repeated pattern reported by tens of thousands of alleged contactees within the last four decades.

THE "TYPICAL" ABDUCTION SCENARIO

In the last four decades, research into alleged alien abductions has been undertaken by a small number of scientists, physicians, and historians, as well as military and government personnel. Two of the most prominent researchers—David Jacobs, Ph.D., in *Secret Life*,[117] and John Mack, in *Abduction: Human Encounters with Aliens*,[118]—point out that while the details of individual encounters differ, nearly four decades of research has brought to light a "typical" abduction scenario.

Information about abductions comes primarily from two sources: spontaneous recollection and hypnotic regression. According to researchers, about a third of the people who report an abduction experience remember large portions of the event spontaneously. The remaining two thirds require some form of relaxation therapy or hypnotic regression to recall the events.

Although no one really knows the number of alleged abductees, numerous researchers estimate that the number may be in the tens of millions worldwide. In his book, *Secret Life*, Jacobs made an extensive study of the magnitude of the abduction phenomenon. In an unpublished survey he conducted of more than 1,200 students at Temple University, he found that 5.5 percent of the students responded to the questionnaire in a way that indicated that they had potentially experienced abduction events.[119] Mack drew similar conclusions in *Abduction*, estimating the number in the hundreds of thousands in the United States alone. Whitley Strieber, author of the bestseller *Communion*, claimed that he received nearly 300,000 letters by individuals who have had abduction experiences.[120]

Abductions typically begin when the victim is either driving late at night or asleep in bed. Individuals driving will report seeing strange lights in the sky or a frank UFO sighting. Many people report feeling a sensation that draws them toward the UFO landing site. There is generally a "blackout" at that point, requiring hypnotic regression to obtain the subsequent events from at least two thirds of the contactees. Spontaneous recall of being taken aboard an alleged UFO is quite rare. Abductees usually report several hours of "missing time." In many cases UFO sightings have been reported by independent witnesses in the same area at the time of a nearby abduction event. In his book *Abduction: Human Encounters with Aliens*, John Mack emphasizes this point as one of the significant proofs for the veracity of abduction events.

Abductees who are taken from their rooms usually describe a bright light outside and a humming noise. This is followed by an encounter with hairless, three- to five-foot tall, gray-skinned entities. Abductees generally report the onset of paralysis and a floating sensation. Many will report being subsequently floated out of their house either through a window or in some cases through the walls or through the roof to an awaiting alien craft.

Once inside the craft, abductees universally report some sort of a physical examination. Generally they report a white room reminiscent of an operating-room-like environment. Once in the examination room, abductees typically report contact with the same gray-skinned aliens who methodically perform head-to-toe examinations with special attention to the genital area. In hundreds of cases, women report being probed with long metallic devices in the abdominal or genitalia area.

Through telepathic communication, female abductees are told that the procedure is being performed to retrieve ovum for the purpose of reproduction. Many female abductees claim that after an abduction they find incisions or scars on their lower abdomen that were not present prior to the encounter. An anesthetic of some kind is generally employed, and the details of the exam are usually recalled under hypnotic regression.

In addition to a "routine" physical exam, male abductees often report procedures for the retrieval of sperm. This procedure is generally painless but is quite humiliating to most of the abductees.

In many cases abductees, both male and female, report the removal of tissue samples with resultant scoop marks on the extremities or torso of the individual.

Insertion of "alien implants" within the body of the abductees is frequently alleged. Abductees report the use of long metal probes used to insert ceramic or metallic implants deep and high up in the nasal passageways. Others report implantations in the torso, the extremities, and the skull cavity. According to researchers, an implant will typically be between one to three millimeters in size. However, detailed analyses of alleged alien implants, which have been surgically removed, have failed to prove an alien origin of the materials found within the implants.

According to some researchers, the retrieval of sperm and ova and the execution of "reproductive procedures," seem to be central to the abduction phenomenon. Abductees who have allegedly experienced such retrievals report being told that their "seed" would be used for the production of hybrid off-spring. David Jacobs and others even claim confirmation (hormonal and ultrasonographic) of pregnancies in female abductees and the subsequent disappearance of fetuses.[121] Of course accounts such as these are impossible to confirm. The social stigma attached to such events compels most alleged abductees to maintain anonymity. Consequently, the only evidence for such events are the anecdotal stories themselves. In addition, there are numerous medical explanations for false pregnancy, false pregnancy tests, and the "mysterious" disappearance of fetuses. These include psychosomatic pregnancy where the woman feels pregnant but in subsequent testing fails to reveal a pregnancy. Spontaneous "absorption" of a deceased fetus in the first few weeks of pregnancy and "molar pregnancy" are but a few of the possible explanations.

DELIVERY OF MESSAGES TO ABDUCTEES

A recurring theme in the abduction scenario is the delivery of detailed messages to abductees. The messages delivered to abductees are typically done by telepathic (mind-to-mind) conversation. Abductees rarely report the use of verbal communication with their captors. In some cases, abductees report being shown scenes or messages on large screens within the alien craft.[122]

These messages are usually horrific prophetic scenarios about impending cataclysmic events on Earth and the destruction of Earth due to environmental degradation. In some cases, overt religious messages are given to abductees. These messages can include the notion that the aliens are our creators, that they are trying to advance our evolution through these breeding experiments, and that mankind must unify—with their assistance—into a system of global governance and religion in order to survive the future cataclysms. We will examine such messages in detail in subsequent chapters.

ABDUCTEE PROFILE

In the last several years, researchers have tried to determine who is "at risk" for an abduction event. While there is not a clear-cut profile of who *is* and who is *not* likely to be abducted, some patterns have emerged which suggest an increased risk.

According to John Mack and others, abduction can occur at almost any age. Many abductees claim that their encounters began at the age of two or three and continued until adulthood. In addition, abductees are most likely to have seen a UFO on numerous occasions prior to the abduction event. Differences in gender, socioeconomic status, and race do not seem to correlate to an increased incidence of abduction. However, C.D.B. Bryan, in his book *Close Encounters of the Fourth Kind,* notes that "contactees were for the most part unchurched people."[123] Bill Alnor, author of *UFOs and the New Age,* and David Allen Lewis, author of *UFO: End Time Delusion,* agree with this conclusion.

It has been called to our attention that there appear to be exceptions in which ostensible Christians have been abducted, such as in the Andreason Affair. However, it also appears that in these cases an invitation was accepted by the abductee. It is the author's belief that Christians cannot be abducted against their will. (See Checklist for Potential Contactees, page 339.)

Abductee surveys have revealed that the overwhelming majority of abductees have shown an interest in paranormal activities, Eastern religions, and New Age world-view. A large percentage of abductees have also reported a history of involvement with Ouija boards, astrology, witchcraft, astral projection, telepathic communication, channeling, past life regressions, and the like. Still others simply agreed to go along with their abductors when approached.

Regarding the profile of abductees Mack reports,

> "I have the impression that abductees as a group
> are usually open and intuitive individuals, less
> tolerant than usual of societal authoritarianism,
> and more flexible in accepting diversity and the
> unusual experiences of other people. Some of my
> cases report a variety of psychic experiences,
> which has been noted by other researchers."[124]

Mack also notes that abductions tend to run in families. An increased risk seems to be associated with individuals who grow up in a severely dysfunctional, abusive home, especially if there is a history of sexual abuse as a child.

PSYCHOLOGICAL EFFECTS

In general, abductees are not physically harmed by these encounters. However, John Mack and others have documented severe psychological and emotional disturbances which can persist for decades after such encounters. According to Mack, abductees often withdraw from society. Fear of ridicule and a sense of hopelessness often result. In some cases, abductees report a sense of being "chosen" for a special purpose. That purpose is usually to bring the message of impending doom or environmental disaster to sleeping populace. According to Mack, some report a sense of overwhelming joy or a feeling of being "home" while on board the alien craft.[125] However, the overwhelming majority of contactees report a sense of dread, humiliation, and hopelessness which can persist for decades.

THE SKEPTICS REPLY

For most of us, reports such as these are exceedingly difficult to swallow. The notion of alien entities abducting people from their cars and bedrooms, performing genetic experiments for the sole purpose of producing hybrid offspring, is suggestive of the deranged tales of a psychotic or grossly disturbed individual. In the case of Betty and Barney Hill, the primary evidence for the abduction was the parallel descriptions of the encounter discovered in separate hypnotic sessions. Ever since the widespread publicity of the Hill's alleged encounter, skeptics have endeavored to systematically debunk such incidents.

In anticipation of these efforts, John Mack has laid out the following series of five tests that he says must be satisfied by anyone who might try to provide an alternate explanation for these events:

1. The high degree of consistency of detailed abduction accounts, reported with emotion appropriate to actual experiences told by apparently reliable observers.

2. The absence of psychiatric illness or other apparent psychological or emotional factors that could account for what is being reported.

3. The physical changes and lesions affecting the bodies of the experiencers, which follow no evident psychodynamic pattern.

4. The association with UFOs witnessed independently by others while abductions are taking place (which the abductee may not see).

5. The reports of abduction in children as young as two or three years of age.

One of the primary skeptics regarding the occurrence of alien abductions was the astronomer Carl Sagan. Shortly before his death in 1996 Sagan authored his final book, *The Demon-Haunted World,* a skeptical inquiry of all things paranormal. In it he devoted considerable space to debunking alien abductions. His objections to the UFO phenomenon and alien abductions are in general fairly representative of the skeptic's positions.

Sagan's primary objection to the abduction accounts is the notorious unreliability of hypnotic regression. He and others rightly point out that numerous studies have shown that hypnotic regression can elicit memories of events that never occurred or of events that are yet future![126] In addition, skeptics argue that if the hypnotherapist has strong opinions about the reality of abductions, those opinions will bias the interview. And, that bias will be reflected in the way the questions are phrased, thus "leading" the subject into "false memories." In defense, John Mack counters that up to one third of abductees recall part or all of their encounters spontaneously, without the aid of regression therapy.

In *Abduction,* John Mack counts as evidence the emotional power of the encounters and the intensity with which contactees report the events. Sagan and others dismiss this as no more reliable than the power and intensity of nightmares and hallucinations.

Another common objection to abduction accounts is a phenomenon called "hysterical contagion." This term refers to the fact that once a description of an unusual event (UFO, alien abduction, apparitions of the Virgin Mary, etc,) become widely publicized, there is an "hysterical" tendency for people to misinterpret a natural phenomenon as such an event. According to skeptics, such "contamination" of the populace by the popular press incites the "psychologically frail" falsely to connect a distant memory of a traumatic event or nightmare to an encounter with aliens.

However, proponents of the reality of alien abduction point out that even before reports of such abductions appeared in books, movies, conferences, and talk show exposes, a significant number of abduction cases had already been reported which fit the prevailing pattern.

Jacques Vallee remarked on the state of abduction research in the early 1970s:

> "There were already a dozen abduction cases in our files by 1970. Some veteran researchers, like Coral and Jim Lorenzen, had accumulated many more. It was clear that abductions had been a part of the mystery since the earliest period. It seemed that the problem we were trying to tackle was a much more formidable one than the arrival on Earth of space visitors, impressive as that possibility might be. The phenomenon challenged not only our definitions of physical objects but our concepts of consciousness and reality. At the same time it brought into question the entire history of human belief, the very genesis of religion, the age-old myth of interaction between humans and self-styled superior beings who claimed they came from the sky, and the boundaries we place on research, science and religion. The abduction experience, in my opinion, is real, traumatic and very complex."[127]

What about the remaining third of alleged abductees who recall their encounters without the aid of hypnotic regression? Skeptics attribute this spontaneous recall to deliberate fabrication, hallucinations, repression of childhood abuse, dream states, sleep paralysis, fantasy-prone personality, psychosis, multiple personality disorder, temporal lobe epilepsy, and any number of psychological abnormalities.

In an effort to assess their psychological stability or lack thereof, researchers in the Department of Psychology at Carlton University examined a group of 49 individuals who reported varying degrees of contact with UFOs or their occupants.[128] In the 1993 study led by Nicholas P. Spanos, researchers compared the psychological and intellectual profiles of UFO reporters with a comparison group comprised of 53 adults from the local community and a group of 74 introductory psychology students from the university.

The results, to the dismay and surprise of many, failed to show any increased incidence of psychological abnormality in the UFO experiencers. In fact, the article states that UFO experiencers "attained higher psychological health scores than either one or both of the comparison groups on five of the psychological health variables." In addition, they found no increased tendency toward temporal lobe instability (a common explanation offered to explain away abductions) and no greater tendency toward fantasy-prone thinking or hypnotizability in UFO experiencers. Furthermore, UFO experiencers were found to have higher intelligence, on the average, than the two comparison groups. "In short," the article stated, "reporting UFO experiences was not associated with either social or intellectual marginality."

Finally, skeptics point out that the lack of independent witnesses to alleged abduction events is a major deficiency of the abduction phenomenon. Considering the dramatic descriptions of alien craft nearby, abductees being floated out of windows, passed through walls, etc., skeptics argue that one would expect many of these encounters to have been witnessed by neighbors or passers by.

Indeed, if recent polls are to be believed, it is estimated that hundreds of thousands if not millions of people have experienced abduction events.[129] To paraphrase one skeptic, "If that many people are being abducted by aliens, then we should see armadas of UFOs floating above the cities of the United States waiting to abduct the millions of people who have alleged such events."

WITNESSED?

On February 1, 1991, abduction researcher Budd Hopkins received a letter he claimed provides the first confirmation of a witnessed abduction. The letter, which Hopkins claimed was from two security officers, "Dan and Richard," recounted an event they claimed to have witnessed on November 30, 1989, at approximately 3:30 A.M. While providing an escort for a "prominent diplomat," they noticed a strange reddish glow coming from the sky. They looked up and saw a glowing oval object hovering above an apartment building two to three blocks up from their location underneath the elevated FDR Drive in Brooklyn, New York. As they watched the object, it descended to the side of the apartment building adjacent to the 12th-floor windows. Both officers observed the event and quickly reached for their binoculars in the glove compartment. What they saw next they could not believe.

While the UFO hovered next to the 12th floor of the apartment building, they observed an adult female wearing a full white nightgown being floated out of the 12th story apartment building accompanied by "three ugly but smaller human like creatures, one above her and two below.[130] The woman was escorted into the bottom of the craft and disappeared inside. After she was escorted up and into the object, it "whisked away" and then plunged into the river adjacent to pier 17, behind the Brooklyn Bridge. In their letter to Hopkins they stated, "Someone else had to have seen what we saw that morning. I know what we saw and we'll never forget it."[131]

Hopkins, who had been studying abductions for many years at this point, had never heard of an abduction account that was witnessed. There were cases where abductees were reported missing when alleged abductions occurred, but an actual eyewitness report had never been filed before.

When Hopkins received the letter from the two security officers, he claims he knew exactly who had been abducted. He had been in contact with a woman named Linda Cortile (an alias for Linda Napolitano), who wrote Hopkins claiming she had experienced frequent abductions in the past. He became acquainted with Linda Napolitano in spring of 1989 as a result of a letter she had written to him. His initial meetings with her centered on UFO abduction experiences that she recalled from her youth. However, on November 30, 1989, Linda Napolitano phoned Budd Hopkins and told him the story of her abduction, only hours before, at 3:30 A.M.

In subsequent months, Hopkins claimed he received additional eyewitness accounts of the Linda Napolitano abduction. Among those accounts was a letter from a woman who was on the Brooklyn Bridge that morning at 3:30. The woman reported that while driving along the Brooklyn Bridge, her car, along with other cars on the same bridge, lost power. She looked out her window and across the bridge, saw the reddish oval object and a woman in a white nightgown being escorted by three humanoid entities into the bottom of the UFO. She reported that others on the Brooklyn Bridge that night saw the event as well. There are many complex and convoluted details to this alleged abduction which Hopkins reported in his 1996 book, *Witnessed*. In addition, Hopkins claimed he has held back a number of details that he believes will help to corroborate the story if additional witnesses come forward. If further corroboration of the Linda Napolitano abduction is forthcoming in the months and years to come, it will undoubtedly prove to be the most significant abduction case in history.

However, in the months and years since Hopkins first made public the story of the Linda Napolitano, the initial excitement regarding this case has been tempered by the discovery of a number of disturbing inconsistencies and intrigues. For example, shortly after the story of Linda Napolitano became public, researchers from the Mutual UFO Network revealed that there are more than a dozen striking similarities between Cortile's story and a book called *Nighteyes* by Garfield Reeves-Stevens, first published in April 1989, only a few months before Linda Napolitano told her story to Budd Hopkins.[132] Even those within the ranks of Ufology have discovered disturbing evidence that the entire event may have been an elaborate hoax. Others believe that the event may have been part of a massive disinformation campaign, perpetrated with top-secret holographic technology, but for what purpose?

THE PURPOSE OF ALIEN ABDUCTIONS

The notion of alien abductions is obviously a highly charged and controversial topic. Verification of such encounters would be incredibly challenging to prevailing scientific, religious, and historical paradigms. It is likely that the proponents and skeptics regarding the reality of these encounters will continue to be debated for years to come. Nevertheless, the experts in the field of abduction research have put forth a number of theories regarding the nature and purpose abduction, as well as the agenda behind this 40-year wave of alleged contact with human kind.

Budd Hopkins, author of *Intruders, Missing Time,* and *Witnessed,* sums up the nature of abductions with the following question:

> "And what is the ultimate purpose of these abductions, these examinations and implants, these genetic attempts to produce hybrids, which have inevitable created emotional havoc among many innocent people? Do the UFO occupants want to lessen the distance between our race and theirs in order to land, eventually, and join us on this

planet? And if so, would this be an operation conducted in the open, or in a more sinister, covert manner? Or do these aliens merely wish to enrich their own [genetic] stock and then depart as mysteriously as they arrived, having achieved their goal and revivified their own endangered species? Or is there yet some other goal which we have not even imagined, something unknowable at this point in our intellectual evolution?"[133]

At the end of his book *Secret Life*, David Jacobs asked the question, "Why are UFOs here?" His answer is disturbing:

"One of the purposes for which UFOs travel to Earth is to abduct humans to help aliens produce other beings. It is not a program of reproduction but one of production. They are not here to help us, they have their own agenda and we are not allowed to know its full parameters."[134]

In his most recent book, *Witnessed*, Hopkins stated:

"Everything I have learned in 20 years of research into the UFO abductions phenomenon leads me to conclude that the aliens' central purpose is not to teach us about taking better care of the environment; instead, all of the evidence points to their being here to carry out a complex breeding experiment in which they seem to be working to create hybrid species, a mix of human and alien characteristics. A careful reading of the various witnesses accounts suggests that here, as in many earlier cases, reproductive issues appear far more frequently than alien ecological concerns."[135]

Some might argue that Hopkins and Jacobs are unqualified from a scientific point of view to make claims about hybridization, genetic engineering, and the production of hybrid half-alien, half-human species. However, this cannot be said of Dr. John Mack. Mack, a psychiatrist for more than 40 years, has extensive training in the biological, medical, and psychiatric sciences. Academically his credentials are unparalleled in the field of UFO and abduction research. Remarkably, Mack came to similar conclusions.

After examining 76 cases of alleged UFO abductions, Mack drew the following conclusions. First, he believes that something definitely happened to the individuals he examined. They did not make up the stories. Secondly, Mack believes that the beings that are abducting humans are interdimensional beings. Based the descriptions of his patients, he believes that the abductions even may occur outside of time and space itself; that is, he believes that it may be some sort of interdimensional transportation to a domain outside of the space-time. Thirdly, Mack believes that one of the primary agendas of the alien entities is to warn mankind of impending ecological catastrophe which has been precipitated by our misuse of resources and destruction of the ecosystem. He noted that the majority of abductees are given these apocalyptic visions of the future catastrophic Earth changes. He also noted that people often take tremendous religious and prophetic significance from these experiences.

While making no assessments about the origin of these entities, he concluded that their nature parallels those of angels, demons, and other supernatural entities. Mack believes that the alien abduction phenomenon may represent the first verification that the dualistic world view—where the spiritual realm is relegated to the field of religion and the scientific and the material realm is separate and distinct and relegated to the scientists—may be breaking down. Indeed, he sees the UFO abduction phenomenon as a merging of science and religion, the appearance of a new paradigm of thought—one in which the lines separating faith and science, religion, philosophy, the material world, and the spirit world are blurred. The result, Mack believes, is a merging and unification of science, religion, philosophy, and the spiritual realm.

Regarding the nature of the aliens and the abductions phenomenon Mack stated:

> "The alien beings that appear to come to us from the sky in strange space craft present a particularly confusing challenge to such a naturalistic or objectivist ideology. For they seem to partake of properties belonging to both the spirit and the material worlds, bridging, as if effortlessly, the division between these realms which have become increasingly sacred and unbreachable since science and religion went their separate ways in the 17th century. On the one hand these beings seem able to be seen by the abductees, who feel their bodies moved and find small lesions inflicted upon them. On the other hand the beings seem to come, like intermediaries from God or the devil, from a nonembodied source, and they are able to open the consciousness of abductees to realms of being that do not exist in the physical world as we know it."[136]

Regarding the purpose of abduction Mack stated:

> "My own impression is that we may be witnessing something far more complex, namely an awkward joining of two species, engineered by an intelligence we are unable to fathom, for a purpose that serves both of our goals with difficulties for each. I base this view on the evidence presented by the abductees themselves."[137]

Mack's belief that the alien beings are interdimensional beings akin to spiritual entities is, he admitted, a staggering blow to the materialistic world view that has emerged in our secular age. He stated:

> "But I believe there is core belief in our culture that is violated by the alien abduction phenomenon, namely the total separation of the spirit and the physical world. We have made that gulf inviolate, relegating to religion the spirit (subjective) world and assigning science to the material (objective) domain. We simply do not know what to do with a phenomenon that crossed that seemingly inviolable barrier. It shocks the foundation of our belief structure, our minds have no place to put such a thing."[138]

Finally, Jacques Vallee, discussed the UFO and abductions phenomenon in its historical cross-cultural contexts. He asked:

> ". . . should we hypothesize that an advanced race somewhere in the universe in some time in the future has been showing us three-dimensional space operas for the last 2,000 years, in an attempt to guide our civilization? If so, do they deserve congratulations? . . . Are we dealing instead with a parallel universe, another dimension, where there are human races living, and where we may go at our expense, never to return to the present? Are these races only semi-human, so that in order to maintain contact with us, they need cross-breeding with men and women of our planet? Is this the origin of the many tales and legends where genetic plays a great role: the symbolism of the virgin in occultism and region, the fairy tales involving human midwives and

changelings, the sexual overtones of the flying saucer reports, the Biblical stories of intermarriage between the LORD's angels and terrestrial women, whose offspring were giants? From that mysterious universe are higher beings projecting objects that can materialize and dematerialize at will? . . . There is nothing to support these assumptions, and yet, in view of the historical continuity of the phenomenon, alternatives are hard to find unless we deny the reality of all the facts, as our peace of mind would indeed prefer."[139]

We are very sensitive to the fact that the material examined in this chapter may disturb many. In this chapter we have endeavored to present a balanced view on the question of alien abductions. However, we ourselves can neither confirm nor refute the occurrence of these alleged alien encounters. At this time the only evidence for these alien encounters is the testimony of the abductees and the experts who have studied them. And yet, to date no one has provided an alternate explanation that can account for the features of these abduction reports. So what is going on? John Mack posed this question at the 1992 M.I.T. Abduction Conference: "If what these abductees are saying is happening to them isn't happening, what is?"[140] This is a question that to date, no one has provided an adequate alternative explanation. However, if in the months and years to come the occurrence of alien abductions is confirmed, we believe that there are historical precedents which may account for the composite view of interdimensional beings that traverse the space-time domain, manifest physically, then interact, abduct and even interbreed with mankind. We also believe that the ultimate agenda of these alien encounters will accompany a global intrigue that may affect the lives of everyone in the years to come.

ALIEN
ENCOUNTERS

SECTION II:

THE
NEW AGE
VIEW

IN THE BEGINNING ET?

". . . Where have you come from? Who are your
creator parents? Who conceived of you, then made
you? The Sumerians understood the visitors from
the stars, who for hundreds of thousands of years
influenced and played with experiments of life
on each continent. . . . The gods watched and
participated with their creations on Earth."

A MESSAGE FROM PLEIADIAN EXTRATERRESTRIALS
IN BARBARA MARCINIAK'S
EARTH: PLEIADIAN KEYS TO THE LIVING LIBRARY?

The notion is a radical one. And yet it has been proposed by serious scientists in recent years—that life on Earth was delivered, some say "seeded," by extraterrestrials in the distant past!

DARWIN'S BLACK BOX

Since the dawn of written history the question of life's origin has been the foremost issue debated by the world's philosophers, scientists and theologians. In 1859 when Charles Darwin wrote his book *The Origin of Species,* he attempted to answer this question when he proposed that life on Earth arose in "some warm little pond" from the random combining of non-living, inorganic chemicals.

This notion, called "spontaneous generation," proposes that life arose when simple molecules combined by chance into more complex molecules and those molecules subsequently combined to form the subsystems of living cells. Ultimately these subsystems came together to form self-reproducing single-celled organisms. In turn, according to Darwin's theory, these single-celled organisms evolved by natural selection into all the life forms on Earth. By the early 20th century, spontaneous generation had become the predominant view of the origin of life in scientific circles.

During the time of Darwin, the living cell was viewed as a mere blob of amorphous, unorganized protoplasm. Consequently the proposal that "simple cells" arose by chance seemed reasonable to the adherents of Darwinism.

However, in the last half of the 20th century, astonishing discoveries regarding the molecular structure and function of living systems have brought the materialistic, random-chance origin of life scenario into serious question. In the field of molecular biology, discovery after discovery has revealed that living systems contain structures which conform in every way to the modern definition of a machine. In fact, the parallel between machines and living systems has now been shown to extend all the way to the molecular level.

In 1986, molecular biologist and evolutionist Michael Denton commented on the remarkable complexity of living cells:

> "Although the tiniest bacterial cells are incredibly small, weighing less than 10–12 grams, each is in effect a veritable micro-miniaturized factory containing thousands of exquisitely designed pieces of intricate molecular machinery, made up altogether of one hundred thousand million atoms, far more complicated than any machine built by man and absolutely without parallel in the non-living world."[141]

In 1996, biochemist Michael Behe described the current predicament of Darwinism to explain the origin of complex of living systems:

> "It was once expected that the basis of life would be exceedingly simple. That expectation has been smashed. Vision, motion, and other biological functions have proven to be no less sophisticated than television cameras and automobiles. Science has made enormous progress in understanding how the chemistry of life works, but the elegance and complexity of biological systems at the molecular level have paralyzed science's attempt to explain their origins. There has been virtually no attempt to account for the origin of specific, complex biomolecular systems, much less any progress. Many scientists have gamely asserted that explanations are already in hand, or will be sooner or later, but no support for such assertions

can be found in the professional science literature. More importantly, there are compelling reasons— based on the structure of the systems them- selves—to think that a Darwinian explanation for the mechanisms of life will forever prove elusive.[142]

The revolution in our understanding of the molecular biology of life began in 1953 when James Watson and Francis Crick elucidated the double helix structure of the DNA molecule.

By the 1970s it became clear that Darwin's notion of a "sim- ple cell" was incredibly naive. Indeed, the suggestion that a liv- ing cell, "far more complicated than any machine built by man and absolutely without parallel in the non-living world" could arise by chance became, to many, a dubious proposition at best.

Ironically, Francis Crick, the man who started the molecular biological revolution by deciphering the structure of the DNA molecule in 1953, began another revolution 20 years later with a simple paper in the scientific journal *Icarus*.[143]

The unparalleled complexity of living systems coupled with our knowledge of the conditions on the early Earth, had rele- gated the notion of spontaneous generation to the realm of the miraculous. By 1982 Crick admitted as much when he stated:

> "An honest man, armed with all the knowledge
> available to us now, could only state that in some
> sense, the origin of life appears at the moment to
> be almost a miracle, so many are the conditions
> which would have had to have been satisfied to
> get it going."[144]

However, Crick was a scientific materialist, committed to the non-miraculous origin of life. If confronted with the personal realization that the spontaneous (non-miraculous) origin of life was impossible, most of us would resort to the theory of intelligent design—that life was the purposeful contrivance of an incredibly intelligent, technologically advanced designer. This is exactly what Crick did, but with an unexpected twist. Life on Earth, Crick argued, had been delivered, or "seeded," by highly advanced extraterrestrial beings billions of years ago! In effect, proponents of this theory believe we are somebody's biology experiment.

In the 1970s, another prominent scientist, astronomer Sir Fredrick Hoyle, was also doing research on the probability of spontaneous generation. Using a super computer and the assistance of graduate students, Hoyle determined that the spontaneous generation of just the simplest bacterium was mathematically impossible, not to mention the generation of an entire human being.

After completing his research, Hoyle stated that the probability of the spontaneous generation of a single bacteria "is about the same as the probability that a tornado sweeping through a junk yard could assemble a 747 from the contents therein."[145]

In 1981, Hoyle expressed the view that life on Earth must be the result of intelligent design:

> "The likelihood of the formation of life from inanimate matter is one to a number with 40 thousand naughts [zeros] after it. It is enough to bury Darwin and the whole theory of evolution. There was no primeval soup, neither on this planet nor on any other, and if the beginnings of life were not random they must therefore have been the product of purposeful intelligence."[146]

However, Hoyle was also committed to a non-miraculous cause for the origin of life. So he joined the list, albeit a small one, of prominent scientists, who asserted that life had been delivered from outer space either by aliens or by a comet "infected" with bacteria. This notion, called "directed panspermia," was a radical new proposal, one which displeased many in the scientific community.

In his book *Darwin's Black Box,* Michael J. Behe discussed the radical theory put forth by Crick and Hoyle:

> "Francis Crick also thinks that life on Earth may have begun when aliens from another planet sent a rocket ship containing spores to seed the Earth. This is no idle thought; Crick first proposed it with chemist Leslie Orgel in 1973 in an article entitled "Directed Panspermia" in a professional science journal called *Icarus.* A decade later Crick wrote a book, *Life Itself,* reiterating the theory."[147]

Francis Crick is by all accounts a brilliant scientist. His elucidation of the structure of the DNA molecule with James Watson in 1953 won them the Nobel Prize for biology. He is considered one of the fathers of molecular biology. And yet, with his background he concluded that the spontaneous origin of life on the early Earth is impossible.[148]

As Michael Behe noted:

> "The primary reason Crick subscribes to this unorthodox view is that he judges the undirected [random chance] origin of life to be a virtually insurmountable obstacle. . . ."[149]

To many scientists the theory of extraterrestrial seeding of planet Earth was an embarrassment. However, it is an idea that will not die. Even as recently as December 1996, Dr. Andrei Arkhipov of the Institute of Radio Astronomy in the Ukraine claims that the ultimate origin of life on Earth began with microbes which had been delivered to the Earth as lumps of "alien waste." He published his view in the respected international astronomical research journal, *Observatory.*[150]

While the notion of human life arising from alien "dung" is rather unappealing, it does point out how intractable the problem of the origin of life has become.

Molecular biologist Michael Denton discussed the irony of the panspermia theory:

> "Nothing illustrates more clearly just how intractable a problem the origin of life has become than the fact that world authorities can seriously toy with the idea of panspermia."[151]

CHARIOTS OF THE GODS?

About the time that Francis Crick began to speculate about an extraterrestrial source of life on Earth, the very same idea became popularized by Erich von Daniken in his book, *Chariots of the Gods*. As evidence for this theory, von Daniken—and more recently Zecharia Sitchin—recounted a number of myths which speak of the ancient visitations of beings from the heavens who came to Earth and interacted with, even interbred with, mankind. In addition, because ancient man worshiped these extraterrestrials as gods, von Daniken and others believe that these ancient astronauts were the very creators of life on Earth.

While many believe that von Daniken and Sitchin have introduced a viable theory into the question of life's origin, in reality it does not come close to solving the problem of life's origin. It only pushes the question back one more planet: If ETs made us, then who made them?

The deficiency of the ancient astronaut theory for the origin of life on Earth was also noted in 1996 by Michael Behe:

> ". . . The interesting part of Crick's idea is the role of the aliens, whom he has speculated sent space bacteria to Earth. . . . This scenario still leaves

open the question of who designed the designer
[the aliens]—how did life originally originate?"[152]

This point is well taken. While the notion that life arose on
Earth by "intelligent seeding" does provide a tentative answer
for the origin of life on Earth, it does not answer the ultimate
question: How did life *first* arise within the dimensions of our
space-time domain?

If the chemical conditions and the laws of nature are insufficient to explain the origin of life on the early Earth, then what
options remain? If we believe that life was delivered here from
ancient astronauts, then how did they arise? If we assume that
they arose by Darwin-like spontaneous generation on another
planet somewhere in the cosmos, then we must assume that
the laws of chemistry, physics, thermodynamics, and mathematical probability are different elsewhere.

The assertion that somewhere else in the universe the laws
of physics and chemistry are more favorable for the origin of
life is not supported by a shred of scientific evidence. To
invoke such an explanation is an appeal to something outside
the bounds of natural laws—i.e., a metaphysical, supernatural
cause. Except under the very exotic boundary conditions of a
black hole, the laws of chemistry and physics appear uniform
throughout the cosmos.

If we are to assume that the laws of physics and chemistry
are essentially uniform throughout the physical universe, and
that those laws alone are insufficient to explain life on Earth,
then we must conclude that life could not have arisen by
chance anywhere in the universe.

Since this is true, then the only other option is that the source
of life in the universe must be an extradimensional one—in
effect, an extradimensional Creator, independent of our space-
time domain.

Even if the laws of physics were found to be more favorable in a distant corner of the universe, and those laws could explain the origin of the incredibly complex biomolecules found in living systems, there would still be no natural explanation for the coded information (which does not arise by chance) that is carried by the DNA molecule. This is a point which is often ignored by origins researchers. The DNA molecule "carries" billions of bits of digital information which, when retrieved, calls for the production of trillions of cellular components, each of which is an "exquisitely designed piece of intricate molecular machinery."[153]

In the real world of engineering, biotechnology, and information science, the amount of information needed to create a machine (which living cells certainly are by any definition of the term) is directly proportional to the complexity of the machine. So if living systems are more complex—as Michael Denton stated, "far more complicated than any machine built by man"—then the "instruction manual" to build life will be more detailed. That is, living systems require *more* information than the one required to build the Space Shuttle or a Cray Super computer![154]

Moreover, the foundational principle of information theory is that information, instructions, blueprints, do not and cannot arise by chance. So even if a DNA molecule (or a substitute suitable for carrying information) could arise by spontaneous Darwin-like chance chemical processes, it would be void of information.[155]

Consequently, since the molecules of life and the information carried by the DNA molecule cannot arise by chance within our cosmos, then the source of living systems must have been an intelligent, extradimensional one—beyond the bounds of space and time.

THE CHURCH OF ET

In the 1960s and 1970s, a bizarre twist was introduced to the UFO question when the UFO movement became a focal point of a number of new religious groups.

The unifying theme of these UFO churches was identical to those of von Daniken and Sitchin. Life on Earth was delivered or created by extraterrestrials. Earthlings are their children and they are returning in these desperate times, at the end of the 20th century, to instruct and guide their children. According to UFO prophets, they have come to give us the answers we need to solve our problems, to unify our purposes, and to help us evolve to the next stage in our evolutionary process.

THE RAELIANS

One of the early but less prominent groups that promotes the notion that God is an ET is the Raelians, which organized in the 1970s. Although the Raelians are a small group, their beliefs are fairly representative of those among religious groups based on a UFO/ET theme. In the mid-1970s, their leader, Claude Vorilhon (born December 30, 1946) began lecturing in the United States and abroad about his remarkable contact with extraterrestrials.

He claimed that his mother, Marie Vorilhon, who was a French citizen, was "selected" by extraterrestrials and inseminated by them on December 25, 1945. Officials of the Raelian movement presented her story:

> "Just after the first atomic bomb explosion of Hiroshima in 1945, the Elohim [the extraterrestrials] selected Marie Colette Vorilhon to be his mother. She was born in Ambert on the 22, October 1922. On December the 25, 1945, they took her inside a UFO and inseminated her. They

then erased it from her memory so as not to psychologically unbalance her, and on the 30th September 1946 Rael [Claude Vorilhon] was born from this union."[156]

After a rather uneventful childhood, Claude Vorilhon claimed, he was contacted by one of the extraterrestrials on December 13, 1973. He claims that while he was hiking near his home in France, on a foggy overcast day, he saw a blinking red light, something like a helicopter hovering nearby. As he approached the craft he noticed a small, childlike occupant. The being was smiling, and there was a glow around his body. On the pilot's green suit was a symbol of a star of David with a swastika in the middle of it. Vorilhon claimed this creature spoke to him in his native tongue of French and even claimed the ability to speak all of Earth's languages. The being claimed to be from another planet and had visited Earth many times on previous occasions.

Vorilhon claimed he was chosen by the extraterrestrials to be a liaison between the ETs and mankind because, as a journalist and a free thinker, they believed he would bring their message to mankind without any "anti-religious bias." (Not to mention the fact that he was one of their offspring!)

Vorilhon claimed he was told to return the next day with his Bible and that he was given extensive commentary on critical portions of the Bible, especially those regarding the origin of mankind.

They had six meetings on successive days, and the notes of those meetings were privately published in the book *The Message Given to Me by Extraterrestrials*. According to Vorilhon, the ETs gave him a new name, Rael, which means "the man who brings light." He was told that he was one of many "light workers" who were chosen to deliver the message to mankind regarding our origin, purpose, mission, and ultimate destiny in the universe.

THE MESSAGE FROM ET

One might expect that such a visitation from our "space parents" would be accompanied by detailed information on how to solve our increasing global difficulties. With their supposed highly advanced technology, surely they would have solved the kinds of political, economic, environmental, and medical problems we now face. And yet, no such message was given. Instead, Rael was given a religious message—in effect, a Bible study conducted by an ET!

The primary message that the extraterrestrials wanted Rael to understand was that they created mankind. According to Rael, the extraterrestrials told him that they created humanity *in their image* by sophisticated genetic engineering techniques.

In *The Message Given to Me by Extraterrestrials*, the extraterrestrials describe for Rael the "true" story of creation. According to Rael, he was given the following interpretation of the creation story in the book of Genesis:

> "Let us start with Genesis chapter 1: In the beginning Elohim created the heavens and the Earth. In Genesis 1:1 the word 'Elohim,' wrongly translated in some Bibles by the word God, means in Hebrew, those who came from the sky, and furthermore, the word is plural. It means that the scientists from our world [the extraterrestrials speaking] searched for a suitable planet to fully realize their projects. They created, or rather discovered the Earth, and realized it contained all of the necessary elements for the creation of artificial life."

Officials of the international Raelian movement, which boasts over 30,000 members, elaborate on this message:

> "The messages dictated to Rael explain how life on Earth is not the result of random evolution, nor

the work of a supernatural 'God.' It is a deliberate creation, using DNA, by a scientifically advanced people who made human beings literally in their image . . . in Genesis, the Biblical account of creation, the 'Elohim' has been mistranslated as 'God' in the singular, but it is a plural, which means 'those who came from the sky.' "[157]

It is important to point out that Hebrew scholars have, for thousands of years, understood the word "Elohim" as one of the names of their God. While this word is a plural form of the name "Eloa," one of the names of God, Biblical scholars have never interpreted the word Elohim in the context of Genesis 1:1 to mean "gods." Rather, the Jews and Christians have always interpreted it to mean one God with a plurality of nature.

ALL ROADS LEAD TO ET

Another aspect of the message to Rael is that all the religions were founded by extraterrestrials and all point to the same "universal" truths. According to Rael, the ETs told him that all religious leaders—Jesus, Buddha, Mohammed, etc.—were half human, half ET prophets who were created by the ETs to bring increasing light and knowledge to mankind in successive epochs. It is interesting to note that many of the UFO churches, as well as some groups identified with the New Age movement, believe that another leader—the New Age Christ, Matreya—will also be a half human, half ET light worker. He is to be the most powerful leader in history, and he will unify the world into a lasting peace through global governance.

Regarding Jesus Christ, the Raelian movement states,

"All the great prophets including Buddha, Moses, Jesus, and Mohammed were messengers of these extraterrestrials. Jesus was born from the union of one of these extraterrestrials and a daughter of man, and his task was to spread the Biblical message in anticipation of the age of apocalypse."[158]

According to official statements by the International Raelian movement,

"The Raelian movement recognizes most other religions because it was our creators, the Elohim who started them. It was they who initiated the prophets whose role was to progressively educate and guide humanity."[159]

While some might embrace this religious philosophy as an enlightened world-view, the messages from these "ETs" is fraught with difficulties, not the least of which is the fact that the religious groups mentioned have radically different and mutually exclusive world-views.

The Eastern religions typically present a pantheistic world-view, where "God is all and in all things." This view, which is also embraced by the New Age movement, is not only incompatible with the Judeo-Christian world-view, it is also incompatible with 20th-century cosmology.

One of the greatest scientific insights of the 20th century is that we now understand that space, time, and matter had a simultaneous origin (called a singularity by physicists) at a finite point in the history of our universe. Among other proofs, this discovery was an outcome of Einstein's theories of special and general relativity at the beginning of this century. So if, as pantheistic religions suppose, the universe is "God," then there was a time when God (the universe) did not exist, because there was a time when the universe did not exist. The existence of a finite universe demands that the cause of the universe must be independent of time and space. This world-view, which is held by Jewish and Christian theologians, is in complete disagreement and mutually exclusive to the Eastern world-view of an eternal pantheistic universe. Apparently the ETs that spoke to Rael either failed their courses in physics and religion, or they have another agenda.

CHANNELED MESSAGES FROM OUR CREATORS?

As we saw in chapter five, one of the more common sources of information from extraterrestrials comes through channelers. Channeling is a process whereby an individual (the channel) allows him or herself to be entered or spoken through by a spiritual entity. This process, which has been used by mediums to contact spiritual entities for thousands of years, is a common occult method. Many modern "channelers" claim that they have acted as channels for numerous highly evolved "extraterrestrial entities" who have the capability to reach them and convey their thoughts by telepathic means. While the reliability of such information is dubious at best, it is surprising how consistent the messages are from the alleged extraterrestrials as given through channelers and mediums.

New Age literature is replete with messages from extraterrestrials who claimed that they are our creators. Depending on the source read, there are at least half a dozen races of alleged extraterrestrials vying for the title of "god." Candidates include the Pleiadians, the Grays, the Reptilians (half human, half reptile-like entities), the Insectoids (insect-like ETs!), the Venusians (from Venus), and others.

In her book *The Extraterrestrial Vision,* New Age author Jeana Lake presents the teachings of Theodore, an extraterrestrial entity which she channels on a regular basis. At the beginning of the book, Theodore discusses the origin of mankind:

> "Human beings did not evolve naturally on Earth, they evolved from genetic engineering of

ape-like primates by beings visiting your Earth millions of years ago. These extraterrestrials were the first intelligent species to discover the Earth besides one former colony of extraterrestrials that had landed here and left when your extraterrestrial forefathers/mothers arrived. That extraterrestrials altered the DNA of certain primates on Earth to create the human species is undoubtedly shocking. And yet, your scientists are beginning to play with the same technology—like father, like son."[160]

This notion that human life was produced by genetically engineering the DNA of a primate ancestor is found extensively in the literature of the New Age movement as well as in the writings of Zecharia Sitchin.[161]

According to New Age author Barbara Marciniak, who channels alleged Pleiadian entities, the creators of mankind were an ancient race of reptilian extraterrestrials:

"Where have you come from? Who are your creator parents? Who conceived of you, then made you? The Sumerians understood the visitors from the stars, who for hundreds of thousands of years influenced and played with experiments of life on each continent. . . . Ancient myths and legends hundreds of thousands of years old tell of the serpents, dragons, and reptilian visitors from the skies. The reptilian race, or Lizzies as we affectionately call them, are an integral part of your ancestral line. . . . Understand that the reptilian energies are creator gods. They are master geneticists. . . . They were some of the prime instigators in putting together the human species on this planet."[162]

ULTIMATE QUESTIONS

As we discussed earlier, if for the sake of argument we grant that life on Earth was seeded by ancient extraterrestrials, then the obvious question is, *Who* or *what* created our extraterrestrial creators? Some would argue that they were, in turn sprinkled (created) by an even more ancient race of extraterrestrials. Well, where did *they* come from? An infinite regression back in time of "alien sprinklings" will not do, because the universe is finite. So, since we cannot invoke an infinite number of such creative events, we must either invoke a transcendent, extradimensional Creator, who is independent of our space-time domain, or we must invoke the belief that somewhere, tucked away in a corner of our cosmos, the laws of chemistry and physics are more favorable to the spontaneous generation of life. As discussed earlier, there is no evidence for this either.

Finally, the speculations of Crick, Hoyle, von Daniken, and others make no attempt to explain the ultimate mystery, the origin of the universe itself—an accomplishment which is well beyond the capabilities of a finite extraterrestrial being.

THE GOSPEL ACCORDING TO ET

"Humanity is learning a great lesson at this time. The lesson is, of course, to realize your godhood, your connectedness with the prime creator and with all that exists. The lesson is to realize that everything is connected and that you are part of it all."

A MESSAGE FROM PLEIADIAN EXTRATERRESTRIALS
TO BARBARA MARCINIAK, EXCERPTED FROM
BRINGERS OF THE DAWN: TEACHINGS FROM THE PLEIADIANS

In our effort to identify their origin, mission, and agenda for mankind, it is important to examine the messages from our extraterrestrial visitors. In the last several decades, tens of thousands of alleged extraterrestrial contactees have received messages from our "space brothers," including detailed information regarding our future destiny, our purpose, and *their* role in our future evolutionary development.

The source of this information has come from abduction experiences, alleged face-to face-contact, channeling, and telepathic messages from the extraterrestrials. Despite the varied nature of contact and ET races encountered, the message to mankind has been remarkably consistent.

DAWN OF A NEW AGE ?

One of the unexpected aspects of the 20th-century UFO phenomenon is that it has been embraced as a source of religious inspiration by more than 10,000 groups in a movement called the "New Age." The New Age movement is not an official organization or religious denomination, but a loose network of organizations worldwide which share a number of common beliefs. In existence for thousands of years, this movement has grown dramatically in the second half of the 20th century. It goes by various pseudonyms such as the age of Aquarius, the New Thought Religion, the New Church, the Third Wave, the New Consciousness, the Transcendental movement, the Human Potential movement, and the New Spirituality.

The foundation for much of New Age doctrine is based on the writings of Helena Petrovna Blavatsky (1836–1891), Alice Bailey (1880–1949), Nicholas Roerich (1874–1947), H. G. Wells (1866–1946), as well as those of Marilyn Fergeson and Robert Mueller (former assistant secretary general of the UN).

The New Age movement is a religion by any definition of that term. It has its own bibles, which include the *Oahspe: The*

Aquarian Gospel of Jesus the Christ; *My Truth, the Lord Himself*; and *My Peace, the Lord Himself.*

Although the New Age movement is a loose network of independent organizations, they share a number of common doctrines including: The belief in a central spirit being known as "the Source" or "the God of Force." The belief in the god within, the divinity of man, the law of rebirth (reincarnation), the belief that Jesus and the Christ consciousness are two separate entities and that the Christ is an office rather than a man.

They share a belief in evolution, the perfectibility of man, the belief in the law of Avatars, which teaches that at the start of every new age the supreme being known as "the Solar Logos " sends the Christ consciousness who overshadows a human being. This Avatar then imparts to the world "new revelation" to help mankind through the coming new age.

New Age groups share the belief that salvation is by works rather than by atonement and grace. They share the belief in the interconnectedness of all things, and many groups share a deep hatred of Judaism, Catholicism, and fundamental Christianity. Finally, they share the belief that Jesus, Buddha, Mohammed, and the great religious teachers of Earth are part of a hierarchy of "Capital Masters" originating from an extraterrestrial environment.

The goals of the New Age movement can be summarized as follows. They share the goal of creating world peace through unification in a one-world spiritual system and a one-world government through a one-world leader of their choosing. Their covert goals are to abolish all systems based on the Bible by the year 2000, which is the beginning of the age of Aquarius. They endeavor to convert Western religious and philosophical belief systems into those of Eastern thought.

The beliefs and goals of the New Age movement are summarized in the writings of Helena P. Blavatsky, the founder of the Theosophical Society in 1875. Helena Blavatsky believed in the notion of ascended masters and gained her information through telepathic communication. According to a brochure published by the Theosophical Society, the goals and beliefs of the Theosophical Society and the New Age movement are . . .

> "To oppose the materialism of science and every form of dogmatic theology, especially the Christian, which the chiefs of the society regard as particularly pernicious; to make known among Western nations the long-suppressed facts about Oriental religious philosophies, their ethics, chronology, esoterism, symbolism; to counteract, as far as possible, the efforts of missionaries to delude the so-called 'Heathens' and 'Pagans' as to the real origins and dogmas of Christianity and the practical effects of the latter upon public and private character in so-called Christian countries."

BE STILL, AND KNOW THAT YOU ARE GOD!

One of the most surprising aspects of the UFO phenomenon is the fact that alleged messages from the extraterrestrials have been primarily of a religious and philosophic nature, rather than scientific and technological. In the previous chapter we saw that extraterrestrials, according to their New Age proponents, claim to be the very creators of mankind and the other life forms on planet Earth. What is even more surprising is the fact that extraterrestrials, through their channels, expound the notion that human beings share in their divinity.

The notion that man is god and that extraterrestrials are god is part of the New Age pantheistic world-view that everything within the universe is deity. The notion of pantheism, which is widespread in the teachings of the New Age movement, denies the existence of a personal transcendent Creator and replaces it with the notion that God is an impersonal life force, a collective of matter and energy.

Among the most prominent teachings from a group of extraterrestrials are the channeled messages of the Pleiadians. The Pleiadians are a "Nordic" type of extraterrestrials who come allegedly from the star cluster of the Pleiades. Barbara Marciniak is one of the better-known authors who channels the teachings of the Pleiadians. She claims that her messages have come from hundreds of hours of channeling over the past two decades.

In her book *Bringers of the Dawn* she describes the message to mankind from our Pleiadian space brothers which was "compiled from more than 400 hours of channeling" and was given to "impart to us the wisdom of the Pleiadians, a group of enlightened beings who have come to Earth to help us discover how to reach a new stage of evolution." Throughout the book we are given a collection of religious and philosophical messages from the Pleiadians with the foremost message being that they are our gods, our creators, and that we ourselves can become gods through a process of evolving to a higher consciousness.

Regarding the nature of God, the Pleiadians told Marciniak:

> ". . . Your history has been influenced by a number of light beings whom you have termed God. In the Bible, many of these beings have been combined to represent one being, when they were not one being at all, but a combination of very powerful, extraterrestrial light-being energies. They were indeed awesome energies from our perspective, and it is easy to understand why they were glorified and worshiped. Who were these gods from ancient times? They were beings who were able to move reality and to command

> the spirits of nature to bend to their will. Humans
> have traditionally called beings God who could
> do things that the human race could not do."[163]

So, according to these alleged Pleiadian entities God is a collective of beings, ancient teachers, extraterrestrial entities, and light-beings.

In the chapter "Ambassadors Through Time," Barbara Marciniak claims that the Pleiadians are a group of highly evolved extraterrestrials from our future who came from a universe that had achieved "completion." That is, they had evolved to the point where they realized that they and their ancestors were indeed the Prime Creator, or the First Cause. They have come to Earth at this time, in the late-20th century, to help us.

According to Marciniak, the Pleiadians told her:

> "Humanity is learning a great lesson at this time.
> The lesson is, of course, to realize your godhood,
> your connectedness with the prime creator and
> with all that exists. The lesson is to realize that
> everything is connected and that you are part of
> it all."[164]

According to the teachings of the Pleiadians, humanity stands at the threshold of a quantum leap of evolution that will abolish religious and governmental systems as we know them. It will bring universal brotherhood of man, the realization that we are part of a gigantic universal entity known as the Prime Creator. This quantum leap, this end run of evolution as expounded by numerous New Age gurus, channelers, and authors is the realization that by our own personal evolution, we can become part of a collective, part of a universal force, and therefore part of the divine being known as God.

Brad Steiger discusses the link between UFOs, science, and religion, in his book, *The Fellowship*:

"As with so many UFO contactees, Moi-ra and
Ra-Ja Dove are convinced that the Aquarian Age
is heralding in a new religion. Even the word religion will not be used anymore. For the main crux
of the matter will have a much deeper sense of
reality. The person will evolve out of believing in
something into becoming that something. The
person will know what the religions of the
ancient age have always tried to demonstrate: to
be still and know that you are god! Indeed, this
is the great new religion! Each and every person
will know that he is god. . . . From their aquarian perspective, Ra-Ja explained, you are god
with respect to the idea that you are an aspect of
god, as the tree, the dog, or the sky all have godly
qualities within. If god is omniscient, omnipo-
tent, and omnipresent, than everything is of god,
therefore is god!"[165]

What is going on here, and what is the agenda?

TRUTH IS RELATIVE

One of the primary teachings of the New Age movement is
the notion that all religions are simply different expressions of
the same God given through different eyes, through different
prophets, at different times in the history of Earth.

Accordingly, Jesus, Moses, Buddha, Mohammed, Krishna,
and Maitreya, are all viewed as ascended masters or "light
workers," who were appointed to be bearers of truth in different generations. The New Age movement teaches that no one
religion is any more correct than any other and that truth is
defined by the individual. That is, there is no absolute basis for
truth; truth is relative to the individual. An obvious outcome
of such logic is that right and wrong, good and evil, are also

defined by the individual. This subjective reality seems hardly applicable to technologically advanced extraterrestrial entities who have "solved all their problems" and spanned the galaxy with interplanetary vehicles. To accomplish such feats of ingenuity would require an advanced knowledge of the laws of physics, chemistry, mathematics, and the like. The problem with such fields is that they tend to be based on inviolate truths, not on fuzzy logic where truth is relative.

THE GAIA HYPOTHESIS

For thousands of years numerous cultures have viewed Earth as a living sentient being. The ancient Greeks worshiped a multitude of gods and goddesses. Among them was the ancient goddess Gaia, which was the spiritual entity, the Earth goddess whose physical body, they believed, was Earth itself. Gaia was believed to be the soul or the spirit of the living planet.

Worshiped for centuries by the ancient Greeks, Gaia has reemerged at the end of the 20th century in the New Age philosophy of pantheism. The American Indians have worshiped Earth for thousands of years as a living being and the mother of all creation. The ancient Babylonians and the ancient Sumerians also believed in the divinity and consciousness of Mother Earth.

On February 6, 1975, scientists Dr. James Lovelock and Dr. Sydney Epton expounded their new theory called the Gaia hypothesis in *The New Scientist*. In this paper and subsequent writings, they note the incredible design and interconnectedness of nature, especially the systems on the Earth. They examined dozens of design characteristics, ecological feedback loops, and the many delicate balances found on Earth. They presented a staggering conclusion that Earth behaved as though it were a living organism. Earth and its biosphere, they stated, "seem to exhibit the behavior of a single organism, even a living creature."

While the scientific community has been slow to embrace the notion that Earth is a sentient being, this notion has been embraced by the New Age movement and other pagan religions of the 20th century. In addition, the notion that Earth is a living organism—a sentient being composed of a material body and a spiritual being—is also expounded by our "space brothers."

In the book *Earth: Pleiadian Keys to the Living Library,* we are told by Pleiadian entities that Mother Earth is "a living biological entity. She is alive."[166] Their concern, we are told, is that if we do not respect our mother [Earth], she will in due time expel us from her surface by cataclysmic upheavals such as earthquakes, volcanoes, and violent storms. We are told that in the late-20th century there will be a return to a belief in "mother goddess energy." As mankind evolves towards a higher vibration, we will all come to realize that we are part of the great universal consciousness and that our Earth mother is part of that consciousness in the form of mother goddess energy.

Regarding the end times, the Pleiadians declare:

> "There will be a return and an awakening to mother goddess energy. You will find in this decade that all of your religions are based on a false ideal. They are all based on a controlling, cold hearted, patriarchal movement, when in actually it is the mother goddess who is behind all things. . . . Your planet must learn who the goddess is as a creator. . . ."[167]

Not surprisingly, this view is echoed in the witchcraft book *The Witches' Goddess* by Janet and Stewart Farrar.

> "Lovelock and Epton's conclusion from this staggering array of scientific improbabilities (which

were nevertheless scientifically demonstrable facts) was that the whole system—the Earth and its biosphere—seemed to exhibit the behaviour of a single organism, even a living creature. They called this creature Gaia, 'the name given by the ancient Greeks to their Earth goddess.' The whole theory deserves careful study by every witch, pagan, or occultist—preferably from Lovelock's easily available book, for it typifies a steadily growing development: the discovery, by the frontiersmen of science, of the coherence of that multi-level reality which occultism has always recognized."[168]

Incredibly, the notion that Earth is a living being, a living spiritual organism, the creator of us all, and worthy of worship is even taught in the public schools. Throughout the United States hundreds of school districts have embraced curriculums which teach the "Earth first" philosophy. Many of the textbooks in public schools teach a brand of Neo-shamanism which embraces the notion that Mother Earth is a living organism, a goddess who is to be honored and reverenced as a living entity. This notion is advanced to the schools primarily by presenting the teachings of Native American shamen and Earth-based religions. To avoid overt criticism about separation of church and state, the Native American Earth based teachings that Mother Earth is a living organism are introduced in classes about the environment and multiculturalism.

In the Capistrano Unified School District, in Orange County California, one of the approved textbooks for high school science teachers is called *Concepts and Challenges in Life Science*.[169] In this book students are taught the Gaia hypothesis that Earth is a living organism, and they are encouraged to study and contemplate the many merits of this hypothesis.

The notion that Earth is a living organism, a sentient being, and a deity composed of body (the physical Earth itself) and spirit (mother goddess' energy) has been a primary doctrine of witchcraft for thousands of years. This presents an incredible irony, because according to recent constitutional interpretations by the Supreme Court, our public schools are to be liberated of religious influence except in its appropriate context in religion and history courses. And yet, even in the biological and natural science courses, we have an ancient pagan religious belief, the Gaia hypothesis, one of the primary doctrines of witchcraft, being taught as a scientifically valid notion in the public schools!

POLITICALLY CORRECT SIN

Within the teachings of the New Age movement is the belief that sin is an archaic concept developed by the patriarchal religious systems to place man in bondage and guilt. The prophets of the New Age claim that we are rapidly headed for a new understanding of our place in the universe and that sin, the notion that we have missed the mark in the eyes of God, is an archaic belief which will have no place in the coming New Age.

Regarding sin, New Age teacher Judy Pope-Ghostwolf stated:

> "Forgive the word sin, because there is no such thing as sin in my spiritual understanding. . . . I would prefer to think that there are some people who chose to commit terrible, horrible acts. . . . I do not believe and cannot accept that there is some long robed male figure somewhere who will render judgment on them. They are going to someplace where they will enter judgment on themselves."[170]

So instead of mankind having a sin nature, as the Judeo-Christian world-view teaches, sin does not exist. Consequently, there is no judgment. Instead, mankind goes to a place to contemplate his evil deeds and to render judgment on himself in the afterlife.

There is one glaring problem with this fuzzy logic. If morality is relative, if we create our own truth, then right and wrong, good and evil, are determined by each individual. So then when we contemplate our deeds in the afterlife, we can simply convince ourselves that we have done no evil, we have not sinned, and therefore no judgment or atonement is necessary! This notion fits well within the New Age world-view of moral relativism, the notion that all roads are equal and lead to God, and the denial of the personal accountability for our deeds on Earth. This type of moral relativism, the warm-fuzzy world-view, is ubiquitous in the teachings of the New Age movement. It represents the effort by New Age thinkers to rid man of guilt and personal responsibility.

THE NEW AGE JESUS

As we saw in the previous chapter, extraterrestrials and their New Age channels have a fascination with Jesus Christ. They teach that Jesus is a half human, half extraterrestrial, who was sent to Earth during the age of Pisces to educate and enlighten mankind.

In the Bible we are told that Jesus Christ was resurrected from the dead after undergoing the crucifixion, one of the most horrible and painful deaths ever invented by mankind. In the book of Acts we are told that Jesus, after giving his disciples their final instructions, ascended into a cloud and up to heaven. Then the disciples were told that he would return "in like manner as you have seen him go up into heaven."[171] When he was asked by his disciples about his Second Coming, he told them that they would see him "coming in the clouds with great glory."[172]

As expected, our "space brothers" have an explanation for all of this. According to Ashtar (the extraterrestrial commander of the Astar Command, a collective of alien entities), Jesus Christ was levitated by spaceship into the cloud, then taken to outer space (heaven) and he will return in like manner! This information was channeled to mankind and is recorded in the book *New World Order* by Timothy Green Beckley:

> "Jesus was taken up into heaven. He was levitated by a spaceship under our command. He will be brought back in a similar fashion. The man you call Jesus of Nazareth has the most powerful aura of anyone born on your planet. He was truly holy. He was truly wise. And yet, many of your people refuse to acknowledge him. There have been other wise men but not of such a high caliber.

> Jesus shall return to your planet in the not-too-distant future. He is waiting and biding his time for his return. Just as your holy book, the Bible, says, everyone will see him descend from the sky. He will come surrounded by a fleet of glittering spaceships, objects which you call UFOs."[173]

Didn't Jesus say he would come in a cloud? Many of the New Age authors take the Biblical words such as cloud, chariot, Jacob's ladder, and others and interpret them as UFOs.

Throughout the New Testament we see that the disciples readily worshiped Jesus as God.[174] For nearly 2,000 years the Church has held the doctrine that Jesus was indeed, God manifest in the flesh and he is worthy of worship. Of course, our space brothers have a different opinion. They believe that we misinterpreted the identity and teachings of Jesus Christ.

Ashtar, through channeled teachings, attempts to set us straight:

> ". . . Jesus rules over this planet [Earth]. He has
> tried for the last 2,000 years to lift you up out of
> the muck and mire humankind has gotten itself
> stuck into. Jesus does not wish to be worshiped.
> He wishes but to teach. He wishes to share his
> knowledge of the kingdom of God with those
> who will listen."[175]

While the worship of Jesus is portrayed as a "mistake" based
on an erroneous interpretation of his teachings, the worship of
Mother Earth is encouraged.

According to the New Age booklet "Shamanism: A Beginners
Guide," the "Earth Mother" is to be reverenced and honored as
the creator:

> "Furthermore, because we understand that Earth
> Mother is alive and conscious, we revere and
> honor Her as the giver and sustainer of life. The
> shamanic path leads us into a loving relationship
> with Earth Mother. We can pray to Her for guid-
> ance, comfort and well being, for She is our
> Mother."[176]

In his book *The Fellowship*, Brad Steiger discussed many
aspects of the life, ministry, and resurrection of Jesus Christ. In
the Bible, information about Jesus' childhood is limited to his
birth and his visit to the Jewish Temple at the age of 12. Steiger
pointed out a common view of the New Age movement regarding the "lost years" of Jesus Christ:

> "Generally speaking, in the Space Beings' teach-
> ings, Jesus of Nazareth is not God but is a Christ,
> an ascended master, who incarnated so that he
> might demonstrate the Christ-pattern for all
> humans to achieve in a like manner. Jesus, most
> extraterrestrials are said to claim, studied with

the Essenes during the lifetime which is reported in the Bible. The 'lost years' of Jesus are no mystery: Between the ages of 12 and 30, according to these sources, he was receiving special training aboard a spacecraft or in a remote area of Earth selected by the space entities."[177]

Needless to say, there is not a shred of Biblical, historical, theological, or archaeological evidence that Jesus spent his "lost years" aboard a spacecraft. However, this is just another example of the bizarre twisting of things Biblical. It seems that no matter what the Biblical doctrine is, the extraterrestrials and their New Age "light workers" have an explanation which is contrary to the historic Biblical view.

INITIATION INTO LUCIFER

One of the most bizarre revelations from alleged extraterrestrials, sprinkled throughout the writings of the New Age movement, are about the "true" origin, nature, and agenda of Lucifer, the one identified in the Bible as Satan.

According to New Age sources, the Biblical authors got it all wrong. Lucifer was not an evil fallen angel bent on rebellion against God and the destruction of mankind. Rather, they assert that Lucifer was a misunderstood ET who had challenged Yahweh, another ET, for the rulership of planet Earth in the days of the giants, known as the Annunaki. One of the most influential writers of the New Age is David Spangler. According to his own writings he receives his insights by channeling a number of extraterrestrial entities. In his 1978 book, *Reflections on the Christ,* Spangler stated that in order to enter the New Age, we must be initiated into Lucifer:

> "Lucifer comes to give to us the final gift of wholeness. If we accept it then he is free and we are free.

That is the Luciferic initiation. It is one that many people know, and in the days ahead, will be facing, for it is an initiation into the New Age."[178]

THE NEW WORLD ORDER

Throughout the history of alleged extraterrestrial contact there is one theme that dominates ETs' messages to mankind. In order to survive, we must unify our resources into a global society, with a world governing body and a global religion.

In his book *The Fellowship*, Brad Steiger emphasizes the "spiritual" aspects of ET contact:

"The Space Beings seem very concerned with the spreading of what has come to be known as New Age concepts—fresh methods of looking at metaphysics, universal laws, brotherhood, and even health and hygiene. The Space Beings appear definitely concerned with seeing that all humankind is united as 'one' on this planet. . . ."[179]

"Contactees have been told that the Space Beings hope to guide Earth to a period of great unification, when all races will shun discriminatory separations and all of humankind will recognize its responsibility to every other life form existing on the planet. The Space Beings also seek to bring about a single, solidified government, which will conduct itself on spiritual principles and permit all of its citizens to grow constructively in love."[180]

The importance of unification is echoed by the ancient alien entity Ashtar:

"It is important that your world unite, for separated as it is now, it will eventually destroy itself. Unity is important. It is probable that this will

not occur, in which case your planet will probably undergo another world war."[181]

AN ALIEN AGENDA

The messages presented to mankind by these alleged ETs
presents a number of questions. First we must wonder why the
contact method of choice is the same as those used by psychics,
mediums, and occultists. Secondly, if they are really highly
advanced, technologically superior physical beings from another
star system, why are they fixated on a religious message?

Doesn't it seem odd that there have been absolutely no specific instructions on how to cure disease, restore the environment, renew civilization, eliminate poverty, war, pestilence and
social unrest? Surely without the elimination of these ills there
can be no "New Age."

Why do the ETs promote an archaic pantheistic world-view
which is scientifically incompatible with the physical history
and nature of the cosmos? Finally, why do the alleged ETs
invest so much energy in flying across the cosmos to promote
New Age concepts that were already prevalent? Couldn't they
just email us?

In their book *The Facts on UFOs,* authors John Ankerberg
and John Weldon ask:

> ". . . Further, in light of the messages given by the
> UFO entities, how credible is it to think that lit-
> erally thousands of genuine extraterrestrials
> would fly millions or billions of light years simply
> to teach New Age philosophy, deny Christianity,
> and support the occult? Why would they do this
> with the preponderance of such activity already
> occurring on this planet? And why would the
> entities actually possess and inhabit people just

like demons do if they were really advanced extraterrestrials?"[182]

What is their agenda? What's *really* going on? According to Jacques Vallee and others, we may be getting set up for a giant deception:

"The UFO phenomenon represents a manifestation of a reality that transcends our current understanding of physics. . . . The UFOs are physical manifestations that cannot be understood apart from their psychic and symbolic reality. What we see in effect here is not an alien invasion. It is a control system which acts on humans and uses humans."[183]

THE QUICKENING

"And ye shall hear of wars and rumours of wars:

see that ye be not troubled: for all these things

must come to pass, but the end is not yet. For

nation shall rise against nation, and kingdom

against kingdom: and there shall be famines,

and pestilences, and Earthquakes, in divers places.

All these are the beginning of sorrows."

MATTHEW 24:6–8

As we approach the dawn of the 21st century, there is a widespread sense that we are living in extraordinary times. To many, the rapid pace of technological and scientific change is an indication that we are on the cusp of a marvelous era of peace, prosperity, and social advancement. To others, the rapid deterioration of moral and ethical standards at the end of the 20th century is an ominous sign of the impending disintegration of societal norms and the reappearance of clan rule that characterized the Dark Ages following the fall of the Roman Empire. Still others see the rapid economic decay, social and political upheavals, widespread corruption, and a dramatic increase in natural disasters as a sign that we are approaching the Biblical end times.

Whatever the interpretation, the fact is that there is a pervasive sense that the pace of events is accelerating and we stand at the threshold of dramatic and irreversible change.

THE QUICKENING

In 1995, Art Bell, a late-night radio talk show host, coined a term to describe the accelerating pace of events in the last few years. He called it "The Quickening." In 1997 Art Bell became the fourth-highest-rated radio talk show host in America, behind Rush Limbaugh, with an estimated weekly audience of nearly 15 million listeners on more than 300 stations nationwide. What is particularly remarkable about this audience is that his program, *Coast to Coast,* is an overnight show during the week. On Sundays he hosts another program, *Dreamland,* which boasts millions of additional listeners worldwide on the internet.

Art Bell's programs are unlike any on radio. In addition to news and politics, Bell deals with a wide variety of unusual topics such as UFOs, alien abductions, crop circles, paranormal phenomena, animal mutilations, alternative religions, and the like. His shows are a magnet for millions of New Age believers, UFO and alien contactees, and those who are simply interested in the bizarre, the arcane, and the outright strange!

In addition, Bell reports nightly on more than a dozen social, governmental, geophysical, and paranormal phenomena which he states are "quickening" as we approach the end of the 20th century.

In his book *The Art of Talk*, Bell describes why he coined the term and the nature of the items he tracks:

> "In all the years I have been on the air with my radio program, I have seen things begin to accelerate in nearly every aspect of American life. . . . The unbelievable violence, the defiance against authority, the blatant looting, and so on. . . . Other evidence of The Quickening, or the acceleration of things, includes the dramatically changing weather patterns; there is more violent weather than ever before. Earthquakes, hurricanes, and other acts of nature are happening with increasing frequency. . . . People everywhere are beginning to feel the hair stand up on the back of their necks as if they realize something is about to happen, perhaps some sort of judgment. I also feel something is about to happen and all these accelerated things seem to point to the same conclusion. After several years of taking note of this accelerated trend (accelerated in mostly a negative way), I finally summed it up one night on the air and just called everything that was going on The Quickening."[184]

Bell is careful not to interpret the signs that he sees. He well recognizes the wide variety of religious, scientific, and philosophical opinions among his listeners and is a master at balancing this tight-rope. And yet, he has put his finger on a feeling that many people share that "something is about to happen, perhaps some sort of judgment."

QUICKENING ITEMS

ECONOMICALLY	The growing American national debt Growing personal debt
SOCIALLY	Rapidly Escalating Crises Riots in numerous cities in the 1990s Gangs who kill for little reason Broken families, little sense of value Lack of respect for other people Increasing crimes of all kinds
POLITICS	Institutionalized deception
WEATHER	More Extreme, More Occurrences Earthquakes Hurricanes Floods

PESTILENCE	Increasing rates of cholera,
	    plague, Dengue fever
	AIDS now pandemic, growing
	    at 25 percent per year
	Hanta virus
	Mad Cow Disease
	Widespread resistance to formerly
	    effective antibiotics

ECO-BIOLOGY	Mutated amphibians and fish Large-scale death of coral reefs and oceanic microbes Deforestation Global Warming Breakup of the Larsen Ice Shelf

WEATHER CHANGES

In recent years, weather experts have noticed a disturbing trend that some connect to a gradual increase in global temperatures. According to global tracking stations, the frequency and intensity of storms has accelerated in the last decade.

In 1995 experts monitored the worst, the most intense weather year in the history of recording weather events. There were more tornadoes, tropical storms, droughts, floods, and other extremes of weather combined in that year than experts had seen since recording began in the mid-1800s.

According to the February-March 1996 edition of *Weather Wise* magazine, an international magazine which tracks weather activity worldwide, 19 tropical storms occurred in 1995—the second-greatest total since records began in 1871. There were 11 hurricanes, only one shy of the record set in 1969. And on August 27 and 28, 1995, a record five tropical cyclones occurred simultaneously in the Atlantic basin.

In May 1995 experts recorded the busiest month for tornadoes in the history of recording these events. There were 391 tornadoes—more than 12 a day, which surpassed the previous record set in 1991 of 68 tornadoes. Not only was there the largest number of tornadoes in history but they hit a total 36 states including California, Idaho, Oregon, Massachusetts, and the District of Columbia. In one day, May 18, 1995, a total of 86 tornadoes cut across the middle Mississippi and lower Ohio valleys with some of the strongest tornadoes in history.

In the July 8, 1996, issue of *Time* magazine, in an article entitled "Global Fever," Eugene Linden asked:

> "Are all the bizarre weather extremes we have been having lately normal fluctuations in the planet's atmospheric system? Or are they a precursor of the kind of climactic upheavals that can

been expected from the global warming caused by the continued build up of carbon dioxide and other so called green house gases? Scientists are still not sure, but one of the effects of the unusual stretch of weather over the past 15 years has been to alert researchers to a new and perhaps more immediate threat of the warming trend—the rapid spread of disease bearing bugs and pests."

In an article in the February 27, 1997, *Los Angeles Times* entitled "Analysis of Winter's Wacky Weather Remains Up in the Air," staff writer Louis Sahagun discussed the dramatic weather changes that flooded Northern California, Oregon, and Washington, and left a snow-pack 200 percent larger than normal in the mountains of seven Western states. According to Sahagun's sources, the dramatic changes may have been due to global warming from man-made greenhouse gasses:

"Kevin Trenberth, a scientist at the National Center for Atmospheric Research at Boulder, Colorado . . . sees a link between global warming and extreme climate changes that seem to be 'enhancing storminess' across the nation and around the world. Trenberth . . . sides with those who believe that the rate of these changes is larger than at any other time during the past 10,000 years. So does Tom Karl, senior scientist at the National Climate Data Center in Asheville, N.C. . . . Flooding along the Mississippi River in 1993 may have been an example of that. With similar trends unfolding in Australia, South Africa, Mexico, and Canada, Karl said, 'We may be witnessing the first discernible impact of human activity on global weather.' "[185]

Bad weather is not the only disaster they could spin off from small changes in global warming. To date, the average global temperature has risen 1.5 degrees centigrade since 1859. With only a few degrees increase in global temperatures some experts believe that a significant melting of the polar ice caps could occur. With only a 33 percent melting of the polar caps the global sea levels could rise as much as 150 feet. This would put a quarter of the world's population base under water.

A startling discovery in 1996 has some experts disturbed that the polar ice caps may indeed be melting at a significantly faster rate than previously believed.[186] Scientists have confirmed that the Larsen Ice Shelf, an 8,000-square-mile portion of ice in Antarctica, is breaking up, possibly due to global warming. While a complete breakup of this ice shelf will not be disastrous, it could be a sign of an even more ominous possibility.

Keep in mind, however, that the entire idea of "global warming" has become suspect to many scientists.

PESTILENCE ON THE RISE

In the last two decades there has been a dramatic increase in the number of infectious diseases worldwide. In the 1980s the "plague of the century," the HIV (AIDS) virus was discovered—a virus which destroys the immune system of its victims, a virus for which there is no cure. According to experts:

> "By mid-1996, cumulative HIV/AIDS-associated deaths worldwide numbered approximately 4.5 million among adults and 1.3 million among children. In 1995 alone, HIV/AIDS-associated illnesses caused the deaths of approximately 1.3 million people worldwide, including an estimated 300,000 children younger than 5 years of age. By the year 2000, an estimated 5 to 10 million children under 10 years of age will be orphaned worldwide because of the premature death of HIV-infected parents."[187]

In northern and central Africa entire nations are on the verge of being wiped out by this virus. According to statistics from the World Health Organization (WHO), at the end of 1994, 17 million adults were living with HIV infection. The majority (66%) of these infections were in sub-Saharan Africa (11.2 million)! In Botswana nearly one out of five people (18.02%) is infected with the HIV virus.

END 1996 GLOBAL ESTIMATES

Persons living with HIV/AIDS	22.6 million
New HIV infections in 1996	3.1 million
Deaths due to HIV/AIDS in 1996	1.5 million
Cumulative number of HIV infections	29.4 million
Cumulative number of AIDS cases	8.4 million
Cumulative number of deaths due to HIV/AIDS	6.4 million

(FROM THE JOINT UNITED NATIONS PROGRAMME ON HIV/AIDS)

While educational efforts among high-risk populations has slowed the pace of infection, the HIV virus continues to infect thousands of additional victims each day in the United States alone. Worldwide, more than 8,000 new HIV infections occur daily.

What is even more staggering are the rates of growth of this pandemic:

"As of 15 December 1995, 1,291,810 cumulative AIDS cases in adults and children have been reported to the World Health Organization (WHO) Global Programme on AIDS from 193 countries. This represents a 26 percent increase from the

> 1,025,073 cases reported in the 3 January, 1995 *Update* (and in the *Weekly Epidemiological Record* of 13 January 1995)."[188]

As of this printing WHO estimates,

> "Through mid-1996, an estimated 27.9 million people worldwide had been infected with HIV, of whom approximately 7.7 million have developed AIDS."[189]

Also by the year 2000, between 30 and 40 million men, women, and children will have been infected with HIV. More than 90 percent of all people with HIV infection will be from developing countries.

A disturbing epilogue to the HIV virus saga is that evidence is mounting that this virus was deliberately "engineered" by scientists who combined strains of the Bovine Leukemia Virus and the Sheep Vishna Virus in a laboratory setting. An increasing number of scientists believe that the virus was introduced into the human population through contaminated vaccines![190]

In the 1990s Americans have been introduced to several additional pestilences which have accelerated in recent years.

The Hanta virus created a panic in the American Southwest when numerous people died from this rodent-borne virus near several Indian reservations in New Mexico. The year 1995 also brought an upsurge of the flesh-eating streptococcus bacteria when a number of people were infected during a summer outbreak in several regions of the United States. In 1996, the Ebola virus reared its ugly head in Africa when it killed dozens of people rapidly and catastrophically by literally dissolving their internal organs in a matter of days. There is no cure for either the Ebola virus or the Hanta virus at this time.

In addition to these threats, a number of bacterial organisms that were once thought controlled made a comeback in the

1980s and 1990s. With the dramatic increase in the use of antibiotics on HIV/AIDS patients, who are frequently infected with multiple pathogenic organisms, there has been a dramatic rise in the incidents of antibiotic-resistant bacteria. The most dangerous among those is the multiple-drug-resistant tuberculosis strains which have begun to crop up around the United States, Europe, and other industrialized nations.

In 1994, the plague, which killed millions of Europeans prior to the invention of antibiotics, made a comeback when India suffered 90 consecutive days of 100-degree weather. The hot weather drove rats into the cities, causing an outbreak of pneumonic plague. The outbreak killed 63 people and ultimately cost India two billion dollars in cleanup, medical bills, and prevention. Paul Epstein, an epidemiologist with the Harvard school of Public Health, stated that "the real threat for people . . . may not be a single disease, but armies of emergent microbes raising havoc among a host of creatures."

EARTHQUAKES IN VARIOUS PLACES

In the last 100 years there has been a dramatic increase in the frequency and intensity of earthquakes worldwide. In the last 15 years, in California alone earthquakes have increased dramatically—with killer quakes, those greater than 6.0 on the Richter scale, increasing to unprecedented levels since 1980.

In 1860, the U.S. Geological Survey and numerous international agencies began cataloging earthquakes worldwide. Between 1890 and 1899 there was one earthquake noted worldwide which was greater than 6.0 on the Richter scale. This frequency remained unchallenged until the decade between 1950 and 1960 when nine earthquakes occurred that were greater than 6.0 on the Richter scale. However, between 1980 and 1989 an unprecedented increase occurred with a total of 86 killer earthquakes greater than 6.0 on the Richter scale occurring worldwide. And in the first three and a-half years of the 1990s there have already been more than 100 killer earthquakes greater than 6.0, according to the U.S. Geological Survey.

Skeptics argue that the increase in frequency of earthquakes is simply due to our improved ability to measure earthquakes

KILLER EARTHQUAKES GREATER THAN 6.0 ON THE RICHTER SCALE

1890–1899	1
1890–1910	3
1910–1920	2
1920–1930	2
1930–1940	5
1940–1950	4
1950–1960	9
1960–1970	13
1970–1979	51
1980–1989	86

In the first 3.5 years of the 1990s, there were already more than 100 killer earthquakes greater than 6.0 (source: U.S. Geological Survey: http://www.usgs.gov/).

worldwide. However, when this objection is carefully examined, it does not stand up. Since the 1960s the number of seismographs has been sufficient to detect any earthquake greater than 5.0 on the Richter scale occurring worldwide. In the last 30 years our ability to detect earthquakes has been so sophisticated that an earthquake of 5.0 or greater will be picked up by a minimum of ten seismographs, usually within a several-thousand-mile radius. Consequently, our ability to detect large earthquakes has been essentially unchanged in the last 30 years. During that period killer earthquakes have increased from 13 events between 1960 and 1970 to more than 100 events between 1990 and 1993.

In California alone from 1980 to 1995 there were 18 earthquakes greater than 5.0 on the Richter scale. That is more than the entire state experienced in the previous 80 years. Since that time, there have been four additional 5.0 or greater aftershocks to the October 1989 Bay area quake which measured 7.1 and the 1994 Northridge quake which measured 6.8.

Damage due to earthquakes in California alone has exceeded 30 billion dollars since 1989. The January 17, 1994, Northridge quake was the largest, most costly natural disaster in U.S. history. However, despite the large quakes in California within the last ten years, seismologists claim that no significant pressure was relieved from the San Andreas fault and they still expect a killer quake of greater than 8.0 to occur sometime in the next 30 to 40 years.

If such a quake occurred in the Los Angeles area it would likely disable the state for several years.

WARS AND RUMORS OF WARS

The 20th century has been labeled by many the century of war and the bloodiest century of all history. At no time during this century has there been peace. At any one time in the 1990s there have been as many as 70 wars and regional conflicts being waged around the world. In recent years there have been more wars and devastation by wars, with several technologies now providing even greater opportunities for mass destruction.

With the fall of the Soviet Union the Western world breathed a sigh of relief as the media and the governments of the world declared that peace was at hand and the cold war was over. However, despite the media glow, the breakup of the Soviet Union brought an even more unstable situation to the Middle East and the Eurasian continent. Currently, there are now more than a dozen countries which possess nuclear weapons, more than two dozen countries presently building intercontinental ballistic missiles, and more than 60 countries who presently have the technology to field a surface-skimming cruise missile. And, they are all mad at each other. The cloud of imminent nuclear attack hangs over all foreign policy negotiations. The nightmare of a virtual wipeout of major civilizations remains only 30 minutes away. The unthinkable lurks behind every major strategic decision.

The threat of nuclear terrorism is of great concern to the U.S. State Department. By smuggling a device just smaller than a footlocker into the United States, terrorists could demolish a city the size of Los Angeles.

Terrorism is a phenomenon which was largely birthed in the 20th century. Splinter groups and factions of numerous political and religious affiliations began to prey upon innocent bystanders by random bombings, kidnappings, mass murders, high-jacking aircraft, etc., for the purpose of political and financial gain. This phenomenon, while rare in previous centuries, has become commonplace at the end of the 20th century.

In addition to nuclear technology, biological and chemical weapons are ever more readily available and easily put into the hands of small, modestly capitalized terrorist groups. Time will tell whether the nightmare scenario of nuclear or biological terrorism will play itself out in the months and years to come.

Never before in history have the means been available—and in place—literally to wipe out mankind. Indeed, "Except those days should be shortened, there should be no flesh be saved: but for the elect's sake those days shall be shortened" (Matthew 24:22).

VIOLENCE ABOUNDS

In the final two decades of the 20th century, an increase in random violence has occurred worldwide. Gang warfare in the inner cities of the U.S. has reached epidemic proportions. The vocabulary of Americans has recently been expanded to include terms such as "drive-by-shooting," "mass murder," "random violence," and the like.

Every day we read stories of unimaginable horror. In the last decade there has been a gradual cheapening of life in industrialized nations. Euthanasia is now legal in many European countries, and it has been approved on ballot measures in a number of states in the U.S. In the last 30 years, more than 30 million abortions have been performed in the United States alone. As a result, the population base of young adults is insufficient to support the Social Security benefits of the aging postwar Baby Boom population.

In the inner cities we read of children killing children for the latest style of sneakers. Teenage violence has reached epidemic proportions with stories of murder, rape, and peer torture appearing daily in the print and broadcast media. It seems as if America has lost its soul. Crimes which were once shocking are now commonplace. Shock has been replaced by numbness in the psyche of Americans, and there seems to be no end in sight to the ever-increasing violence.

FAMINES IN THE LAND

In the last 30 years of the 20th century, despite dramatic technological advances in food production, starvation remains one of the leading causes of death worldwide. Currently experts estimate that 800 million people—nearly one out of every six—suffer from acute or chronic hunger. Approximately two billion of the world's nearly six billion people suffer from chronic malnutrition of some kind. And if recent statistics from United States Department of Agriculture are accurate, the problem will only worsen in the coming months and years.

In the last several years the world's grain stores have decreased dramatically to unprecedented lows. Not since statistics have been kept have the world's grain stores fallen to their current levels.

On September 12, 1995, officials from the U.S. Department of Agriculture estimated grain stores from data that had been compiled for more than 100 agricultural countries and came to a startling conclusion—that the world's grain stores had fallen to their lowest level in history with carryover stocks for 1996 at only 49 days.

The importance of this finding cannot be overstated. Grain is the planet's largest source of food for direct consumption by humans as well as for livestock and poultry. The shortage of grain is compiled by the fact that since 1990 the world's population has grown at a rate of approximately 110 million people per year. This growth has occurred primarily in the countries which can least afford it—the Third World developing nations.

Estimates are that at this rate the populations will reach six billion by 1998, eight billion by the year 2019, and 12 billion by the year 2030. Most experts believe that Earth's capacity to produce food is significantly less than that needed to support the estimated population of 12 billion people in the year 2030.

Adding to the dilemma, studies of the world's water tables have shown that they have shrunk significantly in the last several decades. In addition, the availability of river water has steadily decreased as rivers have been tapped, diverted, and dammed by growing population regions. By the time many rivers reach the ocean there is little or no water left. Consequently, coastal communities are finding river water supplies have decreased dramatically.

In the last several decades, fertilizers have been used to boost grain production. However, since 1990, statistics have shown that the increasing use of fertilizers has *not* increased the production of grains. In a article by Lester Brown in *World Watch* magazine November-December 1995, he stated:

> "Five years ago, we passed a little noticed but fateful turning-point in human history. Though it had worked superbly for half a century, farmers found that increasing crop yields by adding more and more fertilizer to the land is like a baker adding more and more yeast to the dough. The formula began to fail in 1990. In fact, the addition of more and more fertilizers has actually caused a decrease in the production in grain in numerous countries."[191]

DISTRESS OF NATIONS, WITH PERPLEXITY

While the situation we've described sounds grim, in most cases the estimates are conservative. The World Health Organization admits that its statistics on HIV-infected populations may be a gross underestimate of the situation. With nearly two billion people on the verge of starvation and the threat of nuclear war by terrorists groups rising, the leaders of the world face challenges never before encountered on the geopolitical scene.

While government leaders and the media try to put the best possible face on the current world scene, leaders in the private chambers of governments around the world burn the midnight oil looking for solutions to staggering problems. There is a feeling among many that we stand at the edge of a cataclysmic disintegration of society.

THE DAWNING OF THE NEW AGE?

While most people feel a sense of gloom or despair when confronted with this information, our space brothers, through the prophets of the New Age movement, present a wholly different spin on the situation.

MOTHER EARTH IN LABOR

In the last several decades, hundreds of books have been written by contactees who claim that extraterrestrials have predicted this time of Earth changes and have defined its meaning. According to our space brothers the increasing earthquakes, famine, pestilence, wars, poverty, and violence are simply the birth pangs of our Earth Mother as she attempts to usher in a new age of peace and prosperity accompanied by a global governance.

The Earth changes, they claim, are nothing to be feared. They are not the wrath of God, and they will not result in the annihilation of mankind from the planet. Rather, they are something wonderful—something to be desired. They portend a time of hope and joy for the nations of Earth, ushering in the arrival of a world leader who will unify the world in peace and brotherhood with technological answers to solve our problems.

In the spring 1994 issue of *Connecting Link Magazine,* New Age author Kay Wheeler discussed the current Earth changes and their significance. According to the article, she is a "Pleiadian Starseed," that is, a contactee and channeler for extraterrestrials from the star cluster of the Pleiades. In this article she gave us information from the "Souls of Light," a group of extraterrestrials from the seventh celestial plane of life regarding the current Earth changes:

> "There is much happening on your planet at this time. The Mother is cleansing. It is all that she knows to do at this time to clear herself of the

pollution that exists within her bodies. But you as light bearers can help your Mother to cleanse in such a way that does not destroy all life on this planet. . . ."[192]

A number of New Age authors echo this notion that "Mother Earth" is undergoing a beneficial cleansing in order to purge herself of the "pollution" that resides on her body.

According to New Age channeler Barbara Marciniak, the Pleiadians teach that the Earth changes are a test, an exhilarating experience to be embraced and not feared:

". . . It will seem that great chaos and turmoil are forming, that nations are rising against each other in war, and that earthquakes are happening more frequently. It will seem as if everything is falling apart and cannot be put back together. . . ."[193]

"Bless these changes that come to Earth. . . . You will find yourself tested. You will say, 'Am I a victim here? Is the world collapsing around me? Or is it uplifting itself around me while everything is seemingly in the midst of collapse?' "[194]

"The times are changing, and it is not for you to panic over what is coming. It is time for you to feel the exhilaration inside your being. The time you have been waiting for, your purpose, is on the cusp of being fulfilled. . . ."[195]

Despite wars, accelerating earthquakes, famines, pestilence, and "great chaos and turmoil" in general, we are to "bless these changes that come to Earth" and "feel the exhilaration inside [our] being because the time [we] have been waiting for, [our] purpose, is on the cusp of being fulfilled."

This is a rather remarkable view of the current and future Earth changes. Are we supposed to embrace the deaths of tens of millions of HIV victims as something wonderful? Are we to "feel the exhilaration inside our being" when we contemplate the disintegration of society that accompanies the combined impact of pestilence, drought, economic collapse, wars, and governmental corruption that has annihilated sub-Saharan Africa?

If, as the extraterrestrial messengers have predicted, this is our future, "the time [we] have been waiting for," the era that is "on the cusp of being fulfilled," *why are the gurus of the New Age so optimistic?* There is a saying "that an optimist is someone who is simply lacking all the facts." Is this the case, or is there a hidden agenda behind the warm-fuzzy optimism expressed by New Age gurus?

What is the agenda behind such statements? As we will see in the next chapter, the authors and gurus of the New Age believe that our redemption, our salvation from certain destruction, will come at the hands of our extraterrestrial, benevolent space brothers and creators!

THE TIME OF THE SIGNS

Art Bell's choice of the expression "the quickening" to describe the accelerating geopolitical predicament is ironic indeed. "Quickening" is the medical term used by obstetricians to describe the first movement of the fetus in the womb. What is ironic about this choice of idiom is that Jesus Christ used the very same illustration, pregnancy and childbirth, to describe the signs before *his* coming!

As he neared the end of his ministry, Jesus' disciples came to him privately and asked him what would be the sign of his Second Coming and of the end of the age. Jesus' two-chapter answer is recorded in the Gospel of Matthew, chapters 24 and 25.

In this portion of Scripture, Jesus gave an outline of the signs which closely parallel the signs that Art Bell monitors and calls "the quickening." Although Mr. Bell is careful not to interpret the signs, Jesus Christ told us that we should do just that!

> "And Jesus went out, and departed from the tem-
> ple: and his disciples came to him for to shew
> him the buildings of the temple. And Jesus said
> unto them, 'See ye not all these things? verily I
> say unto you, There shall not be left here one
> stone upon another, that shall not be thrown
> down.' And as he sat upon the Mount of Olives,
> the disciples came unto him privately, saying,
> 'Tell us, when shall these things be? and what
> shall be the sign of thy coming, and of the end of
> the world?' And Jesus answered and said unto
> them, 'Take heed that no man deceive you. For
> many shall come in my name, saying, I am
> Christ; and shall deceive many. And ye shall hear
> of wars and rumours of wars: see that ye be not
> troubled: for all these things must come to pass,
> but the end is not yet. For nation shall rise
> against nation, and kingdom against kingdom:
> and there shall be famines, and pestilences, and
> earthquakes, in divers places. All these are the
> beginning of sorrows' " (Matthew 24:1–8).

After telling the disciples that the temple would be destroyed ("There shall not be left here one stone upon another, that shall not be thrown down."), it's interesting to note that first sign Jesus gave them regarding the time of his coming was, "Take heed that no man deceive you." Jesus wanted them to under- stand that one of the primary signs of the times before his coming would be the existence of tremendous deception.

This deception would be characterized by "many" coming in his name. Notice that it is not just one coming in his name but *many!* The mission of these false Christs will be to "deceive many." Deception can take many forms. It can be a false statement or doctrine. It can be a physical deception, such as performing miraculous signs and wonders. Or, these false Christs could purposely misinterpret the signs of the times so that nations of the world will be led away from "the truth." We believe that the deception will involve all three of these forms!

Next Jesus told the disciples that the times preceding his coming would be characterized by "wars and rumours of wars . . . famines, and pestilences, and earthquakes, in divers places." Interestingly, he stated, "but the end is not yet. . . . All these are the beginning of sorrows."

Jesus wanted his disciples, then and now, to understand that the signs would not indicate his immediate return. Rather, the signs would be a precursor to the coming and would be the "beginning of sorrows."

The term "beginning of sorrows" is a provocative illustration. The word translated "sorrows" in the Greek is *odínos* (o-deenos) and means the pain of childbirth, travail pain, or birth pangs. Jesus wanted us to understand that the signs preceding his coming would come upon Earth like the contractions of childbirth.

THE GESTATION AND BIRTH OF THE MAN-CHILD

The duration of a normal pregnancy is 280 days (40 weeks), or about nine months. When the female's ovum is fertilized, it begins a gradually accelerating process of cell division. The fertilized egg becomes two cells in a matter of minutes. The two become four, four become eight, and so on. Within the first 24 hours the fertilized egg has developed into a ball of hundreds of millions of cells.

At about the beginning of the second trimester (between 12–15 weeks of gestation) the mother feels the first movement of the fetus—the "quickening." During the next several weeks the fetus grows rapidly, gaining about an ounce a day. To the mother the activity of the baby is steady, but uneventful.

Toward the middle of the last trimester (32–40 weeks of gestation) the mother starts to feel false labor pangs, called Braxton-Hicks contractions. However, "the end is not yet. . . . All these are the beginning of sorrows." These false contractions are a warning sign that a birth is on the way, but a significant period of time is still left. During this time the mother's realization that "it really is going to happen" sets in. If she is a responsible mother, she will begin to prepare in advance for the real event—the birth of the child.

In the last four weeks of the pregnancy, false contractions increase in frequency and intensity. They can occur every few minutes or hours. However, between events there is a relative calm. Finally, when the fateful day arrives, the false contractions are replaced by a gradual, but rapidly accelerating series of birth pangs.

The birth pangs of "true labor" are indistinguishable from those of false labor. If the expectant mother has not studied a book on childbirth, or been properly mentored, then when true labor begins, the woman is often fooled because of the inadequate preparation.

In the same way, the signs preceding the time of Christ's coming will be misinterpreted by those who are not prepared to recognize them. The Apostle Peter spoke of those who would scoff at the notion of the Second Coming of Christ:

> "Knowing this first, that there shall come in the last days scoffers, walking after their own lusts, and saying, Where is the promise of his coming? for since the fathers fell asleep, all things continue as they were from the beginning of the creation" (2 Peter 3:3–4).

Like the scoffers in the last days the mother may think, "Where is the promise of the child's coming? . . . all things continue as they were from the beginning of conception." However, when true labor pangs begin, the contractions accelerate in frequency and intensity until the child is birthed.

What is fascinating about the idiom of childbirth and the Second Coming of Jesus Christ is that they are both preceded by well-known signs given well in advance of the actual event. And yet, an ill prepared mother, like the skeptic, if she chooses to ignore those signs, will be "caught unaware" when the child is born.

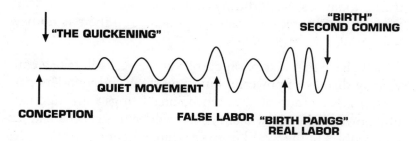

GREAT SIGNS AND WONDERS

In the subsequent verses of Matthew 24, Jesus continues his discussion of the signs with a warning to the Church. He tells his disciples that if anyone comes claiming to be Christ, do not believe:

> "Then if any man shall say unto you, Lo, here is Christ, or there; believe it not. For there shall arise false Christs, and false prophets, and shall shew great signs and wonders; insomuch that, if it were possible, they shall deceive the very elect. Behold, I have told you before" (Matthew 24:21–25).

Again we see the theme of deception. The false Christs and false prophets that arise at the end times will perform "great signs and wonders; insomuch that, if it were possible, they shall deceive the very elect." In the opinion of most Bible scholars, the elect, in this context, is the Church—those who believe that Jesus Christ is the Messiah, the Redeemer of all mankind, and the very Creator of the universe in the flesh![196]

The point is that the coming deception, as presented by these false prophets and false Christs, will be so powerful, so convincing, that even the very "elect" will be deceived, but only for a time. To deceive a believer in Jesus Christ will take more than another belief system, philosophy, or a new scientific discovery. Every philosophy that could ever be invented exists today as well during the time of Christ. As King Solomon said three-thousand years ago, ". . . there is no new thing under the sun."[197]

We believe that deception of the very "elect" will take a convincing display of powerful but lying signs and wonders perpetrated by a group of ultradimensional beings with supernatural powers—beings whose agenda will be to steer the nations and peoples of the world from the transcendent Creator of the universe and his redemptive plan for mankind.

ET TO THE RESCUE!

In the last few decades, a number of Native American shamen, New Age authors, and gurus have connected the accelerating Earth changes to an instantaneous disappearance of millions of people from the face of Earth. This disappearance will be an alien evacuation necessitated by those accelerating changes, which threaten the very existence of the planet. We are told that in order to save "Mother Earth" and her children, alien ships will remove a group of individuals who no longer fit in—those who refuse to return to the matriarchal system, whose very presence threatens the survival of planet Earth and the arrival of the "New Age."

THE COMING EVACUATION!

"Our rescue ships will be able to come in close enough in the twinkling of an eye to set the lifting beams in operation in a moment. And all over the globe where events warrant it, this will be the method of evacuation. Mankind will be lifted, levitated shall we say, by the beams from our smaller ships. These smaller craft will in turn taxi the persons to the larger ships overhead, higher in the atmosphere, where there is ample space and quarters and supplies for millions of people."

A MESSAGE FROM EXTRATERRESTRIALS OF
THE ASHTAR COMMAND, PROJECT WORLD EVACUATION, 1993

By the mid-1960s there were hundreds of alleged UFO contactees who claimed to have received detailed messages regarding the origin, destiny, and future of mankind. Not surprisingly, these messages spoke of a time in the not too distant future when mankind would evolve to a higher consciousness. With the assistance of our "space brothers," we would realize a new era of peace, harmony, and brotherhood of man.

However, the 1960s were marred by war, poverty, racism, famine, and terrible social conflict. The road to the age of Aquarius, it seemed, was being paved with increasing social unrest, economic and environmental calamity, and a general feeling of unrest.

The promise of this "new age of Aquarius," it seemed, was nowhere to be found. Predictably, our space brothers had an explanation. As we saw in the previous chapter, the tremendous upheavals of the latter portion of the 20th century are a precursor of this new age to come. Earth changes, the ETs have insisted, are caused by the presence of pollution within the body of Mother Earth. And like a living organism with an infection, Earth Mother needs to cleanse herself of the pollution as well as the "dark forces" who no longer fit in.

As we will see, according to numerous New Age channelers the "dark forces" are a group of individuals whose thought patterns are of the past. According to our "space brothers," such individuals are keeping Earth and its forces of "light" from evolving to a higher state of consciousness known as the "fifth dimension."

According to hundreds of contactees, Earth changes are part of a cleansing that could be catastrophic if our "space brothers" don't intervene, but they will. The ETs, we are told, have a plan to salvage our planet and prevent Earth Mother from destroying the majority of life as she cleanses herself. The plan is to remove, that is "evacuate," the millions of people who are "out of vibration" with Earth Mother!

Like a surgeon who carefully excises a cancerous lump, making sure not to damage the surrounding tissue, extraterrestrials will "beam up" or levitate these individuals into hundreds of cloaked alien ships that are currently surrounding the Earth. When the global situation reaches a crisis point on Earth, they will evacuate these people in a "twinkling of an eye," then transfer them to larger ships for re-education and initiation into higher levels of consciousness!

BIRTH PANGS AND THE COMING EVACUATION

One of the first channeled messages from alleged extraterrestrials occurred in 1952, when the "space brother" Ashtar spoke through author George Van Tassel. According to Van Tassel, Ashtar is one of the "Council Seven of Lights" pledged to save "mankind from himself. . . . We are concerned about their deliberate determination to EXTINGUISH HUMANITY AND TURN THIS PLANET INTO A CINDER. . . . Our missions are peaceful, but this condition occurred before in this solar system and the planet Lucifer was torn to bits. We are determined that it shall not happen again."[198]

In the 1980s Ashtar clarified the message to Earth through a new channeler named Thelma Terrell, widely known in New Age circles by her "spiritual name," Tuella. In her book *Project World Evacuation*,[199] she compiled the channeled messages of Ashtar, who declared that planet Earth would be spared certain annihilation by an extraterrestrial evacuation of millions of people who threaten the harmony and evolution of Earth. In her book she describes herself as a "messenger of light" who wrote the book for the disciples and initiates of the "Higher

Revelation." The connection to Earth changes and the coming ET evacuation is repeatedly made in Project World Evacuation.

> ". . . We watch diligently, the threat of a polar shift for the planet in your generation. Such a development would create a planetary situation through which none could survive. This would necessitate an evacuation such as I have referred to."[200]

> ". . . Earth changes will be the primary factor in mass evacuation of this planet."[201]

This theme is repeated in the spring 1994 issue of *Connecting Link Magazine*, a quarterly New Age periodical. Author Kay Wheeler—known by her "spiritual name," Ozmana—describes herself as a "Pleiadian star seed" and channeler. In her article she presents the channeled messages from the "Souls of Light," a group of extraterrestrials from the "Seventh Celestial Plane of Life" who are working together to bring "the light of God" to planet Earth. In the article she connects current Earth changes to the removal of "many beings" from the planet.

> "The Mother is desperately fighting for her life. Many of her vortexes have been drained. She is in critical condition at this time and must turn her thoughts to herself if she is to survive. That is why you see the many crises in the world. Many of these you do not hear about on your 'screen of lies.'

> "There is much happening on your planet at this time. The Mother is cleansing. It is all that she knows to do at this time to clear herself of the pollution that exists within her body. But you as light bearers can help your Mother to cleanse in such a way that does not destroy all life on this planet.

"Much of this is necessary. Many of these beings have appointments to leave at this time. Earth's population needs to be decreased to bring forth the necessary changes upon this planet to move into the fourth dimension.

"Your Earth is a fourth-dimensional being at this time. She has moved into this energy pattern, and those upon Earth who plan to stay must be of this vibration."[202]

This is a remarkable claim. A group of individuals, described as "the pollution that exists within her [Mother Earth's] body," have appointments to leave Earth. Why are they leaving, and who are these individuals? According to Wheeler, all those who "keep the Earth held back" because "their thought patterns are of the past" are to be removed:

"Many of these beings who are leaving this planet at this time have completed that which they came to do. It is a time of great rejoicing for them. Do not feel sad about their leaving. They are going home. Many are waiting to be with them again. . . . Many beings must move on, for their thought patterns are of the past. They hold on to these thoughts that keep Earth held back."

THE GREAT SHIFT

In 1995 Barbara Marciniak echoes the theme of Earth changes and the coming disappearance of millions of people in her book, *Earth: Pleiadian Keys to the Living Library*. The book was compiled from 13 trance-channeling sessions in 1991 and 1992 with Pleiadian entities, extraterrestrials from the star system Pleiades. After describing current and future calamities, she encourages the reader to recognize that the Earth changes are here and will accelerate until the "great shift" occurs:

"Some of you want to pretend that the Earth changes are not occurring. However, they are occurring, and there is nothing to fear, for they are part of the process of the great shift. . . . Whether you stay on the planet and alter your vibration, or you check out and sit in the bleachers to watch the show, doesn't really matter. On some level, in some avenue of existence, you will participate and you will learn."[203]

This is a fascinating statement. We will all participate in the coming "great shift"; however, some of us will do so from the bleachers!

Those that are taken off the planet by our space brothers are sometimes identified as the "dark forces." In her book *Revelations of Things to Come,* Earlyne Chaney, a New Age channeler, receives telepathic messages from an extraterrestrial entity named Kut-Hu-Mi. Regarding the coming Earth changes this entity states that "The Mother Deva [Mother Earth] realizes that her matter must be purified. Her akashic ethers must be cleansed of the dark thought forces".[204]

In her book *Bringers of the Dawn: Teachings from the Pleiadians,* Barbara Marciniak returns to the theme of the coming shift and its associated evacuation. The teachings, which were also channeled from Pleiadian entities, discusses a number of specific details regarding the reality of ETs, the coming Earth changes, and the coming evacuation.

At the very outset of this book we are told of the reality of ET contact with planet Earth and the coming shift: "We are here. We are the Pleiadians, a collective of energy."[205] Pleiadian entities, we are told, were some of the "Original Planners" of Earth who seeded Earth with their DNA, "and this DNA became part of the DNA of the human species."

According to the Pleiadian entities, they have come from our future to plant "a seed" to effect change which will affect our future, our present and our past. This seed is the knowledge that they bring, knowledge which will help us to understand that "A major leap is about to take place. There are mother ships surrounding this planet that are acting as literal transducers of energy. . . ."[206]

REACHING FOR A HIGHER FREQUENCY

Throughout New Age literature we are told that the enlightened ones, also known as "light workers," are a group of individuals, millions in number, who are in sync with Earth Mother and "forces of light" who inhabit the universe. These people, known as initiates, have come to realize their connectedness with the universe and the universal "truth" that God is in all, that we possess an inherent deity and that we will, if we attain the highest possible "vibration," evolve into "ascended masters."

According to Pleiadian entities, Earth is also reaching for a higher frequency. However, there are individuals "who pollute the Earth," whose thought patterns are out of sync with the universal consciousness or force, who do not go along with the plan. They will be removed to bring about the higher frequency that the Earth Mother desires.

This theme is abundant in the writings of Barbara Marciniak. In *Bringers of the Dawn*, she stated:

> "If human beings do not change—if they do not make the shift in values and realize that without Earth they could not be here—then Earth, in its love for its own initiation, is reaching for a higher frequency, will bring about a cleansing that will balance it once again. There is a potential for many people to leave the planet in an afternoon."[207]

The people who leave the planet in an afternoon, according to the Pleiadians, no longer fit in and are keeping Earth from evolving to the next plane:

> "The people who leave the planet during the time of Earth changes do not fit here any longer, and they are stopping the harmony of Earth. When the time comes that perhaps 20 million people leave the planet at one time there will be a tremendous shift in consciousness for those who are remaining. . . ."[208]

Where will they go? According to New Age author Timothy Green Beckley, the extraterrestrials state: ". . . Those who refuse to be enlightened and infused with the light of God will be taken to other planets that are uninhabited, but habitable, and there they will make a new start."[209]

How many will go? According to Johanna Michaelson, a spirit guide predicted that two billion people will be removed simultaneously during the coming cleansing:

> ". . . Asher, the spirit guide of John Randolph Price, a moving force behind the New Agers' 'World Instant of Cooperation' (on December 31, 1986, in which thousands of meditators worldwide simultaneously concentrated on world peace hoping to cause a critical mass launching into the New Age) told him that two billion people who didn't go along with the New Age would be wiped off the face of the Earth during the coming cleansing."[210]

THE CONDITIONING

In December 1960, NASA released findings of a study commissioned to evaluate the effect on society if they were to discover and release evidence for intelligent extraterrestrial life on other planets. The report, prepared by the prestigious think tank The Brookings Institute, made an ominous prediction:

> "While the discovery of intelligent life in other parts of the universe is not likely in the immediate future, it could nevertheless, happen at any time. Discovery of intelligent beings on other planets could lead to an all-out effort by Earth to contact them, or it could send sweeping changes or even the downfall of civilization." Even on Earth, the report added, "societies sure of their own place have disintegrated when confronted by a superior society."[211]

In 1960 this was probably an accurate assessment of the situation. Indeed, the reality of UFOs and alien visitors was still a far-off notion to most people, the stuff of science fiction. Such a revelation—the existence of a race of superior alien entities—by official government sources would likely have wreaked havoc on the establishment and populace of that time. However, at the end of the 20th century, we have been conditioned by an unparalleled media fixation with UFOs and extraterrestrials. Now more than 75 percent of Americans believe extraterrestrials exist and have been visiting us for millennia. Furthermore, millions believe that they are our benevolent space brothers who, through their vastly superior technology, are capable of rescuing us from our current predicament.

The dramatic shift in our perceived threat by extraterrestrial life has been highlighted by a number of recent events.

On August 6, 1996, when NASA administrator Daniel Goldin announced to the world that a panel of prestigious scientists had found evidence of microscopic life in an ancient meteorite from the planet Mars, the overwhelming reaction was one of rejoicing. Rather than feeling threatened, the media and scientific establishments of the world greeted the announcement as the greatest discovery of the millennia! Although it was only "circumstantial evidence" of microscopic life, the implications were staggering, according to the "experts." They insisted that if the discovery by NASA scientists stood the test of time and intense scrutiny, life "is likely to be abundant in the cosmos."

The shift in attitude was also highlighted by a recent event in Israel. On January 6, 1997, thousands of Israelis stood on a beach in Haifa, Israel, to greet our space brothers who, they were told, would land that night and make the "first open contact" with mankind. This prophecy was given by the popular Israeli psychic Helinor Harar. Like a scene out of the movie *Independence Day,* they stood for hours awaiting the contact. As music from the *X-Files* was played, Ms. Harar shouted, "Israel will be the center of UFO landings!" Many in the crowd carried signs asking their space brothers to beam them up! However, instead of being vaporized by an alien beamship on a skyscraper in Los Angeles, the restless crowd was bitterly disappointed. At one point the crowd was whipped into a frenzy when an airplane made a low approach nearby. When they realized that it was a terrestrial craft, many in the crowd wept bitterly.

The conditioning by the media and educational establishments has not gone unnoticed by our "space brothers." In fact, according to some authors, this conditioning was carefully orchestrated by them to ease the transition to "ET reality." In the spring 1994 issue of *Connecting Link Magazine,* Yvonne Cole, another channel of the Ashtar command, clearly stated that the governments of the world have been working with "light workers" of the New Age movement to condition the world for the impending contact:

> "Very soon your government, with the assistance
> of our Starseeds, will reveal to the world at large

a truth that they have heretofore been guarding most effectively. Your government and the governments of the other countries have been interacting with what you call extraterrestrials for many years. . . . The public is now ready for the truth. The conditioning by television, newspapers, books, radio, and most importantly the light workers, has done its job and now it is safe to reveal to the inhabitants of planet Earth that WE ARE HERE."[212]

Unfortunately, as far as we can tell, the events foretold in the article entitled "We Will Land in 1994" failed to materialize.

THE "PLAN"

According to "light workers" who are diligently preparing the world for the coming shift and its accompanying evacuation, the Ashtar Command has a detailed plan—already in motion—to systematically remove souls from this planet. Some of these details are given in Tuella's *Project World Evaluation*:

"There is method and great organization in a detailed plan already near completion for the purpose of removing souls from this planet, in the event of catastrophic events making a rescue necessary. . . . [213]

". . . The Great Evacuation will come upon the world very suddenly. The flash of emergency events will be as a lightning that flashes in the sky. So sudden and so quick in its happening that it is over almost before you are aware of its presence. . . ."[214]

". . . Our rescue ships will be able to come in close enough in the twinkling of an eye to set the lifting beams in operation in a moment. And all over the globe where events warrant it, this will be the method of evacuation. Mankind will be lifted, levitated shall we say, by the beams from our smaller ships. These smaller craft will in turn taxi the persons to the larger ships overhead, higher in the atmosphere, where there is ample space and quarters and supplies for millions of people..."[215]

Does this sound familiar?

According to Ashtar, this coming alien evacuation will occur in several phases:

"PHASE I of the Great Exodus of souls from the planet will take place at a moment's notice when it is determined that the inhabitants are in danger."[216]

"PHASE II This second phase immediately following the first. The second phase is vital, as we return for the children of all ages and races. The child does not have the power of choice in understanding nor personal accountability."[217]

This two-phase evacuation is fascinating for a number of reasons. First the adults who no longer fit in, whose "thought patterns are of the past," the "dark forces," are taken up by alien beam ships where there are adequate supplies for millions of people. Then the children of the world are taken up! Why? Because they do not "have personal responsibility."

DON'T WORRY, BE HAPPY!

What is the message to those who have been left behind—those whose children have been taken? Don't worry, be happy. The people who have been taken "have completed that which they came to do. It is a time of great rejoicing for them. Do not feel sad about their leaving. They are going home."

This message is echoed by Ashtar in *Project: World Evacuation*:

> "Do not be concerned nor unduly upset if you do
> not participate in this first temporary lift-up of
> souls who serve with us. This merely means that
> your action in the plan is elsewhere, and you will
> be taken for your instructions or will receive
> them in some other manner. Do not take any per-
> sonal affront if you are not alerted or are not a
> participant in this first phase of our plan. Your
> time will come later, and these instructions are
> not necessary for you at this time. . . ."[218]

What about the "light workers," those adults who have been
initiated into the higher frequency and realized their own
divinity? They are told, "Do not take any personal affront if
you are not alerted or are not a participant in this first phase
of our plan. Your time will come later, and these instructions
are not necessary for you at this time."

According to Timothy Green Beckley, the extraterrestrials
have given us some additional insight on the predicament of
the "light workers" who are left behind:

> ". . . Many of the New Age workers and instruc-
> tors who feel that they will be taken will not be
> taken right away, but left behind to help
> mankind survive through the cataclysmic period.
> This is their mission."[219]

So, the New Age workers are supposed to *rejoice* when they
find out that millions of people, including members of their
own family, have been abducted by aliens and they are "left
behind to help mankind survive through the cataclysmic
period"!

Where do we sign up?

RAPTURE, EVACUATION
OR COSMIC DECEPTION?

What can we conclude about the things we have read in this chapter? New Age prophets speak of a sudden event in which a group of individuals who "no longer fit in," whose thought patterns are of the past, are suddenly, "in a twinkling of an eye," removed—evacuated—from the surface of planet Earth. Incredibly, the Bible speaks of a similar event. In 1 Corinthians 15:52, Paul the Apostle revealed a mystery. In this portion of Scripture he discussed the resurrection of the dead and the conversion of our physical bodies into heavenly bodies:

> "Behold, I shew you a mystery; We shall not all sleep, but we shall all be changed, in a moment, in the twinkling of an eye, at the last trump: for the trumpet shall sound, and the dead shall be raised incorruptible, and we shall be changed. For this corruptible must put on incorruption, and this mortal must put on immortality."

This mystery, we are told, will be a sudden conversion of our bodies; "we shall all be changed" from our corruptible earthly state to an incorruptible heavenly body. According to Paul, this event will occur in "in a twinkling of an eye."

In 1 Thessalonians 4:13–17 Paul elaborated on this event:

> "But I would not have you to be ignorant, brethren, concerning them which are asleep, that ye sorrow not, even as others which have no hope. For if we believe that Jesus died and rose again, even so them also which sleep in Jesus will God bring with him. For this we say unto you by the word of the Lord, that we which are alive and remain unto the coming of the Lord shall not prevent them which are asleep. For the Lord

> himself shall descend from heaven with a shout, with the voice of the archangel, and with the trump of God: and the dead in Christ shall rise first: Then we which are alive and remain shall be caught up together with them in the clouds, to meet the Lord in the air: and so shall we ever be with the Lord."

In his description of this coming event, Paul stated that we will be "caught up" to meet the LORD in the sir. This event, called the Rapture of the Church (from the Latin *rapturo* meaning "caught up"), has been a Biblical doctrine since the Early Church. What's remarkable is that the ETs, through the prophets of the New Age, are apparently attempting to explain away this event as a global alien evacuation of people who no longer "fit in," those whose "vibration" is out of sync with Earth Mother and the universal consciousness! Why? What is behind such claims?

There are those who propose that the Biblical Rapture and the coming alien evacuation are one and the same; that is, they propose that Paul the Apostle and Jesus were both describing a coming evacuation by extraterrestrials, an event that would culminate the age of Pisces and usher in the age of Aquarius. This suggestion, however, will not stand up under scrutiny.

According to the Bible the Rapture of the Church represents the removal of God's elect before he pours out his wrath on a Christ-rejecting world. On the other hand, according to many prophets of the New Age, the coming alien evacuation represents the removal of the evil malcontents (the "dark forces"), whose thought patterns and actions are preventing the evolution of planet Earth and the arrival of the New Age.

Furthermore, according to the Bible, the Church will be taken to the heavenly realm "where neither moth nor rust corrupts."[220]

In the book of Revelation we are told of this place where "God shall wipe away all tears from their eyes; and there shall be no more death, neither sorrow, nor crying, neither shall there be any more pain: for the former things are passed away."

In this heavenly realm there is no death, decay, disease, or pain. All of these are the result of the decay of the matter within our bodies. This occurs because of the irreversible and universal law of decay, the Second Law of Thermodynamics. This law, called the entropy law, acts throughout the dimensions of our space-time domain. The effect of the law is that the universe as a whole is decaying, breaking down, and cooling off with the advance of time.

By definition, heaven must be independent of the space-time domain because within its boundaries the Second Law of Thermodynamics, the law of universal decay, does not function. The nature of heaven is entirely different from that of an alien beamship or any extraterrestrial planet subject to the laws of death and decay.

Consequently, the notion that the Rapture of the Church and the coming alien evacuation are one and the same cannot be true. The coming ET evacuation can be nothing more than a counterfeit explanation for the disappearance of millions of people, meant for those left behind.

ALIEN
ENCOUNTERS

SECTION III:

THE
BIBLICAL VIEW

THE RETURN OF THE NEPHILIM

And as it was in the days of Noah, so shall

it be also in the days of the Son of man.

LUKE 17:26

Among the numerous ancient records of "alien" visitors to planet Earth, none are more significant than the records of the Bible. In fact, the Bible records the first "astronaut" who *left* Earth: Enoch.[221]

THE FLOOD OF NOAH

The reality of the worldwide flood is not the focus of this book. For this discussion, we will set aside the attempts of critics to deny this catastrophe which so manifestly altered Earth so long ago. While not free of its own controversies, there are a number of excellent scientific treatises on this subject.[222]

However, one of the issues which does impact our inquiry is, *why* did God send such a drastic judgment upon planet Earth? There was widespread wickedness, of course. But if that were the only criterion, perhaps we all had better get life jackets! According to the Biblical record, there was much more going on than most people have any idea!

Furthermore, the circumstances which led to the flood are not simply of historical interest. Those conditions are important to us for very practical reasons as well. Jesus left us an ominous warning: "As the days of Noah were, so shall also the coming of the Son of man be."[223] Yet, what were the "days of Noah" like? What made them unique? We must try to understand what was really going on in order to appropriate His warning.

THE DAYS OF NOAH

Most people, including serious students of the Bible, are unaware of the peculiar circumstances that led to the flood of Noah. This has been widely misunderstood (and mistaught) for centuries. The strange but critical goings-on are among the most controversial issues among serious scholars, and we should maintain open minds as we proceed through the murky mists of the deep past.

To understand this astonishing period of prehistory, we need to examine the precedent events as recorded in Genesis 6:

> "And it came to pass, when men began to multiply on the face of the earth, and daughters were born unto them, that the sons of God saw the daughters of men that they were fair; and they took them wives of all which they chose. . . .

> ". . . There were giants in the earth in those days; and also after that, when the sons of God came in unto the daughters of men, and they bare children to them, the same became mighty men which were of old, men of renown" (Genesis 6:1, 2, 4).

This strange passage describes the bizarre circumstances that led to the cataclysmic disaster of the famous flood of Noah. The Hebrew term translated "sons of God" is בְּנֵי־הָאֱלֹהִים, B'nai HaElohim, a term consistently used in the Old Testament for *angels*.[224]

When the Hebrew *Torah,* which of course includes the book of Genesis, was translated into Greek in the third century before Christ (giving us what is known as the Septuagint translation), this expression was translated *angels*.[225] With the benefit of the best experts at that time behind it, this translation carries great weight and it was the one most widely quoted by the writers of the New Testament.

The *Book of Enoch* also clearly treats these strange events as involving angels.[226] Although this book was not considered a part of the "inspired" canon, the *Book of Enoch* was venerated by both rabbinical and early Christian authorities from about 200 B.C. through about A.D. 200 and is useful to authenticate the lexicological usage and confirm the accepted beliefs of the period. The Biblical passage refers to *supernatural beings* intruding upon the planet Earth. (There are alternative interpretations of this, which we will examine shortly.)

"The daughters of men" (בְּנוֹת הָאָדָם, *Benoth Adam*, literally "the daughters of Adam") refers to the natural female descendants of mankind. (Notice that no particular genealogical strain is specified.) The errant supernatural "alien" beings apparently mated with human women and produced unnatural, *superhuman* offspring!

The term translated "giants" is from the Hebrew נְפִילִים, *Nephilim* and literally means "the fallen ones" (from the verb *nephal*, to fall). In the Septuagint translation, the term used was γίγαντες, *gigantes*, or "earth-born."[227] They are also called הַגִּבֹּרִים, Hag Gibborim, the "mighty ones," or "hero," or "chief-man."

THE HEROES OF MYTHOLOGY

Apparently these unnatural offspring, the Nephilim, were monstrous and they have been memorialized in the legends and myths of every ancient culture on the planet Earth. (Some of these were highlighted in chapter 2.) The Nephilim also seem to be echoed in the legendary Greek demigods.[228] Throughout Greek mythology we find that intercourse between the gods and women yielded half-god, half-man Titans, demigods, or heroes which were partly terrestrial and partly celestial.[229] Hercules is but one example. The seductions attributed to Zeus include Thetis, Dione, Leda, Metis, and Europa.[230]

Some scholars attribute certain ancient monuments, such as the Great Pyramid near Cairo, to these ancient giants. Other scholars have even attempted to link the Great Pyramid to the peculiar "face"[231] on the planet Mars.[232]

Why was the presence of the Nephilim so great a threat that God would resort to such an extreme measure as a worldwide flood?

THE GENE POOL PROBLEM

In Genesis 6:9, we encounter another strange reference:

> "These are the generations of Noah: Noah was a just man and perfect in his generations, and Noah walked with God."

The word for "generations" is well understood since it is frequently used to refer to genealogies. But what does "perfect in his generations" mean? The word translated "perfect" is תָּמִים, *tamiym,* which means "without blemish, sound, healthful, without spot, unimpaired." This term is used of *physical* blemishes,[233] suggesting that Noah's genealogy was not tarnished by this intrusion of the fallen angels. It seems that this adulteration of the human gene pool was a major problem on the planet Earth, and apparently Noah was among the few left who were not thus contaminated.

THE ANCIENT AUTHORITIES

The "angel" view of this classic Genesis text is well documented in both ancient Jewish rabbinical literature and Early Church writings.

In addition to the Septuagint translation, the venerated (although non-canonical) *Book of Enoch,* the Syriac Version of the Old Testament, as well as the *Testimony of the 12 Patriarchs*[234] and the *Little Genesis,*[235] confirm the lexicological usage and the extant beliefs of ancient Jewish scholars. Clearly the learned Philo Judaeus understood the passage as relating to angels.[236] Josephus Flavius also represents this view:

> "They made God their enemy; for many angels of God accompanied with women, and begat sons that proved unjust, and despisers of all that was good, on account of the confidence they had in their own strength, for the tradition is that these men did what resembled the acts of those whom the Grecians call giants."[237]

In accordance with the ancient interpretation, the Early Church fathers understood the expression "sons of God" as designating angels. These included Justin Martyr,[238] Irenaeus,[239] Athenagoras,[240] Pseudo-Clementine,[241] Clement of Alexandria,[242] Tertullian,[243] Commodianus,[244] and Lactantius,[245] to list a few. This interpretation was also espoused by Luther and many more modern exegetes including Koppen, Twesten, Dreschler, Hofmann, Baumgarten, Delitzsch, W. Kelly, A. C. Gaebelein, and others.

THE "LINES OF SETH" VIEW

Yet, many able scholars hold a different view. Many students of the Bible have been taught that Genesis 6 refers to a failure to keep the "faithful" line of Seth separate from the worldly line of Cain. The idea is advanced that after Cain killed Abel, the line of Seth remained faithful while the line of Cain became ungodly and rebellious. The "sons of God" are deemed to be referring to the line of Seth, the "daughters of men" to the line of Cain, and the resulting marriages blurred the separation between them. (Why the resulting offspring are called the "Nephilim" is still without any clear purpose.)

The "sons of Seth and daughters of Cain" interpretation obscures the intended grammatical antithesis between the sons of God and the daughters of Adam. Attempting to impute this view to the text flies in the face of the earlier centuries of understanding of the Hebrew text among both rabbinical and Early Church scholars. Substantial liberties must be taken with the literal text to propose this view.

Furthermore, the term "daughters of Adam" does not denote a restriction to the line of Cain, but indicates that many of Adam's descendants seem to have been involved. In fact, these "daughters" are the same as those referred earlier in the same sentence! And what about the "sons of Adam?" Were they innocent? Why were they not spared in the judgment?

Perhaps even more to the point, procreation by parents of differing religious views does not produce unnatural offspring. Believers marrying unbelievers may produce "monsters," but hardly superhuman, unnatural, children! The lexicological antithesis clearly intends to establish a contrast between the "angels" and the women of Earth.

(A more complete discussion of some of the problems with the "Sethite" view has been included in an appendix.)

It should also be pointed out that most conservative Bible scholars reject the "Sethite" view.[246] Among those supporting the "angel" view are G. H. Pember, M. R. DeHaan, C. H. McIntosh, F. Delitzsch, A. C. Gaebelein, Arthur W. Pink, Donald Grey Barnhouse, Henry Morris, Merrill F. Unger, Arnold Fruchtenbaum, Hal Lindsey, and Chuck Smith.

NEW TESTAMENT CONFIRMATIONS

In Biblical matters, it is essential to always compare scripture with scripture. The New Testament appears to confirm the "angel" view in its comments concerning the judgment of these fallen angels. Both the Apostle Peter and Jude comment on these issues in their letters.

> "For if God spared not the angels that sinned, but cast them down to hell [Tartarus], and delivered them into chains of darkness, to be reserved unto judgment; and spared not the old world, but saved Noah the eighth person, a preacher of righteousness, bringing in the flood upon the world of the ungodly . . ." (2 Peter 2:4–5).

Even Peter's vocabulary is provocative. Peter uses the term *Tartarus,* here translated "hell." This is the only place that this Greek term appears in the Bible. *Tartarus* is a Greek term for "dark abode of woe," "the pit of darkness in the unseen world." As used in Homer's *Iliad,* it is ". . . as far beneath hades as the earth is below heaven. . . ."[247] In the Greek mythology, some of the demigods, Chronos and the rebel Titans, were said to have rebelled against their father Uranus and after a prolonged contest were defeated by Zeus and condemned to Tartarus.

Here and in his earlier epistle, Peter's comments even pinpoint the time of the fall of these angels as the days of Noah:

> "By which also [Christ] went and proclaimed[248] unto the spirits in prison; which sometime were disobedient, when once the longsuffering of God waited in the days of Noah, while the ark was a preparing, wherein few, that is, eight souls were saved by water" (1 Peter 3:19–20).

Jude's epistle[249] also alludes to the strange episodes when these "alien" creatures intruded upon the human reproductive process:

> "And the angels which kept not their first estate, but left their own habitation, he hath reserved in everlasting chains under darkness unto the judgment of the great day. Even as Sodom and

Gomorrah, and the cities about them in like manner, giving themselves over to fornication, and going after strange flesh, are set forth for an example, suffering the vengeance of eternal fire" (Jude 6–7).

The allusions to "going after strange flesh," keeping "not their first estate," having "left their own habitation," and "giving themselves over to fornication" seems to fit the alien intrusions of Genesis 6.

It is interesting that the word translated "habitation," οἰκητήριον, oiketerion, refers to the heavenly bodies from which they had disrobed. This term appears only twice in the New Testament, each time referring to the body as a dwelling place for the spirit.[250] The "giving themselves over to fornication and going after strange flesh" seems to have involved their leaving their earlier "first estate," that is, the body which they were initially "clothed with."

THE CAPABILITIES OF ANGELS

We know relatively little about the nature, essence, powers, or capabilities of angels. We know that they seem to have no problem materializing into our space-time. They spoke as men, ate meals,[251] took people by the hand,[252] and were capable of direct combat. One was responsible for the death of the firstborn in Egypt.[253] Another killed 185,000 Syrians.[254] (You don't mess around with angels!)

They always seem to appear as men.[255] The New Testament indicates that many of us may have encountered angels without discerning any uniqueness:

"Be not forgetful to entertain strangers: for thereby some have entertained angels unawares" (Hebrews 13:2).

Some regard Christ's comments regarding marriage in heaven as disqualifying the "angel" view of Genesis 6.

> "But they which shall be accounted worthy to obtain that world, and the resurrection from the dead, neither marry, nor are given in marriage: Neither can they die any more: for they are equal unto the angels; and are the children of God, being the children of the resurrection" (Luke 20:35–36).[256]

In heaven there is no need for procreation. Marriage is a human institution to prevent the extinction of the race by death. This statement by Jesus Christ makes no comment on the capability for sex or other mischief of the fallen angels. They can fall, they can aspire to degeneracy. What limits their technologies? Some ancient traditions attribute the various arts and sciences of the ancient world to the disclosures of angels.[257]

Angels are always rendered in the masculine. Remember, they were attractive targets for the homosexuals of Sodom.[258]

POST-FLOOD OCCURRENCES

Regarding the Nephilim, Genesis 6:4 also includes the haunting phrase, ". . . and also after that. . . ." Apparently these strange events were not confined just to the period before the flood. We find that there seems to be some recurrence of these things which resulted in unusual giants appearing in subsequent periods later in the Old Testament narrative, specifically the giant-races of Canaan.

A number of tribes were giants, among them the Rephaims, Emims, Horims, and Zamsummims.[259] The kingdom of Og, the King of Bashan, was the "land of the giants."[260]

When Moses sent his 12 spies to reconnoiter the Land of Canaan, they came back with the report of giants in the land.[261]

(The term used was *Nephilim*.) Their fear of those terrifying creatures resulted in their being relegated to wandering in the wilderness for 38 years.

When Joshua and the nation Israel later entered the land of Canaan, they were instructed to wipe out every man, woman, and child of certain tribes.[262] That strikes us as disturbingly severe. It would seem that in the land of Canaan there again was a "gene pool problem." These Rephaim, Nephilim, and others seem to have been established as an advance guard to obstruct Israel's possession of the Promised Land. Was this also a stratagem of Satan?

Later, we find more giants: Arba,[263] Anak and his seven sons (the "Anakim"), and the famed Goliath[264] and his four brothers.[265]

THE DESTINY OF THE NEPHILIM

Most students of the Bible tend to assume that the demons of the New Testament are equivalent to the fallen angels. Angels, however, seem to have the ability to materialize, etc. (that is, except those which are presently bound in Tartarus). In contrast, the demons seem desperate to seek embodiment.[266] Angels and demons seem to be quite different creatures.

The Nephilim, the unnatural offspring, are not eligible for resurrection.[267] The bodies of the Nephilim, of course, were drowned in the flood. What happened to their spirits? Could they be the demons of the New Testament?

These may well have continued through the dæmones incubi of the Middle Ages and may be recurring through the UFOs of today. Are the increasing number of "abduction" reports a recurrence of this kind of intrusion?

The New Testament warns of similar events to come. These will be discussed in a subsequent chapter. But first, let's examine why we should take the Biblical record more seriously.

AN EXTRATERRESTRIAL MESSAGE AUTHENTICATED

"There is none like me, declaring the end from the beginning, and from ancient times the things that are not yet done. . . ."

ISAIAH 46: 9–10

It may come as a surprise to learn that we have in our possession a series of documents which are demonstrably a composite message of extraterrestrial origin. It will also become increasingly apparent that this message holds the key to the dilemma
facing us regarding the nature of reality and the beings that are
now apparently intruding into the comfort of our preconceptions.

In the past the Bible has always enjoyed a unique stature, but
in recent years this classic resource has become unfashionable.
However, new discoveries have confirmed it as the only book
on planet Earth that bears a message provably orchestrated
from outside our space-time.

Furthermore, if the Biblical presentation is valid, then we may
well be plunged into the most bizarre drama and delusion of
human history. Since this cataclysm will affect every one of us
and our families, we must determine what is really going on.

Is it possible that the Bible really predicts world events
before they happen? Is it really possible that the future can be
known in advance? Two key discoveries will prove critical to
our understanding:

No. 1: Although the Bible is composed of 66 individual
books penned by 40 separate authors over literally thousands
of years, upon careful inspection it proves to be an integrated
message, evidencing careful and skillful design which transcends those centuries and even our ability to synthesize using
sophisticated computers.

No. 2: The Bible authenticates itself by demonstrating that the
origin of this message is from outside of our dimension of time.

DISCOVERY NO. 1:
AN INTEGRATED MESSAGE

This is an aspect that seems to escape even some of the most
skilled scholars. While they probe the intricacies of various

details of the text, they often lose perspective of the integrated design of the whole.

Any serious Bible student quickly recognizes that the Old Testament lays the foundation for the New Testament. It portrays the predicament of man and the means by which his predicament will ultimately be resolved. It chronicles the origin, the mission, and the ultimate destiny of Israel as God's vehicle to accomplish his broader redemptive purpose. Through a sequence of explicit (and some cryptic) prophecies, the Old Testament further reveals the Coming One through whom mankind's redemption would be accomplished.

As one gains a more complete grasp of the whole, one realizes that every detail—every number, place name, even subtleties of the structure of the text—is the result of skillful design. When this strategic integrity of the whole is grasped, the entire panorama is brought into focus. It has been said, "The New Testament is in the Old Testament concealed, and the Old Testament is in the New Testament revealed."

HIDDEN MESSAGES IN THE TEXT

As we carefully examine the "days of Noah" and the Biblical record of the time before the Great Flood, we will discover some surprising aspects hidden within the text itself.

The events in the days of Noah did not happen suddenly. The intrusions by the alien "space beings" (fallen angels) are believed to have begun in the days of Jared (from the Hebrew verb, *Yaradh*, meaning "descent," or "shall come down"). Four subsequent generations of Jared's descendants—including Enoch, Methuselah, Lamech, and Noah—were apparently called upon to deliver divine warning of the forthcoming flood judgment.

Enoch proves to be one of the most fascinating characters in the Bible and deserves our close attention. Understanding his remarkable life will give us some insights concerning the warning which Jesus used to point us to this strange period.

Enoch apparently had an unusual experience when his son was born. For the rest of his life, it is said that Enoch "walked with God." Enoch named his son Methuselah, which means "his death shall bring." *Methuselah* comes from מוּת, muth, a root that means "death"[268], and from שׁלח shalach, which means "to bring" or "to send forth."[269] Enoch was given a prophecy of the coming Great Flood, and apparently he was told that as long as his son was alive, the judgment of the flood would be withheld; as soon as Methusela died, the flood would be sent forth. (Can you imagine raising a kid like that? Every time the kid caught a cold, the entire neighborhood must have panicked!) Indeed, the year that Methuselah died, the flood came.[270] Methuselah's life was a symbol of God's mercy in forestalling the coming judgment of the flood. Therefore it is remarkably appropriate that his lifetime is the longest in the Bible.[271]

A HIDDEN MESSAGE
IN THE FAMILY TREE

With all of this significance hidden in the name of Methuselah, it's no surprise that there also seems to be a complete message hidden in the genealogy from Adam to Noah. In our Bible, we read a transliteration of the Hebrew names, but what do these names mean in English?

The meaning of proper names can be a difficult pursuit since a direct translation is often not readily available. Even a conventional Hebrew lexicon can prove disappointing. A study of the original roots, however, can yield some provocative insights.[272]

Adam's name, אָדָם means "man." As the first man, that seems straightforward enough.

Adam's son was named Seth, שֵׁת, which means "appointed." At his birth, Eve said, "For God hath appointed me another seed instead of Abel, whom Cain slew."[273]

Seth's son was called Enosh, אֱנוֹשׁ, which means "mortal," "frail," or "miserable." Enosh is from the root *anash*, to be incurable, used of a wound, grief, woe, sickness, or wickedness. As was highlighted in the tenth chapter of this book, men began to defile the name of the Living God during the days of Enosh.[274]

Enosh's son was named Kenan, from קֵינָן, which can mean "sorrow," "dirge," or "elegy." (The precise denotation is somewhat elusive; unfortunately, some study aids presume that Kenan is synonymous with "Cainan.") Balaam, looking down from the heights of Moab, exploited a pun upon the name of the Kenites when he prophesied their destruction.[275]

Kenan's son was Mahalalel, from מְהַלַלְאֵל, which means "blessed" or "praise," and *El*, the name for God. Thus, Mahalalel means "the blessed God." Often Hebrew names include *El*, the name of God, e.g. Daniel, "God is my Judge," etc.

Mahalalel's son was named Jared, יֶרֶד, from the verb *yaradh*, meaning "descent," or "shall come down." Some scholars believe that the intrusions of the "aliens" of Genesis 6 began in Jared's day.

Jared's son was named Enoch, חֲנוֹךְ, which means "teaching," or "commencement." Enoch was the father of Methuselah, whom we have already mentioned. He was the first of four generations of preachers.

Methuselah's son was named Lamech, לֶמֶךְ, a root still evident today in our own English word "lament" or "lamentation." Lamech suggests "despairing." (This name is also linked to the Lamech in Cain's line who inadvertently killed his son Tubal-Cain in a hunting incident.[276])

Lamech, of course, is the father of Noah, נֹחַ, which is derived from *nacham,* "to bring relief," "rest," or "comfort," as Lamech himself explains in Genesis 5:29.

Now let's put it all together:

HEBREW	ENGLISH
Adam	Man
Seth	Appointed
Enosh	Mortal
Kenan	Sorrow;
Mahalalel	The blessed God
Jared	Shall come down
Enoch	Teaching
Methuselah	His death shall bring
Lamech	The Despairing
Noah	Rest, or comfort.

That's rather remarkable:

> "Man [is] appointed mortal sorrow; [but] the blessed God shall come down teaching [that] his death shall bring [the] despairing rest."

This is, of course, a summary of God's plan of redemption for mankind (called the "gospel" in the New Testament) hidden in a genealogy in Genesis. What makes this particularly remarkable is that it is highly unlikely that a group of Jewish rabbis would deliberately contrive to hide an expression of the Christian gospel in a genealogy within their venerated Torah! Unlikely, indeed.[277]

The implications of this discovery are far more profound than is evident at first glance. It demonstrates that in the earliest chapters of Genesis, God had already laid out His plan for redemption from the predicament of mankind. It is a love story, written in blood on a wooden cross which was erected in Judea almost 2,000 years ago. In Genesis 3, when Adam fell, God declared war on Satan and promised a Redeemer.[278] This began a "scarlet thread" of prophetic revelations that would ultimately climax in the book of Revelation. This program has been, and continues to be, the target of the "alien" intrusions.

ENOCH'S LEGACY

As we explore "the days of Noah," it is remarkable to realize that the earliest recorded prophecy was by Enoch and that this prophecy, although given before the flood, deals with the Second Coming of Christ. Jude quoted:

> "And Enoch also, the seventh from Adam, prophesied of these, saying, Behold, the Lord cometh with ten thousands of his saints, to execute judgment upon all, and to convince all that are ungodly among them of all their ungodly deeds which they have ungodly committed, and of all their hard speeches which ungodly sinners have spoken against." (Jude 14–15).

Some believe this makes Enoch the first "astronaut." He was "evacuated." God took him. He apparently was expecting this to happen.[279] What makes this particularly suggestive is that there were three groups of people facing the judgment of the flood: (1) those who would perish in the flood; (2) those who were preserved through the flood, Noah and his family; and (3) those who were evacuated before the flood, namely Enoch. Will this pattern be the same for the climactic judgments that are going to come upon the earth?

Similarly, the New Testament presents three groups of people facing final climactic judgment: (1) the "earth dwellers" who will be the focus of the judgments in the book of Revelation; (2) those who are miraculously preserved through the judgments; and (3) those who are evacuated ("raptured") prior to the judgments.[280]

DISCOVERY NO. 2: ORIGIN FROM OUTSIDE TIME

The second remarkable discovery is that the origin of the Biblical message is demonstrably from outside our time domain.

We discussed our spatial dimensions in the fourth chapter of this book. We also experience a temporal dimension called "time," which we take for granted. We live in an age when the very nature of time is only beginning to be understood. The concepts of time warps, time travel, and the like are no longer the plaything of fiction writers, but the serious study of particle physicists, cosmologists, and other scientists. So, before we go further in our exploration of hyperspace and UFOs, we need to shed the baggage of some additional misconceptions that may hinder our understanding.

THE NATURE OF TIME

While philosophers throughout history have debated almost every idea under the sun since the world began, the one thing that all of them have presumed is that time is linear and absolute. Most of us assume that a minute a thousand years ago is the same as a minute today and that we live in a dimension in which time inexorably rolls onward yet is totally intractable to any attempt to glimpse ahead. We move forward and can look back, but we can't look ahead or move back. (Does anyone "remember" tomorrow?) Traversing the dimension of time remains the ever popular realm of fiction writers—and, apparently, a few strange experiments of the particle physicists.[281] (We explored some speculations concerning "transversible wormholes" in chapter 4.)

This linear view of time is exemplified by our frequent resort to "time lines." When we were in school, our teachers would draw a line on the blackboard. The left end of the line might represent the beginning of something—the birth of a person, the founding of a nation, or an era. The right end of the line would mark the termination of that subject—the death of a person or the end of an era.

BEGINNING ————————————————————————— END

(Now?)

Therefore, when we consider the concept of "eternity," we tend to view it as a line of infinite length—from "infinity" on the left and continuing toward "infinity" on the right. When we think of God, we naturally assume that he is someone "with lots of time."

$-\infty$ ————————————————————————— $+\infty$

But that linear view suffers from the misconceptions of an obsolete physics. Today we owe a great debt to the insights of Dr. Albert Einstein:

> "People like us, who believe in physics, know that the distinction between past, present, and the future is only a stubbornly persistent illusion."

It was the insight of Dr. Albert Einstein, in considering the nature of our physical universe, that we live in more than three dimensions and that time itself is a fourth physical dimension. This insight led to his famous theory of relativity and the discovery that time itself is part of our physical reality.

THE DIMENSIONS OF REALITY

As noted in chapter 4, we live in (at least) a four-dimensional space—that is, the three spatial dimensions of length, width, and height, and the dimension of time.[282] Time is now known to be a physical property that varies with mass, acceleration, and gravity.

A time measurement device in a weaker gravitational field runs faster than one in a stronger field. Near the surface of Earth the frequency of an atomic clock increases about one part in 10^{16} per meter, and, thus, a clock 100 meters higher than a reference clock will have a frequency greater by one part in 10^{14}.

Clocks carried eastward around the world in an airplane will differ (very slightly) from a clock at rest on Earth, or one carried westward, since they are in rotation at different speeds about the center of Earth and there is also a difference in gravitational potential.

In 1971, in experiments with atomic clocks by the U.S. Naval Observatory, atomic clocks were actually sent around the world in airplanes, one eastward and one westward. The eastward-flying clock lost 0.06 microsecond with respect to one at rest, and the westward one gained 0.27 microsecond, confirming the predicted relativistic effects.

WHO CARES?

I once served on the board of directors of a company that was in the process of acquiring a company which specialized in making cesium clocks. I remember when the president proudly announced that their key product was an atomic clock "accurate to within one second in 100,000 years." I couldn't resist asking two questions: "How do you know?" and "Who cares?" It turns out that the accuracy of such a device can be predicted from its molecular behavior. Furthermore, the accuracy of time measurement is a critical factor in the precision of navigation. The precision of their unique product now makes the Global Positioning Satellite navigation system possible.

THE TWIN ASTRONAUTS

Most discussions of the physics of time will also mention the interesting case of two hypothetical astronauts born at the same instant. One remains on Earth; the other is sent on a space mission to the nearest star, Alpha Centauri, about 4.5 light years distant. If his vehicle travels at a speed of half the velocity of light, when our traveler returns to Earth he will be more than two years younger than his twin brother! This example is often used to illustrate the dilation of time.

OUR COMMON MISCONCEPTION

Is God subject to gravity? Is he subject to the constraints of mass or acceleration? Hardly.

God is not someone "who has lots of time." He is outside the domain of time altogether. That is what Isaiah means when he says, "It is he who inhabits eternity."[283]

Since God has the technology to create us in the first place, he certainly has the technology to get a message to us. But how does he authenticate his message? How does he assure us that the message is really from him and not from a fraud or a contrivance?

One way is to demonstrate that the message has its source from outside our time domain. God declares, "I alone know the end from the beginning."[284] His message includes history written in advance. We call this "prophecy."

An illustrative example is that of a parade. We sit on the curb and observe the many bands, marching units, floats, and other elements coming around the corner and passing in front of us. To us, the parade is clearly a sequence of events. However, to

someone who is outside the plane of the parade's existence—
say, in a helicopter above the city—the beginning and the end
are simultaneously in view.

(It is amazing how many theological paradoxes evaporate
when one recognizes the restrictions of viewing our predicament from within our time dimension.)[285]

A MESSAGE OF
EXTRATERRESTRIAL ORIGIN

We are in possession of this collection of 66 books we call
the Bible, written by 40 authors over several thousands of
years, which we now discover is an integrated message from
outside our time domain. The Bible repeatedly authenticates
its uniqueness by describing history before it happens, and
this discovery totally shatters our concept of reality.

There are numerous publications which document the many
amazing examples of Biblical predictions that have been fulfilled in history.[286] However, of primary interest in this particular review are some events on our own immediate horizon. In
fact, you and I are apparently being plunged into a period of
time about which the Bible says more than any other period of
time in history—including the time when Jesus walked the
shores of the Sea of Galilee and climbed the mountains of Judea.

The recognition that we are emerging into a period of history
that has been pre-written in the classic pages of the Biblical
record shatters the comfort of our preconceptions about time,
our universe, and our physical reality.

The entire history of Israel is an astonishing testimony to the
supernatural origin of the Bible. Israel is the lens through which
the Bible presents both the past and the future. One of the greatest miracles in the Bible is before our very eyes: the Jew. The
regathering of Israel to their own homeland—the second
time[287]—is the key to understanding the times in which we live.

The libraries are full of volumes which detail the many incredible examples of how God has repeatedly authenticated his messages through fulfilled prophecies regarding the nation Israel.

Perhaps even more amazing are the detailed prophecies concerning Jesus Christ. More than 300 prophecies concerning his birth, ministry, and sacrificial death are detailed in the Old Testament and fulfilled in the New Testament. Yet, there are several thousand prophecies yet to be fulfilled upon his return![288]

THE MOST AMAZING PASSAGE IN THE BIBLE

We will focus our discussion here to one of the most amazing passages in the entire Bible. It will not only demonstrate the astonishing precision with which the Bible details "history in advance," this passage also holds the key to understanding the period emerging on our horizon just ahead of us.

Four disciples privately came to Jesus for a confidential briefing about his Second Coming. His response was so important that it is recorded in three of the Gospels.[289] In this briefing, Jesus highlighted a passage in the ninth chapter of Daniel as the key to end-time prophecy.[290]

The book of Daniel was part of the Old Testament, and, as such, was translated into Greek in 270 B.C. as part of the Septuagint translation of the Hebrew Scriptures. Although Daniel is one of the most authenticated books of the Bible, this simplifying observation will serve to establish the undeniable existence of the book long before the events it so precisely predicts.

Daniel had been deported as a teenager and then spent the next 70 years in captivity in Babylon. He was reading the prophecies of Jeremiah[291] from which he understood that the 70-year period which had been predicted was about to end, and so he committed himself to prayer. During his prayer, the angel Gabriel interrupted him and gave him the most remarkable

The Seventy Weeks of Daniel

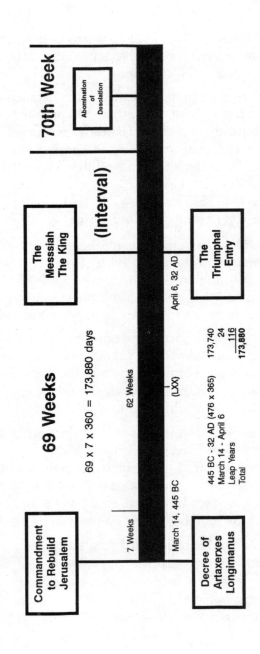

prophecy in the Bible. The last four verses of Daniel 9 are this famed "70-week prophecy of Daniel." Let's examine this passage carefully.

THE 70 WEEKS

The last four verses of Daniel 9 also outline the fourfold structure of the passage:

9:24   the scope of the entire prophecy
9:25   the 69 weeks (of years)
9:26   an interval between the 69th and 70th weeks
9:27   the 70th week

(The key to understanding this passage is to recognize that the 70 "weeks" are not all contiguous and that verse 26 is an explicit interval between the 69th and 70th weeks.)[292]

VERSE 24: THE SCOPE

"Seventy weeks are determined upon thy people and upon thy holy city, to finish the transgression, and to make an end of sins, and to make reconciliation for iniquity, and to bring in everlasting righteousness, and to seal up the vision and prophecy, and to anoint the most Holy Place." (Daniel 9:24).

Seventy *shabu'im* (sevens, or "weeks") speaks of weeks of years. This may seem strange to us, but the Hebrew traditions include a week of days, a week of weeks (*shavout*), a week of months, and a week of years.[293] Seventy sevens of years are determined, or "reckoned" (*hatak*), upon Daniel's people and the city of Jerusalem. Notice that:

1) The focus of the passage is on the Jews, not the Church, nor the Gentile world. Also,

2) There are six major items which have yet to be completed:

to finish the transgressions;

to make an end of sins;

to make reconciliation for iniquity;

to bring in everlasting righteousness;

to seal up (close the authority of) the vision;

to anoint the *Godesh Godashim,* the Holy of Holies.

The fact that not all of these have yet been fulfilled in 2,000 years also demonstrates that the time periods noted are not contiguous.

360-DAY YEARS

Ancient calendars were based on a 360-day year, typically twelve 30-day months. This applies to the Assyrians, Egyptians, Hebrews, Persians, Greeks, Phoenicians, Chinese, Mayans, Hindus, Carthaginians, Etruscans, and Teutons, etc. This also applies to the ancient Chaldean calendar, and it is from this Babylonian tradition that we have 360 degrees in a circle, 60 minutes in an hour, 60 seconds in each minute, etc.

In 701 B.C., all calendars seem to have been reorganized.[294] Numa Pompilius, the second king of Rome, reorganized the original calendar of 360 days per year by adding five days per year. King Hezekiah, Numa's Jewish contemporary, reorganized his calendar by adding a month in each Jewish leap year (on a cycle of seven every 19 years.)[295]

In any case, the Biblical calendar, from Genesis to Revelation, uses a 360-day year.[296]

VERSE 25: THE 69 WEEKS

"Know therefore and understand, that from the going forth of the commandment to restore and

> to build Jerusalem unto the Messiah the Prince
> shall be seven weeks, and threescore and two
> weeks: the street shall be built again, and the wall,
> even in troublous times" (Daniel 9:25).

The city of Jerusalem, at the time, was in ruins, but destined to be rebuilt. Thus, Gabriel gave Daniel a mathematical prophecy:

$$(7 + 62) \text{ times } 7 \text{ times } 360 = 173{,}880 \text{ days}$$

These 173,880 days would occur between the commandment to rebuild Jerusalem until the presentation of the *Meshiach Nagid*. The trigger, the authority to rebuild the city of Jerusalem, was the decree of Artaxerxes Longimanus, given on March 14, 445 B.C.[297]

The target to complete the 69 weeks was the presentation of the *Meshiach Nagid,* the Messiah the King.[298] But when was Jesus ever presented as a king? On several occasions in the New Testament, when they attempted to make Jesus a king, he invariably declined, "Mine hour is not yet come."[299] Then one day, he not only permitted it, he arranged it.[300]

THE TRIUMPHAL ENTRY

Jesus deliberately arranged to fulfill Zechariah 9:9,

> "Rejoice greatly, O daughter of Zion; shout, O
> daughter of Jerusalem: behold, thy King cometh
> unto thee: he is just, and having salvation; lowly,
> and riding upon an ass, and upon a colt the foal
> of an ass.

This was the only day he allowed them to proclaim him King.[301] You and I might not recognize the scriptural significance of what is known as the "Triumphal Entry" in a casual reading. However, whenever there is a danger of us missing a subtlety, the Pharisees come to our rescue!

The enthusiastic disciples were declaring Jesus as the Messiah with Psalm 118.[302] When the Pharisees expressed their concern over the apparent blasphemy, Jesus declared:

> "I tell you that, if these should hold their peace, the stones would immediately cry out" (Luke 19:40).

This was the 10th of Nisan,[303] or April 6, A.D. 32[304] When you convert the Hebrew text into the terms of our calendar, we discover that there were exactly 173,880 days between the decree of Artaxerxes and the presentation of the "Messiah the King" to Israel! Gabriel's prophecy given to Daniel five centuries before—and translated into Greek three centuries before the fact—was fulfilled to the exact day!

This precise anticipation of such historical details is one of the most dramatic demonstrations of the hyperdimensionality of Jesus Christ, the Messiah of Israel. Incredible! (This will be explored further in chapter 14.)

What is also shocking is that Jesus held them accountable to recognize this day. He went on to predict that Jerusalem would be destroyed because the people didn't recognize this day that Daniel had specifically predicted:

> "If thou hadst known, even thou, at least in this thy day, the things which belong unto thy peace! but now they are hid from thine eyes.

> "For the days shall come upon thee, that thine enemies shall cast a trench about thee, and compass thee round, and keep thee in on every side, And shall lay thee even with the ground, and thy children within thee; and they shall not leave in thee one stone upon another; because thou knewest not the time of thy visitation" (Luke 19:42–44).

But there's more.

VERSE 26: THE INTERVAL

> "And after threescore and two weeks shall Messiah be cut off, but not for himself: and the people of the prince that shall come shall destroy the city and the sanctuary; and the end thereof shall be with a flood, and unto the end of the war desolations are determined" (Daniel 9:26).

Verse 26 deals with events after the 62 weeks (therefore, also after the earlier seven, thus making it after the total of 69 weeks), and yet before the 70th week begins, which will be dealt with in verse 27. It is important to recognize that there are specific events specified between the 69th and 70th week, and, thus, not all the weeks are contiguous.

•One of the events is that the Messiah shall be "cut off" (*karat,* execution; death penalty). It comes as a surprise to many to discover that the Old Testament predicts that the Messiah of Israel is to be executed.[305]

Other events that intervene between the 69th and 70th weeks are the destruction of both the city and the sanctuary. Indeed, just as Jesus had predicted, 38 years after the end of the 69th week, in A.D. 70, Titus Vespasian and the 5th, 10th, 12th, and 15th Roman legions laid siege to the city and slaughtered more than a million inhabitants.

Inadvertently, the interior of the Temple caught fire, causing its extensive gold coverings and fixtures to melt, and so the Temple was subsequently taken apart, stone by stone, to recover the gold. The specific prediction of Jesus was precisely fulfilled 38 years after his crucifixion.

While there are specific events that required at least 38 years between the 69th and 70th weeks of Daniel, thus far this interval has lasted more than 1,900 years.[306] This interval is the period of national blindness for Israel[307] which Jesus announced. It is also the period that includes the Church (used here in its mystical or spiritual sense rather than in any organizational sense), a mystery kept hidden in the Old Testament.[308]

(It seems that the Lord deals with Israel and the Church mutually exclusively. A chess clock, with its two interlocked representations, is an illustrative example; one clock is stopped while the other is running.)

Evidence is accumulating that this interval may be about over, and the famed 70th week is about to begin.

There is one remaining verse which details the final 70th week of this prophecy. This seven-year period is the most documented period of time in the entire Bible. Many scholars believe that the chapters 6 through 9 of Revelation are simply a detailing of this terrifying period on the earth. We will explore the Biblical view of this forthcoming period in chapter 13.

First we need to better understand the context which will lead up to it. What will the state of the world be like as this planetary climax approaches? Jesus warned, "As the days of Noah were, so shall the days of the coming of the Son of Man be." The current spate of UFOs and alien intrusions appear to be a key part of what's coming.

Fasten your seat belts!

CHARIOTS OF THE FRAUDS

"Beloved, do not believe every spirit, but test the
spirits, whether they are of God; because many
false prophets have gone out into the world . . .
and every spirit that does not confess that Jesus
Christ has come in the flesh is not of God. And this
is the spirit of the Antichrist, which you have heard
was coming, and is now already in the world."

1 JOHN 4:1, 3

Then material we've examined to this point is indeed bizarre and in some cases unbelievable. And yet, we have seen that there is compelling evidence to believe that we have been visited, some would say "invaded," by aerially adept, shape-shifting, interdimensional beings. The origin and agenda of these beings is a topic of great dispute. Among researchers there are those who believe that the occupants of UFOs are benevolent, highly advanced beings who are here to share their knowledge and genetic material with mankind for the purpose of advancing our evolution. Others believe their behavior and message betray a sinister agenda. Some, like Jacques Vallee, believe that we may be on the threshold of a gigantic cosmic deception perpetrated by interdimensional beings whose purpose and agenda for mankind are unknown.

The UFO literature is replete with speculations about the origin, nature, and intentions of these beings. One thing that is becoming less controversial is the fact that these entities are not mere extraterrestrials, but something much more. As we saw in the third chapter, UFO craft and their occupants, so extensively viewed in the last five decades, have betrayed an interdimensional nature by their ability to dematerialize, change shapes, defy the laws of inertia, etc.

Gordon Creighton, editor of the British periodical *Flying Saucer Review,* a publication that has researched UFOs for over four decades, expresses the official position of FSR as follows:

> "There seems to be no evidence yet that any of these craft or beings originate from Outer Space. The whole phenomenon involves a mass of features that conflict with modern science, and many researchers now believe that more than one type of being may be involved, some of them originating from Outer Space and some of them of an 'interdimensional' nature, and consequently possibly from some unknown aspect of our own World."[309]

Because of the interdimensional nature of UFOs and their occupants, many researchers suggest that the phenomenology that generates UFOs is also responsible for the historical reports of angels, demons, fairies, fauns, sylphs, incubi, succubi, and any number of aerially adept supernatural entities. Indeed, as Jacques Vallee showed in his book *Passport to Magonia,* the parallels between these supernatural entities and the occupants of UFOs are striking. Vallee, a computer scientist who is also trained in astrophysics, is not the type to be given to fads and irrational belief systems. And yet, even he admits that the existence of angels and demons is plausible and may provide a working framework for the UFO phenomenon:

> "I am also tempted to accept as a working hypothesis that in times remote contact occurred between human consciousness and another consciousness, variously described as demonic, angelic, or simply alien."[310]

The UFO phenomenon is perceived as a threat by many because acceptance of the phenomenon and its interdimensional nature seems incompatible with prevailing scientific and religious paradigms. To the scientific "naturalist," the acceptance of interdimensional beings requires the introduction of alternate dimensional realities beyond the four dimensions of space and time that we currently appreciate. To many "naturalists" this thought is anathema because it introduces the very real possibility of angels, demons, and God forbid, GOD!

Astronomer Carl Sagan, the modern-day champion of the naturalistic world-view, eloquently expressed the prevailing scientific paradigm in his book *Cosmos* when he stated, "The Cosmos is all that is, or ever was, or ever will be."[311]

The UFO phenomenon breaks through this barrier of a closed universe, one in which nothing gets in and nothing can escape. According to Dr. John Mack, many abductees sense that their alien captors traverse and perform their experiments outside our space-time domain.

> "Quite a few abductees have spoken to me of their sense that at least some of their experiences are not occurring within the physical space-time dimensions of the universe as we comprehend it. They speak of aliens breaking through from another dimension, through a 'slit' or 'crack' in some sort of barrier, entering our world from 'beyond the veil.' Abductees, some of whom have little education to prepare them to explain about such abstractions or odd dislocations, will speak of the collapse of space-time that occurs during their experiences. They experience the aliens, indeed their abductions themselves, as happening in another reality, although one that is as powerfully actual to them as—or more so than— the familiar physical world."[312]

At the same time, the UFO phenomenon is perceived as a threat by many who hold to the Judeo-Christian world-view— not because it introduces the notion of extradimensional realities, but because the Bible makes no mention of extraterrestrial (non-supernatural) life in the universe. In addition, the Bible teaches that Jesus Christ is our "kinsman redeemer." Unless these aliens are our kinsmen (i.e., fully human beings), then the substitutionary, sacrificial, atoning death of Jesus Christ on the cross is not (as far as we know) efficacious in blotting out the sin of aliens. Some New Age authors suggest that Jesus died many times on many different planets for the sins of God's alien "children." However, the Bible states that Jesus died once and rose only once from the dead.

> ". . . knowing that Christ, having been raised from the dead, dies no more. Death no longer has

> dominion over him. For the death that he died,
> he died to sin once for all; but the life that he
> lives, he lives to God" (Romans 6:9–10).

We believe that it is possible to determine the origin and agenda of these alien entities in a manner that considers their interdimensional character, their message, and the nature of their contact with mankind.

ALIENS, ANGELS, AND DEMONS

In the last several decades a number of experienced UFO researchers have drawn parallels between the nature of angels, demons, and the UFO occupants. Indeed, some—including Jacques Vallee, John Keel, and others—have even suggested that our alien visitors may indeed be fallen angels or demons themselves.

To determine whether aliens are part of the angelic or demonic realm we must first examine some of the attributes of angels and demons. It is commonly believed that fallen angels and demons are one and the same. In fact, they are frequently used as synonyms in the Judeo-Christian literature of the last several hundred years. However, it turns out that ancient rabbis and the Early Church fathers believed that they were separate and distinct entities.

When we examine the Biblical record, we see that the attributes and activities of angels and demons and angels are different. Angels (literally "messengers") are creations of God that have their own physical bodies. They are able to manifest in time and space, and when they do they are usually confused with men!

For example, when God and the two angels appeared to Abraham in the *terebinths* of Mamre in Genesis 18, they are described as having the appearance of men. In fact, they were so convincingly human that the homosexuals of Sodom and

Gomorrah wanted to have intercourse with them.[313] It is unlikely that the men of Sodom would have been sexually interested in the angels had they been semi-transparent, glowing apparitions with wings and halos!

In the New Testament, two angels who were confused with men were at the empty tomb of Jesus after the resurrection. Luke the Apostle stated, "And it came to pass, as they were much perplexed thereabout, behold, two men stood by them in shining garments" (Luke 24:4). After Jesus ascended into heaven, the disciples looked on. "And while they looked stedfastly toward heaven as he went up, behold, two men stood by them in white apparel" (Acts 1:10). These "two men" were angels with physical bodies who advised the disciples that Jesus would return "in like manner." Finally, in the New Testament book of Hebrews we are told, "Be not forgetful to entertain strangers: for thereby some have entertained angels unawares" (Hebrews 13:2).

The nature of demons is entirely different. They are disembodied spirits that seek embodiment. The origin of demons is not commonly known in our time. However, in ancient times it was well understood that demons are the disembodied spirits of the Nephilim. The reader will recall that the Nephilim (the earth-born giants of the days of Noah) were the offspring of fallen angels and the "daughters of men." According to numerous ancient rabbinic and Early Church texts, when the Nephilim died their spirits became disembodied and roamed the earth, harassing mankind and seeking embodiment! This is most evident in the *Book of Enoch*.

The *Book of Enoch* was considered by many ancient Christians and Jews to be an authoritative book of Jewish history. It was probably written in the middle of the second century B.C., but compiled from much earlier material. In the early chapters of the *Book of Enoch* we are told a great deal about the early history of the earth, the days of Noah and the "Watchers." According to the *Book of Enoch* and other ancient rabbinic writings, the "Watchers" were a specific group of angels that God had placed to watch over the earth. According to the *Book of Enoch*, 200 of these Watchers lusted and fell into sin when they married the "daughters of men." The result of this ungodly union was the birth of unnatural offspring, the Nephilim. The destiny of the spirits of the Nephilim is described in chapter 15 of the *Book of Enoch*:

> "Now the giants [Nephilim], who have been born of spirit and of flesh, shall be called upon earth evil spirits, and on earth shall be their habitation. Evil spirits shall proceed from their flesh, because they were created from above; from the holy Watchers was their beginning and primary foundation. Evil spirits shall they be upon earth, and the spirits of the wicked shall they be called. The habitation of the spirits of heaven shall be in heaven; but upon earth shall be the habitation of terrestrial spirits, who are born on earth. The spirits of the giants shall be like clouds, which shall oppress, corrupt, fall, contend, and bruise those upon earth."[314]

In this remarkable text we learn that evil spirits (a common Biblical synonym for demons) appear to proceed from the flesh of the Nephilim. This was, of course, understood to happen after the Nephilim died. Secondly, these evil spirits will "oppress, corrupt, fall, contend, and bruise those upon earth."

Another ancient historical document widely recognized by ancient rabbis and Early Church fathers is the *Book of Jubilees*. In the *Book of Jubilees*, chapter 10, verses 1–5, we find further confirmation that demons are disembodied spirits of the Nephilim.

"And in the third week of this jubilee the evil
demons began to lead astray the sons of Noah and
deceived them and destroyed them. And the sons
came to Noah their father and told him concerning the demons which were leading astray, dark-
ening, and slaying the sons of their sons. And he
prayed before the Lord his God and he said; 'Lord
of the spirits of all flesh thou hast shown mercy
to me and hast delivered me and my children from
the waters of the deluge, and hast not suffered
me to be destroyed as thou didst the children of
destruction [the Nephilim], for thy grace was great
over men, and great was thy mercy over my soul;
may thy grace be exalted over the sons of thy
sons, and may the evil spirits [spirits of Nephilim
implied here] not rule over them to destroy the
earth. And thou hast verily blessed me and my
sons that we increase and multiply and fill the
earth. And thou knowest how the Watchmen [an
idiom for the Watchers], the father of these spirits, acted in my day; and these spirits also which
are alive, cast them into prison and hold them in
the places of judgment. " (Jubilees 10:1–5).

These events are after the flood of Noah. In the Bible we
never read of demons prior to the flood, nor do we find mention of them in any of the ancient historical texts. In summary,
the fathers of the Nephilim are the Watchers, a specific group
of angels (of the "Sons of God") who lusted after the daughters
of men and took them as wives (Genesis 6:1–5). After the
Nephilim died, it seems they became demons who led astray,
harassed, oppressed, corrupted, contended with, and bruised
those upon earth. The relevance of this understanding to our
20th-century alien visitors will become evident as we progress.

THE ANOINTED CHERUB

It is important to point out that there are many types of angels in the Biblical texts. Archangels, Cherubim, Seraphim, and Watchers are but a few. The Bible teaches that Satan was the anointed Cherub before he fell into sin. In the book of Ezekiel we read God's lament regarding the career of Satan:

> "Moreover the word of the LORD came to me, say-
> ing, 'Son of Man, take up a lamentation for the
> king of Tyre,[315] and say to him, 'Thus says the Lord
> GOD: "You were the seal of perfection, full of wis-
> dom and perfect in beauty. You were in Eden, the
> garden of God; Every precious stone was your
> covering: the sardius, topaz, and diamond, beryl,
> onyx, and jasper, sapphire, turquoise, and emerald
> with gold. The workmanship of your timbrels and
> pipes was prepared for you on the day you were
> created. You were the anointed cherub who cov-
> ers; I established you; you were on the holy moun-
> tain of God; you walked back and forth in the
> midst of fiery stones. you were perfect in your
> ways from the day you were created, till iniquity
> was found in you." ' " (Ezekiel 28:11–15).

Although this portion of Scripture is addressed to the king of Tyre, the material covered is obviously not about him. This is a rhetorical device occasionally used by Biblical writers to get to a deeper behind-the-scenes issue; in this case, the tragic career of Satan.

Satan was an angel with tremendous power and beauty, the highest of God's creation. However, he fell into sin when he became envious of God and decided to exalt himself above the place of God. The details of this cosmic intrigue are found in the book of Isaiah.

"How art thou fallen from heaven, O Lucifer, son
of the morning! how art thou cut down to the
ground, which didst weaken the nations! For
thou hast said in thine heart, I will ascend into
heaven, I will exalt my throne above the stars of
God: I will sit also upon the mount of the con-
gregation, in the sides of the north: I will ascend
above the heights of the clouds; I will be like the
most High. Yet thou shalt be brought down to
hell, to the sides of the pit" (Isaiah 14:12–15).

After Satan fell into sin, one third of the angels aligned themselves with him, making themselves the permanent enemies of
God.[316] Satan and his fallen angels are able to manifest physically in time and space, morph themselves into a multitude of
shapes. Incubi, succubi, fauns, satyrs, and sylphs are supernatural entities which many scholars believe are simply different morphological forms of fallen angels. These entities are
found extensively in the folkloric literature of mankind.
According to this literature, these entities have harassed, interbred with, and even abducted humans for thousands of years.

When we compare the attributes and abilities of aliens and
angels, we find some startling parallels. To begin with, they
both have the ability to manifest physically within our space-
time domain in a humanoid form (Genesis 19:1–11; Luke 1:26;
John 20:12; Acts 12:19). In fact, while there are many different
descriptions of alien entities, the vast majority assume some
variation of the humanoid body form. According to contactees
the Reptilians, Pleiadians, Grays, all with the humanoid body
form, are the most common types encountered.

In the Biblical texts we find that angels are able to perform
supernatural signs and wonders. This ability to supersede natural law is shared by alien entities as well. Throughout the

Bible and UFO accounts we find that angels and aliens can materialize and dematerialize at will. We also find that angels and aliens have the ability to manipulate matter. In addition, they share the ability to change their external physical form (Luke 2:9, 13, 15). According to the Bible, even fallen angels can assume a pleasing, attractive, and "godly" form.

In 2 Corinthians 11:14 we are told, "And no wonder! For Satan himself transforms himself into an angel of light." The word translated as transform in the English is the Greek word *metaschematizo*. It means to change the external form of something while its true essence remains unchanged. This ability has some disturbing implications. Because of Satan's sinister nature, many people naturally believe that his physical appearance is evil. However, because of Satan's supernatural ability to change his external form, he could take on a very pleasing, attractive, and even reassuring external form while remaining, in essence, the most evil entity in the universe! It is interesting to note that when Antonio Villas-Boas was abducted in 1957, he described the female alien entity he encountered as the "most beautiful" creature he had ever seen!

Angels and aliens share the ability to control human events and actions (1 Chronicles 21:1; Daniel 10:13; 1 Thessalonians 2:18). They share the ability to manipulate and control the minds of human beings (John 13:2; Matthew 13:19, 39). During abductions people have been shown false images on what they described as screens or holographic projections. This ability was also demonstrated in Matthew 4:8 when Satan showed Jesus the glory of the kingdoms of the earth. Finally, angels and aliens have the power to defy the laws of physics. This is clear from the nature of their flight, their ability to pass through walls and windows, and their ability to miraculously heal their human contactees.

Jacques Vallee catalogues numerous accounts of abductees who have been healed by their alien captors.[317] Those that believe that aliens are benevolent creatures will point to such accounts as proof that they are not evil. However, we know that the ability to heal the sick is not limited to benevolent supernatural entities. Satan himself will manifest this ability when he heals and resurrects the Antichrist from the dead:

> "And I beheld another beast coming up out of the earth; and he had two horns like a lamb, and he spake as a dragon. And he exerciseth all the power of the first beast before him, and causeth the earth and them which dwell therein to worship the first beast, whose deadly wound was healed. And he doeth great wonders, so that he maketh fire come down from heaven on the earth in the sight of men" (Revelation 13:11–13).

It is important to note that holy angels are "messengers" of God who bring glad tidings, warnings, and prophecies. Others are set as guardians of human beings. This was apparently one of the missions of the Watchers. On the other hand, fallen angels attempt to deceive mankind through false messages and lying signs and wonders. Throughout history those who have encountered fallen angels in the form of incubi, succubi, satyrs, sylphs, and the like, report that they deceive their victims by feigning benevolence and virtuous motives for their actions.

It's interesting to note that aliens do the same. During abduction and channeling experiences, aliens give prophetic messages (which often prove to be false), and they profess a benevolent purpose, while doing painful experiments and performing immoral sexual activities with their human victims. Recently Hollywood has gotten into the act with alien-human sexual contact in movies such as *Michael,* where an angel, played by John Travolta, has sexual liaisons with human females.

THE EXPERTS SPEAK

After noting these similarities, a number of UFO researchers have concluded that modern-day aliens may very well be the modern-day equivalent of fallen angels or demonic entities.

Dr. Pierre Guerin, a well known UFO researcher in the 1960s and 1970s, examined the nature and activities of aliens and concluded,

> "UFO behaviour is more akin to magic than to physics as we know it . . . the modern UFOnauts and the demons of past days are probably identical."[318]

John Keel is an internationally renowned UFO investigator and the author of numerous books on the UFO phenomenon. He has done extensive study comparing the nature of aliens, angels, and demons, with startling conclusions. In his book *Operation Trojan Horse,* he stated:

> "Demonology is not just another crackpot-ology. It is the ancient and scholarly study of the monsters and demons who have seemingly coexisted with man throughout history. Thousands of books have been written on the subject, many of them authored by educated clergymen, scientists and scholars, and uncounted numbers of well-documented demonic events are readily available to every researcher. The manifestations and occurrences described in this imposing literature are similar, if not entirely identical, to the UFO phenomenon itself. Victims of demonomania (possession) suffer the very same medical and emotional symptoms as the UFO contactees. . . . The Devil and his demons can, according to the literature, manifest themselves in almost any

> form and can physically imitate anything from
> angels to horrifying monsters with glowing eyes.
> Strange objects and entities materialize and
> dematerialize in these stories, just as the UFOs
> and their splendid occupants appear and disap-
> pear, walk through walls, and perform other
> supernatural feats."[319]

Keel's observations are quite disturbing. Later in his book,
Keel discusses the supernatural nature of UFOs and the fact
that many contactees have been deceived and lied to on many
occasions.

> "The UFOs do not seem to exist as tangible, man-
> ufactured objects. They do not conform to the
> accepted natural laws of our environment. They
> seem to be nothing more than transmogrifica-
> tions tailoring themselves to our abilities to
> understand. The thousands of contacts with the
> entities indicate that they are liars and put-on
> artists. The UFO manifestations seem to be, by
> and large, merely minor variations of the age-old
> demonological phenomenon. Officialdom may
> feel that if we ignore them long enough, they will
> go away altogether, taking their place with the
> vampire myths of the Middle Ages."[320]

While the attributes of aliens and fallen angels seem to parallel one another, this does not necessarily mean that they are
one and the same. We must compare alien and angelic contact
to further examine the possible connection.

ALIEN CONTACT

The interdimensional nature and seemingly benevolent
behavior of our alien visitors has caused many to speculate that

they are angelic beings of the noble variety doing God's bidding. However, when we examine the nature of their contact, we find some disturbing parallels to contact with demons and fallen angels. As we have seen, our interdimensional visitors prefer to interact and communicate with mankind by two primary methods, abduction and channeling (telepathic) communication.

According to the Bible, angels are supposed to be our guardians and messengers of God. Yet, what we find in abduction phenomena is that these powerful alien entities take people against their will, paralyze, probe, and inspect them with painful metallic objects. They plant thoughts in the abductees' minds, perform sadistic sexual acts on them. They impregnate women, then re-abduct them only to "harvest" the fetuses for the purpose of creating a hybrid race! This sounds like a science-fiction thriller in which humans are nothing more than lab animals.

After examining the UFO and abduction phenomena, Stuart Goldman concluded his research with the following comments:

> ". . . the unpleasant fact is, 50,000 people can not be lying. Something is here—probing people, inspecting them, and planting thoughts in their minds, manipulating their bodies—treating them, in a sense, like so many cattle. Is it all simply a gigantic cosmic joke, or is there a more sinister plot at hand? Are we seeing the formation of a new and highly destructive cult, one whose view posits the elimination (the New Agers call it 'spiritual cleansing') of people who are 'unfit' to exist in the coming New World? Are there really demonic entities hovering about, searching for likely candidates whose brains and minds they can invade, filling them full of fairy tales and

lies—fattening them for the kill? The answer is not easily forthcoming. But whichever scenario you may choose, the ominous statement of John Keel must—for all but the most hardened skeptics—ring in our ears. 'The earth is not inhabited,' says Keel. 'It's infested.' "[321]

Science fiction writer Whitley Strieber wrote extensively of his encounters with aliens in his best-selling books *Communion* and *Transformation.* In *Transformation,* his second book about alien contact, he recounted his numerous contacts with alien entities and considers their origin and agenda for mankind:

> "Increasingly I felt as if I were entering a struggle that might even be more than life and death. It might be a struggle for my soul, my essence, or whatever part of me might have reference to the eternal.

> "There are worse things than death, I suspected. And I was beginning to get the distinct impression that one of them had taken an interest in me.

> "So far the word demon had never been spoken among the scientists and doctors who were working with me. . . . Alone at night I worried about the legendary cunning of demons. . . . At the very least I was going stark, raving mad."[322]

After discussing the paralysis and sense of helplessness induced by the alien entities Strieber stated:

> "I felt an absolutely indescribable sense of menace. It was hell on earth to be there [in the presence of the entities], and yet I couldn't move, couldn't cry out, couldn't get away. I lay as still as death, suffering inner agonies. Whatever was there seemed so monstrously ugly, so filthy and dark and sinister.

Of course they were demons. They had to be. And they were here and I couldn't get away."[323]

In later years, Strieber apparently changed his mind. While careful not to be too dogmatic, Strieber at times stated that he believed the alien entities may be benevolent space brothers who are here to help mankind with our spiritual and physical evolution. This kind of reversal is common in abduction cases. People who often report the most hideous, sadistic experiences imaginable will later come to identify with their captors as moral beings with a "higher cause." This same phenomenon was seen by psychiatrists after the holocaust of World War II. Some Jews who had been treated worse than lab rats eventually came to identify with their Nazi captors.

"WALK-INS"

There is an additional, albeit little-known, alien life form called "Walk-ins." Walk-ins make contact with human beings by entering (some would say "possessing") a willing subject. According to New Age authors, these entities roam the universe seeking embodiment. They are said to be some of the most "highly evolved" alien life forms in the cosmos. They are so highly evolved, according to New Age authors, that they have shed the limitations of a physical form and taken on the nature of a purely "spiritual" entity.

The good news is that Walk-ins must be "invited in." However, when a person enters a state of altered consciousness—such as astral projection, telepathic communication, channeling, hypnosis, mediumship, etc.—the entities may attempt to fill the void left by the altered state. Nothing we have found in alien contact phenomena more closely parallels demonic possession, where disembodied entities enter a human being and take over the bodily functions of the host.

Demonic possession, as a theme, appears numerous times in the New Testament. The indwelling of human beings by demons can begin in childhood (Luke 9:39) and can cause great physical harm including dumbness, blindness, epilepsy, and a host of other disabilities (See Matt. 9:32–33; 12:22; 17:15, 18). Tragically, many abduction researchers have uncovered cases of probable childhood abduction as well.

There are many who will argue that because some people have a "good time" during their abduction experience, it is unfair to label these events as demonic encounters. The fact that people come to identify with their alien captors and view them as highly evolved spiritual entities who bring them closer to God is supposed to be proof that they are morally upright and benevolent creatures.

However, one of the attributes of deception is that on the surface it looks like truth and benevolence. The most skilled deceivers are the ones that can perform a deception and make us think that they are benevolent, friendly, and acting on our behalf. False prophets will, we are told, will appear as sweet, benevolent, and harmless "wolves in sheep's clothing":

> "Beware of false prophets, which come to you in
> sheep's clothing, but inwardly they are ravening
> wolves" (Matthew 7:15).

A soft, cuddly lamb can be "fun" to be around. But allow the lamb to paralyze you, insert long metallic objects into your genitals for the purpose of extracting your seed, take tissue samples, then fill your head with horrible images of impending doom and anti-Biblical messages, and you might begin to suspect that underneath the wool is an evil entity that is set on your personal destruction!

Finally, Jacques Vallee in characteristic fashion draws many parallels between the demonic nature of abduction experience.

> "I pointed out in *Invisible College* that the structure of abduction stories was identical to that of occult initiation rituals. Several years before, I had shown in *Passport to Magonia* that contact with ufonauts was only a modern extension of the age-old tradition of contact with nonhuman consciousness in the form of angels, demons, elves, and sylphs. Such contact includes abduction, ordeal (including surgical operations), and sexual intercourse with the aliens. It often leaves marks and scars on the body and the mind, as do UFO abductions."[324]

Vallee has received a lot of criticism for his radical views on the nature of the UFO phenomenon and the alien abduction scenario. His conclusions that they are interdimensional beings akin to angels and demons, who harass, even abduct and physically harm human beings, has made him few friends in the UFO or scientific community. The primary reason is that the interdimensional theory offends two groups with one "stone." To the scientific community, which prefers to think of the universe as a closed system, Vallee's theories introduce the distinct possibility of the supernatural realm—something that is anathema to the high-priesthood of science. On the other hand, the UFO research community is disturbed because Vallee's theories deny the extraterrestrial hypothesis which asserts that these are "nuts and bolts" ships from within our universe. The interdimensional theory along with the sadistic activities of the alien entities shatters these views and introduces the very real possibility that Satanic forces are here and they are not friendly!

ALIEN MESSAGES

In previous chapters we examined numerous messages given through contactees and channelers. Curiously, these messages are primarily of an apocalyptic, religious, and anti-Biblical nature. This begs the question that if these aliens entities are highly evolved space brothers who are concerned with our well-being, why don't they provide solutions to the socioeconomic and environmental problems we face? Why don't they share their scientific know-how so we can end hunger, poverty, war and disease? Instead, they enter the bodies and minds of people and fill their heads with anti-Biblical messages.

Why do they profess an Eastern Mystical, New Age worldview which claims that all religions emanate from and point to the same universal truths? The Bible—which teaches the notions of a finite universe, a transcendent Creator and salvation through Jesus Christ alone—is contradictory and mutually exclusive to the Eastern religious views.

However, if the aliens are indeed demonic messengers or fallen angels, this is exactly the kind of message we would expect them to profess. The Apostle Paul warned that in the last days people would give heed to evil, seducing spirits who would teach anti-Biblical messages:

> "Now the Spirit speaketh expressly, that in the
> latter times some shall depart from the faith, giv-
> ing heed to seducing spirits, and doctrines of
> devils" (1 Timothy 4:1).

What is interesting about Paul's statement is that these deceivers will be "seducing spirits." A seducing spirit is one that tries to win over the person with affection, "good" motives, and the promise of personal enrichment or spiritual transformation This is exactly what our alien visitors do.

Secondly, Paul states that people will "give heed" to these spirits. In the Greek language the word translated "give heed," is *prosecho*. This means to "bring near," "give attention to," or "to be given or addicted to." The scary implication of this verse is that in the last days, human beings will have contact with physically embodied Satanic spirits. These spirits will appear benevolent, and they will preach a "seducing message" which will cause people to stray from the Biblical truth of our origin, destiny, and salvation through Jesus Christ.

Dr. John Mack notes that people who are involved in the hybridization program are often given "enlightenment" about coming cataclysmic earth changes and the failure of mankind to protect the environment:

> "Furthermore, for most abductees the hybridization has occurred simultaneously with an enlightenment imparted by the alien beings that has brought home forcibly to them the failure of the human experiment in its present form. Abduction experiencers come to feel deeply that the death of human beings and countless other species will occur on a vast scale if we continue on our present course and that some sort of new life-form must evolve if the human biological and spiritual essence is to be preserved."[325]

> "It is difficult to ignore the fact that the UFO abduction phenomenon is taking place in the context of a planetary crisis of major proportions. . . . Abductions seem to be concerned primarily with two related projects: changing human consciousness to prevent the destruction of the earth's life, and a joining of two species for the creation of a new evolutionary form."[326]

Why are these alien entities connecting the hybridization process to the coming earth changes? As we saw in chapter 8, Jesus foretold that cataclysmic Earth changes would be one of the signs that would precede his Second Coming. In the book of Revelation we are told that the earth changes will be divine judgments poured out by God upon a Christ-rejecting world.

In the last several decades, dozens of contactees have delivered messages from alien entities which state that Earth changes are not the wrath of God; they are the birth pangs of our Earth Mother who is trying to expel the "dark forces" from her surface so she can evolve to a higher dimension of existence.

It seems to us that our alien visitors wish to set up the world for an alternate explanation for coming Earth changes. Instead of God's wrath, the Earth changes are connected with a coming cleansing of Mother Earth and the arrival of a new, highly evolved humanoid-hybrid species. This new hybrid species will, according to our space brothers, be in harmony or vibration with Mother Earth.

So with one carefully crafted explanation, the aliens have explained away the coming wrath of God and their hideous hybridization program. Rather than fearing Earth changes and the abduction-hybridization process, they declare, we should embrace them as something wonderful.

Even more incredible is the fact that the Earth changes and mankind's coming evolutionary quantum leap are connected with a future evacuation of millions of people by alien beamships. This evacuation, we are told, is to remove those who no longer fit in, those whose thought patterns are of the past. By removing these less-fit malcontents, Mother Earth, we are told, can evolve to a higher "vibration" without destroying all life on her surface. The hybridization program will, from the New Age perspective, help to facilitate the evolution of mankind and Mother Earth. When enough people of the "right vibration" (which the hybrids supposedly have) populate the earth, the New Age of peace, harmony, and brotherhood will arrive.

This carefully crafted triad of deception has taken thousands of years to set up. At the end of the 20th century we have hundreds of millions of people who will embrace such teachings as a rational explanation for the wrath of God, the interbreeding of aliens with man, and the Rapture of the Church.

The paradoxical nature of the religious messages has not gone unnoticed by researchers. John Ankerberg and John Weldon have asked the obvious questions:

> ". . . Further, in light of the messages given by the UFO entities, how credible is it to think that literally thousands of genuine extraterrestrials would fly millions or billions of light years simply to teach New Age philosophy, deny Christianity, and support the occult? Why would they do this with the preponderance of such activity already occurring on this planet? And why would the entities actually possess and inhabit people just like demons do if they were really advanced extraterrestrials? Why would they consistently lie about things which we know are true, and why would they purposely deceive their contacts?"[327]

Finally, there is the question of channeling itself. Numerous researchers have noted that channeling is identical to the process whereby demonic spirits contact mediums and psychics.

Ankerberg and Weldon drove the point home with these statements:

> ". . . If the UFO phenomena were actually extraterrestrial, it seems a bit odd that the advanced beings associated with them would act in their communications in the same manner that demons do with their human hosts—as in seance mediumism, channeling, and other forms of spiritism."[328]

In a UFO research document commissioned by the U.S. Government, author Lynn Catoe notes the remarkable linkage between UFOs and occultic and demonic phenomenon:

> "A large part of the available UFO literature is closely linked with mysticism and the metaphysical. It deals with subjects like mental telepathy, automatic writing and invisible entities as well as phenomena like poltergeist manifestation and 'possession.' Many of the UFO reports now being published in the popular press recount alleged incidents that are strikingly similar to demonic possession and psychic phenomena."[329]

Finally, on February 28, 1997, an incredible claim regarding the nature of UFOs and their messages to mankind was made by Lord Hill-Norton, the former head of the British Armed Forces. He was admiral of the British Fleet and chief of Defense Staff from 1971–73. In an article in the prestigious British newspaper *The London Times,* Lord Hill-Norton indicated that he believed that UFOs were of Satanic origin and "definitely antithetical to orthodox Christian belief." He has helped to form an international group, UFO Concern, to bring awareness of the Satanic origin of UFOs and their associated alien entities. Also quoted in the article was the Reverend Paul Inglesby, who is secretary of UFO Concern. He said that the truth about UFOs has been suppressed for many years and that the messages coming from alien entities are "anti-Christian, or demonic."

Surprisingly, Gordon Creighton, editor of the British periodical *Flying Saucer Review* agreed with Lord Hill-Norton stating, "I do believe that the great bulk of these phenomena are what is called Satanic."[330]

THE SONS OF GOD RETURN!

As we read in chapter 5, Harvard University professor John

Mack, M.D., and other researchers believe that one of the primary purposes for the alleged alien abductions is the production of hybrid (half-alien, half-human) offspring. While the current evidence for this breeding program is anecdotal at best, as we stated previously, there are indeed historical precedents in the book of Genesis that shed light on the issue.

In chapter ten we read that during the days of Noah the "sons of God" took human women (the daughters of men) as their wives. According to the story related in Genesis 6:2, ". . . the sons of God saw the daughters of men that they were fair; and they took them wives of all which they chose." In the text there is a subtle sense that the women were chosen ("of all which they chose") against their will. The result of these ungodly unions was a race of very wicked and very powerful hybrid (half-fallen angel, half-human) offspring—the Nephilim—who corrupted, harassed, even killed mankind. Now, at the end of the 20th century, we have the return of "alien" entities with apparent supernatural powers.

Like the "sons of God," our modern alien entities "choose" their sexual cohorts against their will. With reassuring telepathic communication they convince their captives that they mean them no harm and their program is for our benefit.

Incredibly, these alien entities are said to enter in ("Walk-ins") and "possess" their human contacts and fill their heads with a pantheistic world-view which denies the God of the Bible and all of the essentials of the historic Christian faith. From the deity of Jesus Christ to the coming Earth changes and the Rapture of the Church, they deny it all.

It's interesting to note that Zecharia Sitchin, Erich von Daniken, and many popular authors in UFO circles promote the notion that the "sons of God" who interbred with the "daughters of men" in Genesis 6 were indeed extraterrestrial aliens. Zecharia Sitchin has referred to them as the Anunnaki—"those who from the heavens came."

Although these authors recognize the remarkable parallels between the "sons of God" and the alien entities, they fail to point out that for centuries the majority of Jewish, Christian, and secular scholars knew them to be fallen angels—the minions of Satan himself. In addition, Sitchin and von Daniken seem to be committed to the "nuts and bolts" extraterrestrial hypothesis, since they choose to ignore the interdimensional nature of UFOs and their alien "pilots."

While today many Christians can accept the notion that such Satanic unions might have occurred in the murky past of the days of Noah, the notion that these same events could occur in our "days of enlightenment" causes many to recoil at the thought. But didn't Jesus state that the world's predicament would be as it was in "the days of Noah"? He did, indeed!

While the days of Noah were also characterized by widespread disobedience, violence, and rejection of God, the Holy Spirit has chosen to emphasize in the Biblical narrative of Genesis 6 the fact that fallen angels, "Watchers," took the daughters of men and created hybrid offspring. For what purpose? To give a historical framework by which we might evaluate the "alien" activities of our day and the arrival of a coming great deception.

In addition, we know from many Biblical passages that the time of the end would be Satanically energized, very dark times. Why do some assume that the capabilities and plan of Satan and his fallen angels would be any different in our day? Not only has Satan's plan not changed, but we can expect that in the days to come his assaults on mankind and the plan of God will accelerate and the nations of the world will likely see "alien incursions" that will stagger the minds of men. Indeed, the book of Revelation tells us that in the last days Satan and his fallen angels will be "cast down to earth" in preparation for the final conflagration, the Battle of Armageddon.

> "And the great dragon was cast out, that old serpent, called the Devil, and Satan, which deceiveth the whole world: he was cast out into the earth, and his angels were cast out with him" (Revelation 12:9).

A COMING DECEPTION?

As we approach the end of the 20th century, the interest in extraterrestrial life and UFO phenomena has reached an all-time high. While the scientific community, lead by NASA and various national scientific academies, look for confirmation of the existence of microbial life forms on our local planetary bodies, hundreds of millions of people look to the skies for our space brothers to make contact and save us from our advancing planetary predicament.

The prevailing view that they are our highly evolved ancestors with incredibly advanced technology has prepared the world to receive them as our technological saviors. With their enormous powers, their answers for mankind, and some surprising connections to the Coming World Leader, we believe that the stage is set for the worship and reverence of alien entities as our 20th-century technological saviors in a global religion which will culminate in the greatest deception in the history of mankind.

ALIEN ENCOUNTERS

SECTION IV:

QUO VADIS: WHERE ARE WE HEADED?

COSMIC DECEPTION

"For there shall arise false Christs, and false prophets, and shall shew great signs and wonders; insomuch that, if it were possible, they shall deceive the very elect."

MATTHEW 24:24

"Even him, whose coming is after the working of Satan with all power and signs and lying wonders."

2 THESSALONIANS 2:9

Adeception of cosmic proportions is coming. It won't be just a false doctrine, a defective world-view, or one of the tragic "isms" so prevalent today. It will include a comprehensive global leadership backed by supernatural powers and capabilities that will overwhelm the imagination of the world at large. And it will be authenticated by miracles—great signs and lying wonders.

The Bible has more to say about this coming period than it does about any other period of history, including the time when Jesus walked the shores of Galilee and climbed the mountains of Judea. Much has been written, from many viewpoints, about the conditions which will be pending at the "end times" as predicted in the Bible. Few things are as controversial. But if one considers the texts seriously, some clear perspectives emerge. We believe that the arrival and involvement of "aliens" will likely play a key role.

THE INTIMATE BRIEFING

Four disciples approached Jesus privately to inquire about his Second Coming, and this resulted in a detailed answer which is so important that it is recorded in three of the four Gospels.[331] Jesus opened this famous discourse with the admonition,

> "Take heed that no man deceive you" (Matthew 24:4).

The first thing Jesus wanted the disciples to understand is that the primary sign that will accompany the days before he comes is DECEPTION. Jesus went on to give the signs that would precede his coming:

> "For many shall come in my name, saying, I am Christ; and shall deceive many. And ye shall hear of wars and rumours of wars: see that ye be not

troubled: for all these things must come to pass, but the end is not yet. For nation shall rise against nation, and kingdom against kingdom: and there shall be famines, and pestilences, and earth-quakes, in divers places. All these are the beginning of sorrows" (Matthew 24:5–8).

It's important to note that Jesus said that many would be coming in his name and that they "shall deceive many." It is often assumed that a single individual, the "Antichrist," will come on the scene to deceive the world. However, in this text Jesus points out that there will be many coming in his name, claiming to be "a Christ," and will undertake a deception of unimaginable proportions. The Coming World Leader will likely be the leader of those who, claiming to be a Christ, will deceive the world with supernatural power.

In 2 Thessalonians, the Apostle Paul amplified the nature of the coming deception:

"Now we beseech you, brethren, by the coming of our Lord Jesus Christ, and by our gathering together unto him, that ye be not soon shaken in mind, or be troubled, neither by spirit, nor by word, nor by letter as from us, as that the day of Christ is at hand. Let no man deceive you by any means: for that day shall not come, except there come a falling away first, and that man of sin be revealed, the son of perdition; who opposeth and exalteth himself above all that is called God, or that is worshipped; so that he as God sitteth in the temple of God, shewing himself that he is God" (2 Thessalonians 2:1–4).

Paul was attempting to comfort the Christians in Thessalonica because they had heard a rumor that Jesus had already come a second time. In the letter he tells them that Jesus will not come until two things occur. First there is to be a great "falling away." This falling away (*apostasia* in the Greek), according to the structure of the language, seems to suggest a sudden forsaking or defection from the Biblical world-view.

Regarding the coming apostasy Hal Lindsey states,

> "The first event which precedes the Day of the Lord is 'the apostasy.' This word (*apostasia* in Greek) means to deliberately forsake and rebel against known truth from and about God. The definite article before the term 'apostasy' clearly indicates that it is a definite event, not just a progressive rebellion. The article also points out that this fact had been taught to them before. There are many New Testament warnings about a progressive apostasy in the last days which would grow in intensity within professing Christendom. . . . But 'the apostasy' is a reference to a climactic event when the professing church will completely revolt against the Bible and all of its historical truths.

> "This ultimate act of apostasy on the part of professing Christendom sets the stage for the second great sign, which apparently happens almost simultaneously . . . the unveiling of the Antichrist."[332]

While the exact nature of this event is not revealed by the Apostle Paul, the result is that millions of ostensible Christians will be deceived into believing that the Biblical world-view is wrong. They will forsake God, the Bible, and faith in Jesus Christ.

The second event that must occur before the return of Jesus Christ is the coming of the "man of sin . . . the son of perdition." This Coming World Leader will be so powerful and so cunning that he will exalt himself above all that is worshiped. This is a remarkable statement. This includes Jehovah, Allah, Buddha, and Krishna, etc. Incredibly, he will be received and worshiped by the world as the savior—the one that is able to bridge the gulf that has separated religions, science, and philosophy for thousands of years. How will he accomplish the feat?

After the great falling away, Paul tells us, the Coming World Leader will accomplish the deception with lying signs and wonders:

> "And then shall that Wicked be revealed, whom the Lord shall consume with the spirit of his mouth, and shall destroy with the brightness of his coming: even him, whose coming is after the working of Satan with all power and signs and lying wonders, and with all deceivableness of unrighteousness in them that perish; because they received not the love of the truth, that they might be saved. And for this cause God shall send them strong delusion, that they should believe a lie: that they all might be damned who believed not the truth, but had pleasure in unrighteousness" (2 Thessalonians 2:8-12).

The effects of the signs and wonders are catastrophic. For those who would not receive the love of the truth, Jesus Christ, God will send them a "strong delusion" so that they would believe a lie. The effect of the lie is discussed by Paul in the book of Romans:

> "Because that, when they knew God, they glorified him not as God, neither were thankful; but became vain in their imaginations, and their foolish heart was darkened. Professing themselves to be wise, they became fools, and changed the

glory of the incorruptible God into an image made like to corruptible man, and to birds, and four footed beasts, and creeping things. Wherefore God also gave them up to uncleanness through the lusts of their own hearts, to dishonor their own bodies between themselves: who changed the truth of God into a lie, and worshipped and served the creature more than the Creator, who is blessed for ever. Amen" (Romans 1:21–25).

The effect of believing the lie is that men will worship the creation ("the creature") rather than the Creator.

Finally, regarding the coming deception Jesus said that it would be so powerful that even his elect (believers in Jesus Christ) would be deceived for a while.

"Then if any man shall say unto you, Lo, here is Christ, or there; believe it not. For there shall arise false Christs, and false prophets, and shall shew great signs and wonders; insomuch that, if it were possible, they shall deceive the very elect. Behold, I have told you before" (Matthew 24:23–25).

Again we see that Jesus wants us to understand that there will be many false Christs who will perform signs and wonders.

The fact that Biblically literate followers of Jesus Christ will potentially be deceived is very disturbing. What kind of deception could deceive even the very elect? For reasons that will become evident, the widespread deception associated with the forthcoming climax will be more than simply philosophical or theological deviations promulgated on the unsuspecting masses. Every belief system that has ever existed or could exist is here now; and yet, God's elect are not led astray by these mere "isms." We believe that it will take a powerful display of visible, even palpable supernatural signs and wonders. In effect, we believe that the deception will involve a worldwide series of physical manifestations by Satanic forces in a convincing display that will persuade the five senses that what one is seeing is indeed true.

We believe that one's five senses will not help in discerning whether the events are a Satanic deception or a benevolent God-ordained revelation. Only spiritual discernment will betray the true nature of the lying signs and wonders that will come upon Earth in those days.

Ultimately, the deception will involve the entire world-view of the planet Earth—even to bringing the nations of Earth into a climactic, ostensibly interplanetary war! And the armies of the world will be gathered by specific spirit beings established for that very purpose.

THE RUSH TOWARD GLOBALISM

Earlier we highlighted the emergence of a major global empire as the time of "end" approaches. It would seem that the tide toward a socialistic, centralized, "New World Order" is setting the stage. It has become fashionable—especially in the U.S. and in Europe—to deem the sovereign "nation-state" as obsolete, to promote multiculturalism over any traditional heritage, and to assume that the ultimate destiny of the planet Earth is for a unified global governance.

The reader will recall that one of the primary messages given to alien contactees is that mankind must unify into a one world government. While the Bible is clear that this global unity will ultimately be brought about by the Coming World Leader, all over the world hundreds of millions of people look to the arrival of highly advanced benevolent alien entities to accomplish this goal. Could there be a connection here?

KING NEBUCHADNEZZAR'S REMARKABLE DREAM

In Daniel 2, Daniel interprets a troubling dream of King Nebuchadnezzar of Babylon. (Fortunately, the interpretation of this strange dream is quite explicitly laid out for us in the text. The reader is encouraged to review this very readable chapter for himself.)

In this dream there was a large, shiny metallic image with a head of gold, arms and chest of silver, belly and thighs of brass, and legs and feet of iron. The feet were further notable in that there the iron was mixed with "miry clay."

A stone "cut without hands" struck the image at its feet, it crumbled, and then the stone grew into a mountain which filled the whole earth. Strange dream, indeed.

Fortunately, Daniel interprets this for us. In fact, later in Daniel's life, he received another series of visions (recorded in Daniel 7) which, although using entirely different idioms, covered the same subject matter. These visions yield much of the essential background which illuminates the book of Revelation.[333]

The large metal image turns out to be a time line of the sequence of four major empires which will dominate the planet Earth until the time when God sets up his own government. The era covered is referred to as "the times of the Gentiles."[334]

The head of gold represented Babylon under the rulership of Nebuchadnezzar.[335] This was the empire extant at that time.

The silver portion of the image referred to the empire which would conquer Babylon, that is, the Persians.[336] The fall of Babylon is detailed in Daniel 5. (Daniel himself rose to prominence in the Persian Empire. The magi visiting Bethlehem some centuries later would reflect Daniel's tutelage.)

GOLD   BABYLON

SILVER   PERSIA

BRASS   GREECE

IRON   ROME I

IRON + CLAY   "ROME II"

The brass portion of the image represented the empire that would subsequently conquer the Persians, namely the Greeks.[337] (Alexander the Great's career was so detailed in Daniel 8 that when that passage was presented to him upon entering Jerusalem, he spared the city.[338])

The iron of the image represented the empire which would ultimately conquer the Greeks, namely the Romans.[339] It is interesting that the Roman Empire ultimately split into two (two legs of the image?). More significantly, who conquered the Romans? The answer: no one.

About A.D. 476, the Roman Empire broke into pieces. Throughout subsequent European history, each piece has made a bid for global dominion without fully succeeding. The Dutch, the French (under Charlemagne and later Napoleon), the Germans (under Bismarck and later Hitler), the Spanish with their Armada, the English as "mistress of the seas," all have had their day in the sun. But none of them really established suzerainty in the sense that the Romans did.

Daniel's portrayal suggests that these "pieces" will ultimately recombine before the end.[340] This theme is echoed in many other passages and is one of the reasons that some Bible commentators have, for centuries, looked for an ultimate "revival" of the Roman Empire, in some form, at "the time of the end." (Some suggest that the current moves within the European Union may be setting the stage for this final government.[341])

This final empire—represented by the ten toes of iron mixed with miry clay—is the subject of many passages dealing with the final climax.[342] It will be in the days of the ten toes that the "stone cut without hands" will smite the image and set up God's own government upon the earth.[343] This "stone" will be reviewed in chapter 14.

THE RETURN OF THE NEPHILIM?

Even our common expression "the idol has feet of clay" apparently comes to us from this classic passage. But what is represented by the "miry clay?" It seems to be strangely mixed—but not completely—with the iron in the dream. The term "miry clay" refers to clay made from dust,[344] a Biblical idiom which suggests death. (The *Rephaim,* a tribal term for some of the giants, is also a term often translated "death."[345]) What makes this famous prophecy especially suggestive for our exploration here is the strange allusion in verse 43:

> "And whereas thou sawest iron mixed with miry
> clay, they shall mingle themselves with the seed of
> men: but they shall not cleave one to another,
> even as iron is not mixed with clay" (Daniel 2:43).

Switching to a personal pronoun, *they* "shall mingle themselves with the seed of men. . . ." This is extremely suggestive
when viewed in the light of the warning of our Lord heading
this chapter, ostensibly directing us to look more closely at
Genesis 6. Just what (or who) are "mingling with the seed of
men?" Who are these Non-seed? It staggers the mind to contemplate the potential significance of Daniel's passage and its
implications for the future global governance.

Could this be a hint of a return to the mischief of Genesis 6?
Are "aliens" and their hybrid offspring part of the political
makeup of this emergent world empire? Are the UFO incidents part of a carefully orchestrated program to lead us
toward a political agenda?

Or has it started already? Are the UFOs and increasingly
widespread abductions part of the preparations for this scenario? Is the alleged "hybridization program" on which John
Mack and others expound part of a Satanic plan to infiltrate
the coming global government with "alien" Satanic forces? Are
these aliens or their offspring part of the move toward a global
government that we already see in motion, both here in the
U.S. and in Europe?

THE COMING WORLD LEADER

The centralized global government, not surprisingly, will
ultimately be taken over by a dictator the likes of which the
world has never seen. He apparently will be the most attractive, commanding, winsome presence ever to command the
world stage. He is alluded to by 33 different appellations in the
Old Testament and 13 in the New Testament.

Unfortunately, he is commonly called by one of the most misleading of these labels, "the Antichrist." This is widely misunderstood as it would focus on the idea that he is "against Christ," which he, indeed, will be. However, the Greek term *antichrist* really means "pseudo-Christ" or "in place of" Christ. He will be an impostor, posing as Christ.

THE GENEALOGY OF THE ANTICHRIST

History is littered with speculations as to the identity of this final Coming World Leader. There are numerous justifications to assume he will be a Gentile. There are also many reasons to view him as Jewish. Others have suggested that he will be Judas Iscariot resurrected from the dead. Some have even promoted President John Kennedy or Henry Kissinger. Surprisingly, a number of prominent Bible teachers—Hal Lindsey and Dave Hunt as examples—have publicly stated their view is that this leader will either be an alien or he will boast of alien connections! Remarkably, in addition to Daniel 2:43 there are many startling clues in the Bible that seem to connect the Coming World Leader to Satan and his "alien" forces.

THE SEED OF THE SERPENT

In the first book of the Bible we find an intriguing clue to the possible lineage of the coming Antichrist. In Genesis 3 we find the story of the fall of man. The setting is the garden of Eden, where God had placed a tree called "the tree of the knowledge of good and evil." God had placed Adam in the garden and told him that he could eat of the fruit of every tree except the tree of the knowledge of good and evil (Genesis 2:17). However, one day Satan (the serpent) came to Eve and tempted her to eat of the forbidden tree.

It's interesting to note that the first thing Satan said to Eve was, "Hath God said, Ye shall not eat of every tree of the garden?" This is the first tactic of the enemy—to question the word of God. Satan went on to promise Eve that if she would eat of the tree she would not "surely die." Instead, she would be like God; she would have incredible knowledge, "knowing good and evil." Immortality, deity, and incredible knowledge. What a deal Satan promised Eve! So, she ate of the forbidden fruit and so began the fall of mankind.

In Genesis 3:14–15 we read the response of God as he, so to speak, takes Satan to the woodshed:

> "And the LORD God said unto the serpent, Because thou hast done this, thou art cursed above all cattle, and above every beast of the field; upon thy belly shalt thou go, and dust shalt thou eat all the days of thy life: And I will put enmity between thee and the woman, and between thy seed and her seed; it shall bruise thy head, and thou shalt bruise his heel" (Genesis 3:14-15).

This is one of the most pivotal portions of scripture in the entire Bible. It sets up the battle between the seed of the woman (a prophecy of the virgin birth of Jesus Christ) and the seed of Satan. A casual reading of this text will miss a disturbing textual insight. The Hebrew word translated seed is the word *zera,* meaning "offspring, descendants, posterity, and children." Satan is going to have seed! Who is the seed of Satan and what is his future destiny? We get another hint in the New Testament.

THE SON OF PERDITION

We saw earlier, in Paul's second letter to the Thessalonians, a description of the Coming World Leader:

> "Let no man deceive you by any means: for that day shall not come, except there come a falling

> away first, and that man of sin be revealed, the
> son of perdition; who opposeth and exalteth
> himself above all that is called God, or that is
> worshipped; so that he as God sitteth in the tem-
> ple of God, shewing himself that he is God"
> (2 Thessalonians 2:3–4).

After the falling away Paul states that "the man of sin . . . the son of perdition" will be revealed. This is a fascinating insight that may relate to the very parentage of the Antichrist himself. The word translated "son" is the Greek word *huios*, which is used in a general sense to mean "a male offspring." In a wider sense it means "descendant, posterity, child." The word translated "perdition" is the Greek word *apoleia*, meaning "utter destruction, destroy." This word comes from the same Greek root from which we get "Apollyon," one of the names of Satan found in Revelation 9:11.

> "And they had a king over them, which is the angel
> of the bottomless pit, whose name in the Hebrew
> tongue is Abaddon, but in the Greek tongue hath
> his name Apollyon" (Revelation 9:11).

According to Greek scholars this one called Destroyer, Abaddon, and Apollyon is the "minister of death and the author of havoc on the earth"—none other than Satan himself!

The composite we can draw from these verses is disturbing indeed. We have examined in detail the intrigues of Genesis 6, where the fallen angels consorted with the "daughters of men" and produced supernatural offspring, the "mighty men which were of old, men of renown." If the fallen angel interpretation is indeed a valid description of the state of affairs in Genesis 6, then it is likely that Satan, as a fallen angel himself, must also have the ability to cohabit with a human female. By definition any offspring produced by such an ungodly union would be the seed of the serpent and the son of perdition!

While this scenario may seem farfetched, it is neither unique nor without additional Biblical support.

DEMONIALITY

The notion that the Antichrist would be born by the union of an incubus and a human female dates back at least several hundreds of years to the Middle Ages. During the Middle Ages there were hundreds of recorded accounts of men and women who had allegedly consorted with demonic forces. This fact is even confirmed by St. Augustine of Canterbury (b.?-d.604), founder of the church in southern England.[346]

> "It is a widespread opinion, confirmed by direct or indirect testimony of trustworthy persons, that the Sylvans and Fauns, commonly called Incubi, have often tormented women, solicited and obtained intercourse with them. There are even Demons, which are called Duses [i.e., lutins] by the Gauls, who are quite frequently using such impure practices: this is vouched for by so numerous and so high authorities that it would be impudent to deny it."[347]

Such unions, called demoniality, were forbidden by the Church and frequently resulted in excommunication, witch trials, and being burned at a stake.

At the end of the 17th century, Fr. Ludovicus Maria Sinistrari de Ameno (1622–1701) of the Franciscan Order wrote a lengthy treatise on the copulation of demonic entities with human beings. In the manuscript *De Daemonialitate, et Incubis, et Succubi* he discussed the historical fact of such unions and showed that a number of Early Church fathers supported the view that the "sons of God" in Genesis 6 were indeed fallen angels. Regarding the parentage of the Antichrist Fr. Sinistrari states:

"To theologians and philosophers, it is a fact, that from the copulation of humans (man or woman) with the demon, human beings are sometimes born. It is by this process that Antichrist must be born, according to a number of doctors [theologians]: Bellarmin, Suarez, Maluende, etc., . . . the children generated in this manner by the incubi are tall, very strong, very daring, very magnificent and very wicked. . . ."[348]

In *Passport to Magonia*, Vallee points out a fascinating statement by the 18th-century theologian R. P. le Brun regarding the offspring of such unions (Nephilim) and the origin of the Antichrist:

"If the body of these children is thus different from the bodies of other children, their soul will certainly have qualities that will not be in common to others: that is why Cardinal Bellarmin thinks Antichrist will be born of a woman having had intercourse with an incubus."[349]

The notion that fallen angels can consort with a human female and produce viable offspring is quite startling and indeed foreign to most of us in the 20th century. However, in the Middle Ages it was a common-enough occurrence that there was much discussion among theologians regarding the physical mechanism employed by such spirit entities.

There will no doubt be many who will find the entire thesis (that angels can manifest physically and consort with humans) presented herein impossible to believe. The skeptic will likely argue that "angels are spirit beings that have no physical bodies, so the entire thesis is absurd." While we don't know how it is done, we should not underestimate the power of Satan and his minions. If Satan and his minions were capable of this in the days of Noah, there is every reason to believe that they still are.

The fact is that angels do manifest themselves in physical form throughout the Bible and the annals of history. How they do it is not explained. However, angels, including fallen ones, do have the power to manipulate matter and reshape it into a multitude of forms, including life! (We will discuss this in detail in the next chapter.) Suffice it to say that if angels can appear physically; take men by the hand; fight with men; and form eyes, ears, skin, etc., then the manifestation of reproductive organs is also within their capabilities.

THE RETURN OF THE NEPHILIM

If the Antichrist does arise from such a union, then from a Biblical perspective, he would be a Nephilim ("fallen one"). While this notion may seem radical, it turns out that there is additional Biblical evidence that the Nephilim will play a major role in the end-times scenario.

In the book of Isaiah, chapters 13 and 14, we read of the destruction of the city of Babylon in the context of the last days of planet Earth. During the time of Daniel and Ezekiel (6th century B.C.) the city of Babylon was the greatest city on Earth. Its walls were reportedly over 200 feet tall and so thick that the Babylonians conducted chariot races on the top of the city walls.

Over a hundred years before the Babylonian empire was replaced by the Medo-Persian Empire, the prophet Isaiah foretold that the city of Babylon would be destroyed. It is commonly assumed that the destruction of Babylon occurred centuries before Christ by the Medo-Persian, Greek, and Roman Empires. However, this was not the case. The city was never destroyed; it simply decayed into ruin over many centuries. One of the major prophetic themes of the end times involves the sudden destruction of the rebuilt city of Babylon.

Regarding those days the prophet Isaiah wrote,

> "The burden of Babylon, which Isaiah the son of
> Amos did see. Lift ye up a banner upon the high
> mountain, exalt the voice unto them, shake the
> hand, that they may go into the gates of the nobles.
> I have commanded my sanctified ones, I have also
> called my mighty ones for mine anger, even them
> that rejoice in my highness" (Isaiah 13:1–3).

The term "mighty ones" is the Hebrew word *gibborim* and is
the same term used in Genesis 6 for the Nephilim. It was
understood by ancient scholars to be a synonym for the giants
(Nephilim) of old.

This is evident in the Greek translation of Isaiah 13:

> "The vision which Esaias [Isaiah] son of Amos saw
> against Babylon. Lift up a standard on the moun-
> tain of the plain, exalt the voice to them, beckon
> with the hand, open the gates, ye ruler. I give com-
> mand and I bring them: giants are coming to ful-
> fill my wrath, rejoicing at the same time and
> insulting. . . . For behold! the day of the Lord is
> coming which cannot be escaped, a day of wrath
> and anger, to make the world desolate, and to
> destroy sinners out of it . . . . And Babylon, which
> is called glorious by the king of, the Chaldeans,
> shall be as when God overthrew Sodoma and
> Gomorrah. . . . It shall never be inhabited, nei-
> ther shall any enter into it for many generations:
> neither shall the Arabians pass through it—nor
> shall shepherds at all rest in it. But wild beasts
> shall rest there; and the houses shall be filled
> with howling; and monsters shall rest there, and
> devils shall dance there and satyrs shall dwell

there; and hedgehogs shall make their nests in their houses. It will come soon, and will not tarry" (Isaiah 13:1-3, 9, 19–22, Septuagint Version).

If the ancient translators' understanding of the Hebrew text of Isaiah is correct, then it seems to follow that the Nephilim will be returning in the last days of planet Earth and the city of Babylon will become the habitation of "monsters, devils and satyrs!" These are terms which for centuries have been understood to be synonymous with physical manifestations of fallen angels!

This disturbing look at the future of Babylon is echoed in the book of Revelation:

"And he cried mightily with a strong voice, saying, 'Babylon the great is fallen, is fallen, and is become the habitation of devils, and the hold of every foul spirit, and a cage of every unclean and hateful bird!' " (Revelation 18:2).

Could it be that the city of Babylon, which was the original region of Satan's rebellion against God, will be inhabited in the last days by Satanic entities masquerading as modern-day aliens? Time will tell.

NIMROD: A "TYPE" OF ANTICHRIST?

Throughout the Bible we see that the Holy Spirit uses dramatic stories that scholars call "types" or "models" as a way of revealing the nature, mission, or destiny of Jesus Christ. God even declares this through the prophet Hosea:

"I have also spoken by the prophets, and I have multiplied visions, and used similitudes [models or types], by the ministry of the prophets" (Hosea 12:10).

The lives of Moses, Joseph, and the sacrifice of Isaac in Genesis 22 are but a few examples. However, in the book of Genesis we have the story of Nimrod who, according to many scholars, is a typological model of the Antichrist.

Nimrod, whose name means "the rebel," was the son of Cush and lived after the flood. Nimrod's rebellion, which was in open revolt against God, was exemplified by his leadership of a great confederacy of peoples. This confederacy consisted of a unified "one world" government with a common language. He was founder of an ungodly, idolatrous, pagan religious system from which most of the subsequent pagan religions emerged. ExtraBiblical records indicate that he set himself up as god and was even worshiped by the ungodly nations as the "god of gods."[350]

Nimrod, the king of Babylon, had his headquarters in Babylon. It is interesting to note that the Coming World Leader is called "the king of Babylon" (Isaiah 14:4), and in the book of Revelation he is connected with "mystery Babylon" (Revelation 17:3-5). Nimrod's supreme ambition was to make a name for himself. All of these characteristics parallel the resume of the Coming World Leader, who will "exalt himself above all that is called God, or that is worshipped; so that he as God sitteth in the temple of God, showing himself that he is God" (2 Thessalonians 2:4).

There is an additional aspect of the story that we find very provocative. Nimrod is called a "mighty one" in the text of Genesis 10:8.

> "And Cush begat Nimrod: he began to be a mighty
> one in the earth" (Genesis 10:8).

This is provocative because the title "mighty one" is the very same Hebrew word, *gibborim*, that is frequently used as a synonym for the Nephilim! While we do not know whether he was a Nephilim,[351] it is interesting that in order to complete the typology of the Antichrist, the Holy Spirit inspired Moses, the author of Genesis, to use the very same synonym for the Nephilim!

THE ALIEN CONNECTION

In addition to the Biblical evidence for Antichrist's lineage, some striking parallels emerge when we compare the nature and mission of the Antichrist with the reported nature of our 20th-century alien visitors.

As we plunge into the literature regarding the nature and purpose of our modern-day alien visitors, we find that they are usually viewed as having the answers we need to resolve our predicament and survive into the centuries to come. This belief emerges because of their incredible mastery over the laws of physics and the seemingly supernatural powers they possess.

The ability to perform "signs and wonders" and provide answers for mankind's problems are characteristics shared by the Antichrist as well. He will have a global plan that is so incredible that he will be embraced as a technological savior.

Finally, when we examine the message given to alien contactees, we find they promote globalism, ecumenism, personal immortality (reincarnation), pantheism ("you will be like gods," Genesis 3:15), moral relativism, and the notion that the Bible is not the word of God. These are beliefs that Satan himself, through the ministry of the Antichrist, will promote during the coming global confederacy.

When we think about the supernatural characteristics of the Antichrist, an interesting question arises. What will he tell the world about the source of this power and knowledge? If he were to state that his power came from God, he would likely be rejected by those in the secular, scientific community. If he were to boast that his power was from the forces of darkness, his would not likely be well received by the masses. We believe that it is very likely that the Coming World Leader will boast of a connection with the powerful, god-like alien entities who have, it is believed, overcome the problems of poverty, famine, disease, war, and the pain of cultural and religious division.

These "saviors" will have a plan to unify mankind, and they will provide the Coming World Leader with the answers we need to solve our global predicament. The plan will be backed up by the power to supersede the laws of physics and perform, in effect, supernatural signs and wonders. When such a man arises on the scene with a message of love, unity, and peace, along with the answers we need backed up by supernatural signs and wonders, the peoples of the world will willingly set aside their differences, lay down their weapons to follow him, and even worship him as god!

Even a casual perusal of the UFO and New Age literature reveals that millions of people are expecting the coming New Age Messiah to have an alien connection. Many, including a number of UFO cults, believe that the Coming World Leader will be a hybrid, half-human, half-alien Avatar. According to these groups, this was the case with Jesus, Buddha, Mohammed, etc. So the pattern is set.

In his book *The Day the Gods Came,* George King discusses the origin, power, and mission of the Coming World Leader. According to King, the information about the coming Avatar was "telepathically relayed" to him from "the voice of God—Itself."

> "There will shortly come Another among you. He will stand tall among men with a shining countenance. This One will be attired in a single garment of the type now known to you. . . . He will approach the Earth leaders. They will ask of Him, His credentials. He will produce these. His magic

will be greater than any upon the Earth—greater than the combined materialistic might of all the armies. And they who heed not his words shall be removed from the Earth. This Rock is now Holy—and will remain so for as long as the world exists. Go ye forth and spread My Word throughout the world, so that all men of pure heart may prepare for His Coming."[352]

There is a lot we can glean from this message. According to King, the coming Avatar will apparently be of tall stature. Secondly, he will be endowed with magic powers, and those who do not heed "his words shall be removed from the Earth." Again we see the theme of the coming evacuation of the malcontents, the "dark forces" who refuse to go along with the plan!

The extraterrestrial origin of this coming Avatar is clearly implied by King only a few paragraphs later:

"The Declaration states quite definitely that there will be no mystery about the birth of the next world Avatar as there was about the birth of Krishna, Buddha, Jesus and others. This majestic Being will come among men dressed in the one piece suit usually worn by the Intelligences from other Planets. . . . He will openly approach the Earth leaders; He will make His origin known to them but they will not believe Him. However, He will have great powers which, by Karmic Law, He will be allowed to use in order to demonstrate to all men beyond all doubt, the Authority empowering Him to carry out His great Mission on Earth. . . . The power of this Being will be greater than mankind has ever seen before in any single humanoid frame. So vast will it be as to be almost terrible, for, as the Declaration states: 'They who heed not His words, shall be removed from the Earth.' This means that those who cannot follow the teachings of Truth. Peace and Spirituality will pass from this Planet on to a younger One in order to learn from the experiences they deserve for those who will not follow the next Avatar will not be ready for the Golden Age. . . . The Initiation [sic] of Earth has been given. Mankind should spare no efforts to help prepare the way for the next great Cosmic Event—for the next Master. Who—WILL COME."[353]

The belief expressed by King that the Coming World Leader will have an extraterrestrial connection is obviously implied by his statement that they will not believe him when he tells the world leaders his origin. This claim is illustrative of the New Age literature regarding the origin and nature of the Coming World Leader and can easily be confirmed by a casual perusal of this literature. Indeed, the New Age literature often declares that the supernatural power and knowledge of the Coming World Leader is a direct result of his connection with "highly evolved" extraterrestrial entities.

THE TIME OF HIS COMING

We happen to be among those who believe that the Coming World Leader will not be revealed until after the Rapture (evacuation) of the Church.[354] As we have seen, this view is not inconsistent with the messages given by New Agers declaring that the New Age and its Messiah cannot occur until the dark forces (the Church) are removed.

In chapter 9 we discussed the doctrine of the Rapture (*rapturo* in the Latin) of the Church. This mystery, we are told, will be a sudden conversion—"we shall all be changed"; our bodies will be changed from a corruptible, earthly state to a heavenly, incorruptible state. According to the Apostle Paul, this event will occur "in a twinkling of an eye." What we did not discuss was the timing of this event in relation to the arrival of the Coming World Leader. This is discussed by Paul in his second letter to the Thessalonians.

> "Do you not remember that when I was still with you I told you these things? And now you know what is restraining, that he may be revealed in his own time. For the mystery of lawlessness is already at work; only he who now restrains will do so until he is taken out of the way. And then the lawless one will be revealed, whom the Lord will consume with the breath of his mouth and destroy with the brightness of his coming" (2 Thessalonians 2:5–8).

We believe that the restrainer referred to in this verse is the Holy Spirit working through the Church. Paul states that once "he who now restrains . . . is taken out of the way . . . the lawless one will be revealed." We know that the Holy Spirit will not be taken out of the world, because during the Tribulation (the last three and one-half years of Daniel's 70th week) he will be working in the lives of Christians who are converted after the Rapture. The point is that the Holy Spirit—working through the Church—is restraining the forces of darkness, and he may be restraining far more than we can imagine! The removal of this restraining force (the Church empowered by Holy Spirit) will allow Satan free reign once the troublemakers are removed.

We can't help but point out that Satan has not spent any time trying to explain away the view that the Church will be taken out after the arrival of the Antichrist and the completion of the Tribulation!

THE "MISSION" OF
THE COMING WORLD LEADER

As we examine the Biblical text, we discover that the primary goals and purposes of the Coming World Leader are to set himself up as the leader of a global confederacy of nations,[355] to cause people to fall away from the Biblical world-view and to usurp the worship[356] and adoration due to Jesus Christ, to exalt himself above all that is called God,[357] and to bring the world to battle against Jesus Christ and his followers in the Battle of Armageddon.[358]

To accomplish these goals he must bridge the gaps created by nationalism, religion, science, and philosophy. At the same, he must discredit, ostensibly, the Christian world-view of a personal Creator and saving faith in Jesus Christ. The Coming World Leader must also somehow convince the world that Jesus Christ is the enemy when Christ returns in the clouds!

WHEN THE WORLD WILL BE AS ONE

Throughout the centuries many have attempted to unify the world into a cohesive, global confederacy. However, these attempts at world empires have fallen short. Although it's an oversimplification, one of the primary reasons for this failure is that previous dictators attempted to win the world over by military force. Obviously, this method has proved incapable of accomplishing world unification. Though it may result in considerable territorial gains, rather than unifying disparate groups, subversion by military means only serves to deepen the divisions and resentment between those with ethnic and religious differences.

For the Coming World Leader to rise to prominence and unify the world will require him to exploit, at a minimum, the following four stratagems.

First, it is well-known that out of the ruins of catastrophe and anarchy there arises a desire for a strong leader who can unify the masses and heal the wounds of conflict. Consequently, a global shock that shakes the foundations of existing paradigms is almost certain to be introduced (or exploited) by Satan to take advantage of this instinct in order to raise up his global leadership in the last days.

Second, after the initial shock a powerful plan and a "rational" explanation for the global events will be needed to soothe the fears of the masses and bring order, understanding, and hope for the future out of the existing chaos. Without hope the plan will not be embraced. Without understanding there can be no sense of order or unity, and fear will remain prevalent. In effect, he must shock but reassure at the same time.

Third, for any global scheme to take hold the Coming World Leader must have a plan to deal with the malcontents.

Finally, because there will be skeptics among the religious and scientific communities, unification behind the Coming World Leader must and will be accompanied by supernatural signs and wonders. Without such signs he would likely be viewed as just another politician.

UNIFICATION THROUGH PEACE

Remarkably, unlike previous would-be world dictators, the Coming World Leader will rise to power primarily by peaceful methods. This is confirmed in the eighth chapter of Daniel:

> "And in the latter time of their kingdom, when the transgressors are come to the full, a king of fierce countenance, and understanding dark sentences, shall stand up. And his power shall be mighty, but not by his own power: and he shall destroy wonderfully, and shall prosper, and practise, and shall

> destroy the mighty and the holy people. And
> through his policy also he shall cause craft to pros-
> per in his hand; and he shall magnify himself in
> his heart, and by peace shall destroy many: he
> shall also stand up against the Prince of princes;
> but he shall be broken without hand" (Daniel
> 8:23–25).

The precarious nature of this peace is confirmed by Paul the
Apostle in his first letter to the Thessalonians:

> "For when they say, 'Peace and safety!' then sud-
> den destruction comes upon them, as labor pains
> upon a pregnant woman. And they shall not
> escape" (1 Thessalonians 5:3).

The peace and safety temporarily accomplished in the first
half (3.5 years) of Daniel's 70th week will likely be ushered in
by the Coming World Leader after a global disturbance.
Although the employment of peace as a part of his plan will
certainly reassure the masses and help to quiet the noncon-
formists, this peace will, however, prove to be false and short-
lived. Ultimately, the result of this "peace plan" will be the
death and destruction of many. The question we would like to
consider is, what kind of catastrophe or global disruption will
precede the unification and false peace brought by the Coming
World Leader?

Of course the number of possible scenarios is endless. Some
suggest that a global economic collapse or war in the Middle
East will necessitate the Antichrist's arrival. Others suggest a
global environmental crisis as the source of unification. Still
others suggest that it will be the Rapture of the Church or open
alien contact that will be so shocking and so disruptive that a
leader with answers will arise.

THE EFFECT OF OPEN ALIEN CONTACT

An occurrence of open ET contact would obviously have staggering sociological and psychological effects on mankind. While we can only speculate what these effects might be, a number of prominent people have expressed their belief that it would be a powerful unifying force for the nations of the world.

On September 21, 1987, President Reagan, in his address to the 42nd General Assembly of the United Nations made a startling statement regarding the unifying effect of an "alien threat":

> "Perhaps we need some outside, universal threat to make us recognize this common bond. I occasionally think how quickly our differences world-wide would vanish if we were facing an alien threat from outside this world. And yet, I ask you, is not an alien force already among us?"[359]

More recently, in an address to the Bilderbergers meeting in Evian, France, on May 21, 1992, according to *USA Today* and other newspapers, Henry Kissinger stated:

> "Today Americans would be outraged if UN troops entered Los Angeles to restore order; tomorrow they will be grateful! This is especially true if they were told there was an outside threat from beyond, whether real or promulgated, that threatened our very existence. It is then that all peoples of the world will pledge with world leaders to deliver them from this evil. The one thing every man fears is the unknown. When presented with this scenarios, individual rights will be willingly relinquished for the guarantee of their well-being granted to them by their world government."

Even Hollywood promotes the notion of global unification through open extraterrestrial contact. In the 1996 movie *First Contact*, members of the Star Trek team discuss the effect of the first open contact with aliens in the year 2063. Regarding the importance of this first contact, Counselor Troi, the Star Trek team's resident New Age counselor, states that the first open contact with extraterrestrials "unites humanity in a way that no one ever thought possible when they realize that they're not alone in the universe. Poverty, disease, war; they'll all be gone in the next 50 years."

In his book *Messengers of Deception*, Jacques Vallee discusses the power of the UFO phenomenon to change lives, inspire awe, and the hope of "salvation from above":

> "I believe there is a machinery of mass manipulation behind the UFO phenomenon. It aims at social and political goals by diverting attention from some human problems and by providing a potential release for tensions caused by others. The contactees are a part of that machinery. They are helping to create a new form of belief: an expectation of actual contact among large parts of the public. In turn this expectation makes millions of people hope for the imminent realization of that age-old dream: salvation from above, surrender to the greater power of some wise navigators of the cosmos.[360]

Here Vallee has put his finger on the mystical and religious side of the UFO phenomenon. Recognizing our inability to rescue ourselves from the human predicament of poverty, pain, suffering, death, and disease, there is a inherent tendency for us to seek salvation from a "greater power," a higher, nonearthly source. In times past this yearning was primarily fulfilled by a relationship with God. However, with the widespread, institutionalized abandonment of Judeo-Christian principles in the 20th century, millions of people have begun to look to the supernatural UFO phenomenon and their associated, god-like alien entities as the higher source of salvation for mankind.

Tragically, on March 26, 1997, this was played out in the suicide-deaths of 39 members of the "Heaven's Gate" UFO cult in Rancho Santa Fe, California. Led by Marshall Applewhite, known as "Do," the 39 members of the cult believed that aliens from the "kingdom of heaven" were about to make open contact with mankind by evacuating the "faithful" from the surface of the planet. Believing that the world is on the threshold of global cataclysms, they decided to expedite their exit by "shedding their containers" in an effort to join a UFO they believed was traveling behind comet Hale-Bopp!

The tragic lesson here is that the while the UFO phenomenon has the ability to engender tremendous personal devotion and self-sacrifice, it also has the ability perpetrate massive deception.

As we have seen, the UFO phenomenon has come to be seen by many as a scientifically acceptable replacement for God. Logical constraints of the "God is an astronaut belief" notwithstanding, for those that have rejected traditional religious beliefs, the UFO phenomenon has become an elixir for millions. This deception is a replacement to fill the God-shaped void possessed by all mankind and a powerful device to which stirs emotions and thoughts of salvation from above.

We believe that the cultural preparation (or deliberate conditioning) of the world to view our alien visitors as powerful and highly evolved saviors makes the UFO phenomenon the perfect motif for the Antichrist to exploit when he ascends to power. His ability to perform supernatural signs and wonders, his comprehensive plan for the peaceful unification of mankind, and his connection to or origin from god-like alien entities will engender the masses to follow him into the biggest deception in history.

OPEN ET CONTACT AND THE CHURCH

In chapter 8 we pointed out that the pace of events (wars, pestilence, earthquakes, famine, etc.) in the last days was likened by Jesus to the process of pregnancy, labor, and childbirth. This presents a potentially disturbing scenario for the Church in the last days.

We pointed out that long before the true labor ensues there will be a period of very intense, potentially deceptive, false labor pains that are virtually indistinguishable from the real thing. This presents the frightening scenario that at least a portion of the quickening pace of events (the false labor pains) will be experienced by the Church.

Does this mean we will see extensive persecution, global cataclysms, and the early stages of a well-orchestrated global deception that will cause men to doubt the Biblical world-view and exchange it for something more socially and scientifically palatable? We already are! Worldwide, Christians are being killed by the thousands annually. As we read earlier, the pace of events is quickening dramatically as we approach the end of the 20th century.

But could this scenario mean that we may see proof of alien reality or open contact before the Church is taken out? We believe that this is a distinct and disturbing possibility.

Jesus said that the coming deception would be so powerful that it would deceive, if possible, the very elect. As we have said, we believe to deceive the very "elect" it will take a convincing display of powerful, but lying signs and wonders. While this deception will be associated with an ecumenical, universalistic, "all roads are the same" message, such a message alone is not sufficient to explain the effect on the Church. Indeed, something radical, even unbelievable, must happen to cause millions of Bible-believing Christians to abandon their faith for a while.

Jesus spoke of such an event near the end of his ministry when asked about the signs before his coming. As he was enumerating the signs before his coming Jesus said,

> "And there shall be signs in the sun, and in the moon, and in the stars; and upon the earth distress of nations, with perplexity; the sea and the waves roaring; men's hearts failing them for fear, and for looking after those things which are coming on the earth: for the powers of heaven shall be shaken. . . . And when these things begin to come to pass, then look up, and lift up your heads; for your redemption draweth nigh" (Luke 21:25–26, 28).

"Looking after those things which are coming on the earth." What a remarkable statement by Jesus! What things are going to be coming on Earth? What catastrophe would cause men's hearts to fail them? What would it take to cause millions of believers to seriously doubt and "fall away" from the Biblical world-view? While we can only speculate about the nature of these events, one thing is for certain, the appearance of alien ships in the skies of planet Earth would be the greatest shock in the history of mankind. It would shake the foundations of religious, scientific, and philosophical paradigms. It would cause many of God's elect to abandon, for a time, the Biblical world-view. It would indeed cause the hearts of many men to fail!

According to Richard Boylan, Ph.D., a well-known UFO researcher, the effect of open alien contact on "Christian fundamentalists" has also been a point of concern among government operatives in the super-secret UFO research unit known as "the Aviary." According to Boylan, the Aviary is a "shadowy group of defense industry scientists and active/former military and intelligence officers, who have complete access to closely held UFO information."[361]

> "One of the predictions is that there will be a very large rift in human society as a result of ET contact becoming publicly known. . . . The Aviary are quite concerned that fundamentalist Christians will experience spiritual, if not ontological, shock at the revelation of ET visitation, and over the reported contents of the Red and Yellow Books, which contain information that suggests that Jesus had some connection with the extraterrestrials. . . . Some within the Aviary are concerned that the theological and religious social implications may be the most serious ones resulting from open extraterrestrial contact. . . . Adding more fuel to Aviary concerns, [there are] reports that a European television station reported that Vatican experts on the Fatima Prophecies held a reported briefing for government representatives from the U.K., France, Germany and the U.S., concerning the third remaining publicly unannounced Prophecy. This Prophecy is rumored to deal with ET Visitation. A spokesman for the Vatican reportedly confirmed that such a briefing took place."

Although many millions of God's elect would, for a time, be deceived, millions more would see through the miracles performed by these Satanic forces and understand that what they are seeing is a carefully crafted deception. Their reluctance to accept alien entities as benevolent space brothers would, no doubt, result in significant persecution.

When the Church is raptured the Antichrist will most likely explain it away as an alien evacuation necessitated to achieve and preserve peace and facilitate the reeducation of the misguided malcontents! With the malcontents taken out of the way, his plan for global unification and ecumenism can go forward. To those left behind this explanation will seem very plausible.

The bottom line is that the sudden apostasy of millions of believers, a strong desire for unified global leadership, and "men's hearts failing them" from fear could all be "accomplished" by the occurrence of open ET contact before the Church is taken out.

In the event that the Church is taken out before open ET contact, there will be tremendous confusion and fear. The chaos and uncertainty will facilitate the appearance and rise to power of a charismatic leader. His ability to explain away the disappearance of millions of people, coupled with his plan for the peaceful unification of the nations, backed by his ability to perform signs and wonders, will bring about widespread worship and devotion to the Coming World Leader and his plan for mankind. Ultimately, this "Idol Shepherd"[362] will draw the nations of the world to battle against Jesus Christ in the Valley of Megiddo.

THE WAR OF THE WORLDS

Many books have been written about the "Battle of Armageddon," which itself has become an idiom of our language, even among non-Biblical writers. What is astonishing about this final conflict is that the world will be taking up arms against God!

> "Why do the heathen rage, and the people imagine a vain thing? The kings of the earth set themselves, and the rulers take counsel together, against the Lord, and against his anointed, saying, 'Let us break their bands asunder, and cast away their cords from us.' He that sitteth in the heavens shall laugh: the Lord shall have them in derision"[363] (Psalm 2:1–4).

The notion that the kings of the earth would even attempt to war against God is an aspect of the end times that has puzzled Bible scholars for centuries. Indeed, the psalmist tells us that "He that sitteth in the heavens shall laugh" at the notion. What could possibly compel the leadership of planet Earth to be drawn into such a senseless scenario? Will these leaders really believe that they are going to battle against God, or are they victims of "bad intelligence"? According to David Allen Lewis, author of *UFOs: End Time Delusion,* we get a hint of possible extraterrestrial involvement in the Battle of Armageddon in the book of Revelation.

As we have read, there are different categories of "aliens" recognized by researchers. In chapter 6 we read about the Reptilians, a group of humanoid alien entities with frog-like faces that some in the New Age movement believe were our creator gods. In the book of Revelation the Apostle John gives us a disturbing look at the final global conflict which is apparently orchestrated by entities that closely resemble descriptions of the Reptilians:

> "And I saw three unclean spirits like frogs come out of the mouth of the dragon, and out of the mouth of the beast, and out of the mouth of the false prophet. For they are the spirits of devils, working miracles, which go forth unto the kings

of the earth and of the whole world, to gather them to the battle of that great day of God Almighty" (Revelation 16:13-14)

Like a scene out of the movie "V," these "spirits of devils" convince the world that they are our benevolent creator-saviors by performing lying signs and wonders for the kings of the earth. Once the kings of the earth are fully convinced of their deity, these fallen angels, masquerading as Reptilian "aliens," begin to describe the coming of a "bad ET" who will come in the clouds with ten thousands of his followers. With their awesome power and the persuasive leadership of the Antichrist, they will draw the kings of the earth into a battle against Jesus Christ, whom they will have portrayed as that "bad ET" who must be stopped at all costs!

Is it possible that the preparations for this cosmic conflict have already begun? Is the gigantic delusion already being positioned? Are the UFOs, alien intrusions, and "New Age" rationales the beginning of the demonic preparation for this "interplanetary" conflict?

FINAL THOUGHTS

In the book of Acts the Apostle Paul encourages us to be like the Bereans, who were "more noble than those in Thessalonica, in that they received the word with all readiness of mind, and searched the scriptures daily, whether those things were so" (Acts 17:11). This is where Paul encourages you not to believe anything that *we* tell you, but to check it out for *yourself.*

Throughout this chapter we have endeavored to present a thesis which is based on our understanding of Scripture and our belief that our 20th-century alien visitors are none other than fallen angels who have invaded our culture for the purpose of distracting and deceiving mankind.

There will be those who will no doubt argue that Satan and his cohorts are incapable of creating alien ships and masquerading as extraterrestrials. However, when we look carefully at the capabilities of angelic beings, as we will in the next chapter, we find that angelic beings have extraordinary ability and power to manipulate matter within our space-time domain.

Others will argue that the UFO phenomenon is incapable of generating a global ecumenical religious belief system. And yet, even without open extraterrestrial contact, tens of millions of people embrace ETs as our saviors with a fervor seldom matched by most Christians. In his foreword to Jacques Vallee's book *Dimensions,* Whitley Strieber discusses the profound religious implications of the UFO phenomenon:

> "It is a social issue of the utmost importance, because it has all the potential of a truly powerful idea to enter unconscious mythology and there to generate beliefs so broad in their scope and deep in their impact that they emerge with religious implications for the surrounding culture. The only thing now needed to make the UFO myth a new religion of remarkable scope and force is a single undeniable sighting."[364]

With our insights into the nature, agenda, and purposes of Antichrist, Strieber's observation presents the chilling possibility that a global, ecumenical religion that generates "beliefs so broad in their scope and deep in their impact" could be built around the UFO motif. All that is needed, according to Strieber, is "a single undeniable sighting."

The power of the UFO phenomenon to inspire religious awe is even confirmed by Jacques Vallee:

> "I think the stage is set for the appearance of new faiths, centered on the UFO belief. To a greater

degree than all the phenomena modern science is confronting, the UFO can inspire awe, the sense of the smallness of man, and an idea of the possibility of contact with the cosmic. The religions we have briefly surveyed began with the miraculous experiences of one person, but today there are thousands for whom the belief in otherworldly contact is based on intimate conviction, drawn from what they regard as personal contact with UFOs and their occupants."[365]

That Satan will exploit this power in the near future we believe is certain, but the good news is told by the Apostle John:

"And the seventh angel sounded; and there were great voices in heaven, saying, The kingdoms of this world are become the kingdoms of our Lord, and of his Christ; and he shall reign for ever and ever" (Revelation 11:15).

Amen!

THE ULTIMATE
HYPERDIMENSIONAL

The capabilities of angels are obviously quite

formidable, yet there is One who eclipses even

them beyond all comprehension. He is clearly

the ultimate remedy we have against these strange

forces, but let's attempt to get the entire picture

in perspective.

THE SCARLET THREAD

God declared war on Satan and announced his plan for the redemption of all that Adam had lost.[366] In Eden, God promised a redeemer, the "seed of the woman," through whom mankind would be freed from the power of Satan and death.[367] This began a string of Messianic promises, each with incremental additional revelations of the details of God's plan of redemption. This was God's love letter, ultimately written in blood on a wooden cross which was erected in Judea almost 2,000 years ago.

God's program will also result in a final cosmic collision and an open warfare between the physical and spiritual worlds. Some have conjectured that the UFOs are, somehow, a preparation for that coming conflict.

A revealing perspective of the Biblical panorama emerges when one recognizes that the entire cosmic drama is one in which Satan repeatedly attempts to thwart God's plan. As God incrementally reveals each additional detail, Satan more closely focus his subsequent attacks.

God has a destiny for mankind—Mr. and Mrs. Man—that is so fantastic that Adam's fallen race could not attain it unaided. To enable mankind, God established a program through which he would substitute his own eligibility on man's behalf. But God's plan required a pure kinsman of Adam to fulfill the requirements of God's nature (reflected in God's laws) on Adam's behalf. Thus, one of Satan's initial stratagems was an attempt to adulterate the human genealogies—and the potential Messianic line—by the incursions of the fallen angels, as we reviewed in chapter 10. However, God's gambit with Noah thwarted this early attempt.

As God revealed that his plan would be accomplished through Abraham,[368] Satan singled Abraham out for special attacks on his seed, etc.[369]

As we encounter Pharaoh's attempts to destroy the Jewish babies[370] and his later attempts to wipe out the entire nation,[371] we can again see Satan's invisible hand behind it all.

When Israel is to enter the Promised Land of Canaan, they find that it has been populated with "giants" (the Rephaim, et al) in apparent anticipation of their arrival.[372]

When God reveals that his plan will be established through the house of David,[373] Satan focuses his attack on David's line. As one carefully analyzes the details of the continuing narrative, when Jehoram kills his brothers,[374] when the Arabians slew all the heirs but Ahazariah, when Athaliah kills all (except Joash),[375] in each instance we see the Satanic intrigues continuing. When Hezekiah is assaulted, etc.,[376] the same theme is being played out.

When God pronounces a blood curse on the royal line in the days of Jeconiah,[377] there may have been celebration within the counsels of Satan. They probably assumed that God was now over a barrel. The Messiah was to be eligible for the throne of David, of the lineage of David, yet now there was a curse on the royal line. (I always imagine God saying to the heavenly angels, "Watch this one!")

We then find this apparent paradox resolved when we compare the genealogies of Matthew and Luke. Matthew, as a true Jew would, presents Jesus as the Messiah the King. Consequently, he initiates his genealogy with Abraham, the "first Jew," and continues through David, Solomon, etc., to Joseph, the legal father of Jesus.

Luke, however, as a physician, focuses on Jesus as the Son of Man, and so his genealogy starts with Adam. From Abraham to David they are identical. However, when Luke gets to David, he takes a surprising turn. Instead of going through Solomon, he connects through Nathan, the second son of

Bathsheba. This line continues to Heli, the father of Mary, the mother of Jesus.[378] Thus, by means of the virgin birth, Satan's hopes are again foiled! Jesus is, indeed, of the house and lineage of David, thus eligible for the throne, but not subject to the "blood curse" upon the descendants of Jeconiah!

These intrigues are even visible in the days of the Persian Empire, with Haman's attempts to eradicate the Jews in the days of Esther.[379] Again, God's hand delivers his people.

The drama continues in the New Testament with Joseph's fears regarding Mary's pregnancy,[380] Herod's murder of the babes in his attempt to eradicate the potential heirs,[381] etc. In Jesus' early ministry, a mob attempts to throw him off a cliff.[382] Even the several storms on the Sea of Galilee seem to have supernatural aspects.[383]

The climax occurs at the cross at Golgotha. (These attempts by Satan to thwart God's plan are also summarized in Revelation 12.) Nor is Satan through yet! The UFOs and the apparent alien intrusions could be a continuing part of his plan. Indeed, all this may be included in the warning which the Lord Jesus gave us:

> "As the days of Noah were, so shall the days of the coming of the Son of Man be." (Matthew 24:37)

SUPER ANGEL OR E.T.?

There are some that view Jesus as a kind of "Super Angel" or hyperdimensional "Extraterrestrial." Clearly, he did demonstrate many hyperdimensional capabilities. His ability to materialize and dematerialize, while yet being tangible, within a closed room, indicates that he possesses a dimensionality which is independent of the limitations of our three-dimensional spatial "reality." His ability to foretell the future indicates his nature is independent of our time domain.[384] Conquering death, as validated by his resurrection, was, of course, the crowning achievement and is evidence of supremacy over the laws of physics.

There are some who have conjectured that Jesus' resurrection body enjoys at least 11 dimensions: nine spatial dimensions (which mathematically would permit "rotation" in and out of three-dimensional spaces) and at least two dimensions of time.[385] There is also the more appealing assumption that Jesus enjoys the dimensionality of what mathematicians call a Hilbert space, a hyperspace of infinite dimensions.

Jesus' hyperdimensional nature is further exemplified by a cryptic statement he made to his disciples in the Gospel of Matthew. After discussing aspects of heaven Jesus stated, "For where two or three are gathered together in my name, there am I in the midst of them" (Matthew 18:20).

This is a fascinating insight into his extradimensional nature. Because Jesus possesses additional dimensions (or their equivalent) of spatial reality, he is able to be at all places simultaneously. This attribute, called omnipresence, is exclusively applied to God throughout the Biblical text and is further proof of Jesus' deity.

After just a brief examination of the scriptural claims regarding Jesus Christ, it becomes obvious that regarding him as a "Super Angel" is an untenable position. The writer of the epistle to the Hebrews anticipated this view:

> "Being made so much better than the angels, as he hath by inheritance obtained a more excellent name than they. For unto which of the angels said he at any time, Thou art my Son, this day have I begotten thee? And again, I will be to him a Father, and he shall be to me a Son? And again, when he bringeth in the firstbegotten into the

world, he saith, And let all the angels of God worship him. And of the angels he saith, Who maketh his angels spirits, and his ministers a flame of fire. But unto the Son he saith, Thy throne, O God, is for ever and ever: a sceptre of righteousness is the sceptre of thy kingdom" (Hebrews 1:4-8).

Although Jesus shares a hyperdimensional nature with angelic beings, the writer of Hebrews makes it clear that his nature is "so much better than the angels." Indeed, the Bible is consistent as presenting Jesus as the very Creator of the physical universe and its life forms, including the angels!

The Apostle John opens his Gospel with this declaration, using "the Word of God" as His supreme title:

"In the beginning was the Word, and the Word was with God, and the Word was God. The same was in the beginning with God. All things were made by him; and without him was not any thing made that was made. . . . And the Word was made flesh, and dwelt among us, and we beheld his glory, the glory as of the only begotten of the Father, full of grace and truth" (John 1:1-3, 14).

Here the Apostle John indicates that Jesus Christ (the "Word," *Logos*) is not only the very Creator of all things, but that Jesus revealed his glory when he physically manifested himself in time and space. This portion of Scripture also reiterates the fact that Jesus Christ is independent of time. When time began ("in the beginning") the Word (Jesus) already was. He preexisted the time domain which, according to the insights of Einstein and others, we now know had a finite beginning.

His independence of the time domain is echoed by Paul the Apostle in 2 Timothy:

> "Who hath saved us, and called us with an holy
> calling, not according to our works, but accord-
> ing to his own purpose and grace, which was
> given us in Christ Jesus before time [*chronos* in
> Greek] began" (2 Timothy 1:9).

Can someone go back in time? Jesus did! He went back, not
to modify the past, but to fulfill both the past and the future—
our future.

His role is amplified in Paul's letter to the Colossians:

> "Who is the image of the invisible God, the first-
> born [a term of position, not origin] of all cre-
> ation: For by him were all things created, that are
> in heaven, and that are in earth, visible and invis-
> ible, whether they be thrones, or dominions, or
> principalities, or powers [these terms in the
> Greek refer to angelic ranks]: all things were cre-
> ated by him, and for him: and he is before all
> things, and by him all things held together
> [cohere; compacted together; constituted with]"
> (Colossians 1:15–17).

This passage can be applied to the structure of the atoms.
There is an active force imposed upon the universe which
actively holds the very atoms of the material together moment-
by-moment, day-by-day, century-by-century. Similarly, the
accelerated electrons circling the nucleus should quickly radi-
ate their energy away and fall into the nucleus unless there
existed an invisible energy source to counteract this.
According to this verse, Jesus literally "sustains the universe by
his mighty word of power."[386]

The disciples' belief that Jesus is, indeed, God "manifest in
the flesh," is unequivocally proclaimed by the Apostle Paul in
1 Timothy 3:16:

"And without controversy great is the mystery of godliness. God was manifested in the flesh, justified in the Spirit, seen by angels, preached among the Gentiles, believed on in the world, and received up in glory" (Timothy 3:16).

When was God "received up in glory"? In the first chapter of the Acts of the Apostles, Jesus Christ ascended into heaven from the Mount of Olives 40 days after his resurrection.

In these few scriptures we see that there is a vast gulf between the nature of Jesus and mere angels. Jesus Christ as the eternally existent God "manifested in the flesh" created all things, including the angels and holds the very atomic structure of the universe together!

Those who would make Jesus an ancient astronaut or an extraterrestrial also err by failing to recognize the vast difference between his nature and the nature of alien entities. Even though our alien visitors seem to exhibit interdimensional, god-like capabilities (materializing, defying certain laws of physics, etc.), the Bible teaches that Jesus Christ is the Creator of all things—including the fallen angels who may now be masquerading as aliens in the 20th century. Jesus Christ himself claimed to be the Creator of the universe and the very voice of the burning bush which confronted Moses:

"Jesus said unto them, Verily, verily, I say unto you,
Before Abraham was, I am [ego eimi]" (John 8:58).

The title "I Am" was the name that God applied to himself when he spoke to Moses at the burning bush in Exodus 3:14. After Jesus applied this name to himself, the Jews that heard him picked up stones to kill him for equating himself with God. However, according to the text, "Jesus hid himself and went out of the temple, going through the midst of them, and so passed by."[387]

The fact that Jesus continually professed his deity did not get past the Jewish leadership of his day. After claiming that he and God his father "were one," they took up stones to kill him.[388] Jesus then asked them, "Many good works I have shown you from my Father. For which of those works do you stone me?"

Their answer leaves no doubt that Jesus had continually professed his deity in their presence.

> "The Jews answered him [Jesus], saying, 'For a good work we do not stone you, but for blasphemy, and because you, being a man, make yourself God' " (John 10:33).

Claims by Jesus such as these leaves us only three possibilities:

1) That Jesus wasn't God and just thought he was. That would make him a lunatic or a New Ager! This hardly deals with the facts.

2) That Jesus wasn't God and knew he wasn't. That would make him a liar, a notion which is also totally inconsistent with the facts.

3) That Jesus *was* who he said he was. That would make him Lord of the Universe.

Lunatic? Liar? Or Lord? Which is it? And how can you tell? Not by miracles! They can be—in fact, are going to be—simulated, counterfeited, and replicated.

As we saw in chapter 13 of this book, the last days of planet Earth will be characterized by supernatural signs and wonders performed by Satan and his minions. In fact, most of the miracles performed by God will be counterfeited by Satan and the forces of darkness. The healing and resurrection of the "Antichrist" are but a few of the miracles Satan will yet perform.

This presents a problem. If Satan can duplicate the miracles of God, then "signs and wonders" cannot be used as the arbiter of truth. That is, we cannot determine whether someone or something is good or evil based on ability to perform "signs and wonders." So what *can* a person rely upon to determine truth from error? Jesus gives the key in his response to the Jewish leadership when they asked him for a sign to authenticate his messianic claim:

> "Then certain of the scribes and of the Pharisees answered, saying, Master, we would see a sign from thee. But he answered and said unto them, An evil and adulterous generation seeketh after a sign; and there shall no sign be given to it, but the sign of the prophet Jonas: for as Jonas was three days and three nights in the whale's belly; so shall the Son of man be three days and three nights in the heart of the earth" [a prophecy!] (Matthew 12:38).

Jesus disparaged signs and wonders to authenticate his messianic claim. Why? Because signs and wonders will be counterfeited by the coming Antichrist. So instead of a sign to authenticate his messianic claim, Jesus gave them a prophecy.

We see powerful examples of Satan's power in the Old Testament. In Egypt, for example, after Moses and Aaron turned their rod into a serpent, Pharaoh's magicians Jannes and Jambres turned their rods into serpents, too!

> "And Moses and Aaron went in unto Pharaoh, and they did so as the LORD had commanded: and Aaron cast down his rod before Pharaoh, and before his servants, and it became a serpent. Then Pharaoh also called the wise men and the sorcerers: now the magicians of Egypt, they also

did in like manner with their enchantments. For they cast down every man his rod, and they became serpents: but Aaron's rod swallowed up their rods" (Exodus 7: 10).

Many Bible teachers assume that Satan cannot create life, believing instead that this ability belongs to God alone. However, in this scripture we find that Satan, acting through the sorcerers and magicians, was able to convert nonliving matter into (apparently) living serpents. In the subsequent verses we find that the magicians and sorcerers were also able to create a plague of frogs and turn the Nile to blood!

In the book of Revelation we find another disturbing account, where the false prophet brings an inanimate idol of the Antichrist to life:

"He was granted power to give breath to the image of the beast, that the image of the beast should both speak and cause as many as would not worship the image of the beast to be killed" (Revelation 13:15).

The purpose of giving life to the image was to cause people to worship the Antichrist, the "son of perdition," and vicariously to Satan himself. Obviously such miracles will convince the multitudes that the Antichrist is a "god," and the promised Messiah who is worthy of worship. Several prominent Bible teachers, including Hal Lindsey and Dave Hunt, have suggested that this Coming World Leader may either be an "alien" or boast of an alien connection.

The deceitfulness of miracles and the superiority of prophecy is a prominent theme in the Bible.

The Apostle Peter, an eyewitness to hundreds of Jesus' miracles, nevertheless elevates prophecy over signs and wonders, even over "eyewitness" accounts!

> "For we have not followed cunningly devised
> fables, when we made known unto you the power
> and coming of our Lord Jesus Christ, but were
> eyewitnesses of his majesty. For he received from
> God the Father honour and glory, when there
> came such a voice to him from the excellent
> glory, This is my beloved Son, in whom I am well
> pleased. And this voice which came from heaven
> we heard, when we were with him in the holy
> mount. We have also a more sure word of
> prophecy" (2 Peter 1:16–20).

This is a remarkable claim. Peter had personally seen Jesus heal multitudes of blind, deaf, lame, and leprous individuals. He had even seen Jesus raise the dead! And yet, Peter said that we have "a more sure word of prophecy." Why?

It turns out that God's ability to foretell history distinguishes him from Satan and the powerful forces of darkness. It demonstrates his total independence and transcendence of our time domain—something which neither Satan, nor the fallen angels, nor any alien entity can do.

It's fascinating to note that God appeals to this prophetic ability as the proof of his deity. He mocks the false prophets and their gods for their inability to match this ability:

> "'Present your case,' says the LORD. 'Bring forth
> your strong reasons,' says the King of Jacob. 'Let
> them bring forth and show us what will happen;
> let them show the former things, what they were,
> that we may consider them, and know the latter
> end of them; or declare to us things to come.
> Show the things that are to come hereafter, that
> we may know that you are gods; yes, do good or
> do evil, that we may be dismayed and see it
> together'" (Isaiah 41:21–23).

Realizing that no one can counterfeit his prophetic ability, God highlights the implications of this unique ability:

> "Behold, the former things have come to pass, And new things I declare; before they spring forth I tell you of them" (Isaiah 42:9).

> "Remember the former things of old: for I am God, and there is none else; I am God, and there is none like me, declaring the end from the beginning, and from ancient times the things that are not yet done, saying, My counsel shall stand, and I will do all my pleasure" (Isaiah 46:9–10).

PROPHECY:
THE TESTIMONY OF JESUS

During the intimate gathering of Jesus with his disciples at the Last Supper, on the night before he was crucified, Jesus also appealed to his prophetic ability as the proof of his deity. While breaking bread, Jesus foretold his betrayal by Judas Iscariot and his coming crucifixion. Jesus then told the disciples, "Now I tell you before it comes, that, when it is come to pass, ye may believe that I am" (John 13:19). The disciples were to understand that by predicting the one who would betray him, they should understand that he is God, the "I Am" who spoke to Moses at the burning bush.

We believe that the importance of this insight cannot be over emphasized. Jesus Christ elevated the importance of the prophetic word far above the performance of signs and wonders. According to the Apostle Peter, faith in the messianic claim and deity of Jesus Christ was to come by the Word of God. This is echoed by Paul the Apostle: "So then faith cometh by hearing, and hearing by the word of God" (Romans 10:17). Faith does not come by sight and the performance of signs and wonders. Faith comes by hearing the Word of God! This is why it is important for churches to emphasize the Word of God—so that faith can be built in the heart of the believer in Jesus Christ. This is also why God rarely uses signs and wonders to convince people of his existence. If someone can be converted by signs, they can be led away by them as well. But the Word of God has the power to convert the soul to the true and living God, Jesus Christ. Finally, according to the book of Revelation it is prophecy—not miracles—that testifies of Jesus.

> "And I fell at his feet to worship him. And he said unto me, See thou do it not: I am thy fellowservant, and of thy brethren that have the testimony of Jesus: worship God: for the testimony of Jesus is the spirit of prophecy" (Revelation 19:10).

FALSE PROPHETS SHALL ARISE

Now the skeptic will argue here that aliens and psychics have indeed told the future. However, there are many examples of false prophecies that have been given by contactees over the last 40 years. The first edition of Project World Evacuation stated that the alien evacuation of planet Earth would take place in the early 1980s. As we saw in chapter 13, John Keel, in his book *Operation Trojan Horse,* pointed out that numerous contactees have been told false predictions by alien entities:

> "The UFOs do not seem to exist as tangible, manufactured objects. They do not conform to the accepted natural laws of our environment. They seem to be nothing more than transmogrifications tailoring themselves to our abilities to understand. The thousands of contacts with the entities indicate that they are liars and put-on artists. The UFO manifestations seem to be, by and large, merely minor variations of the age-old

demonological phenomenon. Officialdom may feel that if we ignore them long enough, they will go away altogether, taking their place with the vampire myths of the Middle Ages."[389]

Keel pointed out that in the 1960s many people were told of catastrophic events that would shortly come to pass by their alien contacts. As a result, many people quit their jobs, moved out of state, and arranged their lives in order to avoid the events. When they did not occur, the lives of those who were deceived were so disrupted that many took years to recover. Such false prophecy is commonplace in the annals of UFO contact. This points out the fact that Satan and his minions, though able to transcend the spatial limitations of our three-dimensional universe, are not independent of, nor can they supersede, the time domain. Thus, true prophecy is not within the capability of Satan or the forces of darkness.

What about psychics? In the 1990s the popularity of psychics has risen enormously as people look for answers for their problems. The "Heaven's Gate Cult" is but one grim example. How do we explain a psychic's apparent ability to know intimate details about a person's past. Satan and his minions are apparently confined to a knowledge of the past and the present as we are. Unlike God, they cannot see forward in the time domain to gain a detailed knowledge of the future. But, Satan does have the resources and ability to know history! We can presume that Satan, like a well-equipped intelligence department chief, has his agents strategically placed to gather necessary information to reveal an individual's past. While they ostensibly display a limited proficiency at telling one's past, psychics are woefully inadequate at predicting the future. If Satan and the forces of darkness actually knew minute details about the near future, then investment institutions would need only consult their staff psychic on tomorrow's price of every stock on the NYSE and we could all be billionaires!

Furthermore, if Satan had a detailed knowledge of the future then he would never have inspired Judas Iscariot to betray Christ. This was the biggest blunder he ever made, because it resulted in the vicarious, sacrificial death of Jesus on the cross, providing the way of atonement for the sins of mankind and fulfilling the very program that Satan had been trying for centuries to thwart.

In the Bible we are given an "acid test" we can apply to anyone claiming to be a prophet of God. Anyone who is a true prophet of God must prophesy with 100 percent accuracy!

> "But the prophet who presumes to speak a word in my [God's] name, which I have not commanded him to speak, or who speaks in the name of other gods, that prophet shall die. . . . When a prophet speaks in the name of the LORD, if the thing does not happen or come to pass, that is the thing which the LORD has not spoken; the prophet has spoken it presumptuously; you shall not be afraid of him"[390] Deuteronomy 18:20, 22).

All of this is why it is of such paramount importance to discover what is God's plan, how has it been fulfilled to date, and what is on the horizon! It is time for each of us to rediscover the Bible and do our own homework!

HIS RETURN

In the interpretation of King Nebuchadnezzar's famous dream, we saw the "stone cut without hands" strike the image at its feet and become a "mountain" which filled the whole earth. Strange as it may seem, this "stone" is a commonly employed idiom for the Messiah.[391] As we previously reviewed, it will be in the days of this final empire that the Messiah intervenes and establishes his reign upon the earth.

Even among many ostensible Christians, this will be doubted:

> "Knowing this first, that there shall come in the last days scoffers, walking after their own lusts, and saying, Where is the promise of his coming? for since the fathers fell asleep, all things continue as they were from the beginning of the creation" (2 Peter 3:3–4).

(Note how this skepticism is linked with the theory of evolution. Both views deny the involvement of the Creator in his program from the beginning to the end.)

When Jesus Christ comes with his armies,[392] he will be recognized by his wounds!

> ". . . and they shall look upon me whom they have pierced" (Zechariah 12:10).

Even secular researchers have concluded that the UFOs and their occupants are demonic. Their message reveals their reality and their agenda. They deal in deception, they are part of an ultimate deception of cosmic proportions, and *you* are one of their ultimate targets! Are you prepared? Or are you a sitting duck?

The strange reports reviewed in this book are only a prologue. The cosmic (spiritual) battle is going to become increasingly visible. The strange entanglements of the Heaven's Gate cult and other groups are only a beginning.

YOUR OWN ACTION PLAN

Many of the readers of this book will shrug all this off and join the vast majority embracing the New Age notions of neo-paganism, pantheism, or other politically correct ideologies. Jesus anticipated this. He said,

> "Wide is the gate, and broad is the way, that lead-
> eth to destruction, and many there be which go
> in there at; but strait is the gate, and narrow is the
> way, which leadeth unto life, and few there be
> that find it" (Matthew 7:13–14).

Are you going to be among those few? Or among the many?
If you are going through a popular gate, you may have chosen
the wrong one!

The mystery of death throws shadows over even the most care-
free human life. None of us is truly indifferent to the possible
issues concerning our personal eternity. The fall and eternal ruin
of an immortal spirit is the most dreadful tragedy imaginable.

Yet, God's mercy is unobligated and sovereign:

> "I will have mercy on whom I will have mercy,
> and I will have compassion on whom I will have
> compassion" (Romans 9:15).

We do well not to murmur at this. The incarnate God, who
has suffered vicariously and personally more than anyone else
ever will or could, surely has the right to determine the
method and extent of his own self-immolating compassion.
The transgressor who assumes redemption as something to
which he is entitled needs to consider God's rebuttal:

> "Is it not lawful for me, to do what I will with
> mine own?" (Matthew 20:15).

He made this whole place. He is in command.

"Salvation" presupposes a prior damnation. In order to
escape any danger, one must recognize and believe in the danger. Disbelief is sure destruction. We are commanded to fear
hell. We need to be just as plain, solemn, and tender as Christ
himself was on this topic.

Denial is no remedy. Denial is an error which obstructs repentance from sin, which in turn bars any pardon.

Consequently, no error is more fatal than universalism, the idea that there are many paths to God. While this is the current politically correct theology, those who advocate universalism, or the neo-paganism of the New Age, are gambling their eternity that the Bible is wrong!

> "Jesus saith unto him, I am the way, the truth, and the life: no man cometh unto the Father, but by me" (John 14:6).

If there were any other path to the throne of God, then the Father didn't answer Christ's prayer in Gethsemane.[393] and he died in vain. Universalism attempts to mask retributive justice; it transmutes sin into misfortune instead of guilt; it translates suffering into mere chastisement; it converts the completed work of Christ into mere moral influence; and it makes salvation a debt due to man rather than an unmerited gift from God.

Fortunately, we are each the beneficiaries of God's love letter—a love letter written in blood on a wooden cross erected in Judea almost 2,000 years ago. This event has turned out to be the most cataclysmic event in the entire universe, and it directly impacts every one of us in more ways than we can possibly imagine.

C. S. Lewis gathers all this up very well in these words from *Mere Christianity*:

> "God is going to invade this earth in force. But what is the good of saying you are on his side then, when you see the whole natural universe melting away like a dream, and something else— something it never entered your head to conceive—comes crashing in; something so beautiful

to some of us, and so terrible to others, that none of us will have any choice left? For this time it will be God without disguise; something so over-whelming that it will strike either irresistible love or irresistible horror into every creature. It will be too late then to choose your side. There is no use saying you choose to lie down when it has become impossible to stand up. That will not be the time for choosing; it will be the time when we discover which side we have really chosen, whether we realized it before or not. Now, today, this moment, is our chance to choose the right side. God is holding back, to give us that chance. It will not last forever. We must take it or leave it."

CAN A CHRISTIAN BE ABDUCTED?

This question will prove to be among the most controversial of any which we have addressed. We have received letters from those who claim they are examples of those who *have* been abducted. We have been contacted by experts and senior exec-utives of organizations who have had substantial experience in this strange arena. However, being "churched" is not enough to be adequate or even relevant to the potential of being abducted.

Demonic access of any kind requires the lowering of the gate of one's will. This can be initiated by a subtle "entry"—involve-ment in a seemingly "harmless" pursuit or game such as a "ouija" board, a seance, a party game, or something more serious. This can make you prey for the forces of darkness and eligible for the types of events or pseudo-events described in this book.

What's the remedy? You presently have access to the most powerful resource in the cosmos! You have direct access to the Throne Room of the Universe. And you have a prearranged appointment. Right now.

There is One who is waiting to release you from the clutches of these strange malevolent forces. He is the One who has already demonstrated His victory, even over death itself. He is the *only* One who can set you free.

> "If it were possible, they would deceive the very elect."[394]

Are you one of the "elect"? You can elect to be. Where do you presently stand? The church you attend has little to with it.

> "Many will say to me in that day, Lord, Lord, have we not prophesied in thy name? and in thy name have cast out devils? and in thy name done many wonderful works? And then will I profess unto them, I never knew you: depart from me, ye that work iniquity" (Matthew 7:22–23).

A personal relationship with Christ is your only protection. And right now He stands waiting for your response. Right now, in the privacy of your own will, you can seal your eternal destiny and put yourself out of reach of these strange plots against your own well-being.

1) Approach God's throne—right now—in the authority which Christ has already granted you, pleading the blood that was shed for you on that cross.

2) Acknowledge and renounce any and all previous involvement with the occult, with the forces of darkness, with Satan, or any of his minions.

3) Explicitly accept the pardon Christ has already purchased for you on that cross 2,000 years ago; then,

4) Share this commitment with someone you feel a deep trust spiritually.[395]

Recognize that if you have made this commitment you are God's and "they" cannot touch you. They very well may attempt to bluff you, but they cannot violate your own will unless you explicitly let them!

If you see a UFO, immediately call on God and plead his blood as your basis for immunity. And don't let yourself become hypnotized. It's serious business. Your eternal destiny is at stake. It's time to do your homework. It is our prayer that this book is but a beginning to the most exciting adventure in the history of the universe. (See also our appendix)

Drop us a line so that we can pray for you and send you some study materials.[396] There should also be a gift certificate in the back of this book for a provocative monthly intelligence journal you may find helpful. If it isn't there, just call us: (800) 546-8731.

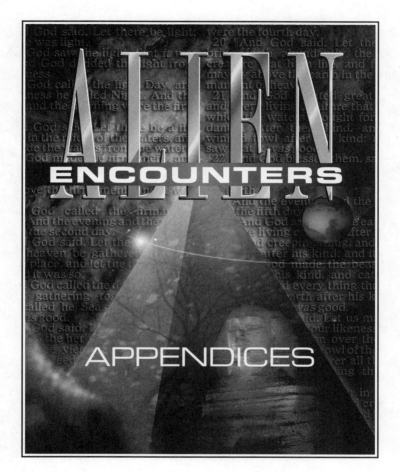

ALIEN ENCOUNTERS

APPENDICES

THE "SETHITE" VIEW

And it came to pass, when men began to multiply on the face of the earth, and daughters were born unto them, that the sons of God saw the daughters of men that they were fair; and they took them wives of all which they chose.

There were giants in the earth in those days; and also after that, when the sons of God came in unto the daughters of men, and they bare children to them, the same became mighty men which were of old, men of renown.

GENESIS 6:1, 2, 4

As highlighted in Chapter 10, the "Sons of God" of Genesis 6 was understood as referring to (fallen) angels by the ancient rabbinical sources, by the Septuagint translators, and by the early church fathers. However, many students of the Bible have been taught that passage in Genesis 6 refers to a failure to keep the "faithful" lines of Seth separate from the "worldly" line of Cain. The idea has been advanced that after Cain killed Abel, the line of Seth remained separate and faithful, but the line of Cain turned ungodly and rebellious. The "Sons of God" are deemed to refer to leadership in the line of Seth; and the "Daughters of men" is deemed restricted to the line of Cain. The resulting marriages blurred an inferred separation between them. (Why the resulting offspring are called the "Nephilim" remains without any clear explanation.)

ORIGIN OF THE SETHITE VIEW

Both the ancient Hebrew scholars and the early church fathers understood the text to refer to fallen angels procreating with human women. However, it was in the fifth century A.D. that the "angel" interpretation of Genesis 6 was increasingly viewed as an embarrassment when attacked by critics.

(Furthermore, the worship of angels had begun within the church. Also, celibacy had also become an institution of the church. The "angel" view of Genesis 6 was feared as impacting these views.)

Celsus and Julian the Apostate used the traditional "angel" belief to attack Christianity. Julius Africanus resorted to the Sethite interpretation as a more comfortable ground. Cyril of Alexandria also repudiated the orthodox "angel" position with the "line of Seth" interpretation. Augustine also embraced the Sethite theory and thus it prevailed into the Middle Ages. It is still widely taught today among many churches who find the literal "angel" view a bit disturbing.

PROBLEMS WITH THE SETHITE VIEW

Beyond obscuring a full understanding of the events in the early chapters of Genesis, this view also clouds any opportunity to apprehend the prophetic implications of the Scriptural allusions to the "Days of Noah." Some of the many problems with the "Sethite View" include the following:

1. THE TEXT ITSELF

Substantial liberties must be taken with the literal text to propose the "Sethite" view. (In data analysis, it is often said that, "if you torture the data severely enough it will confess to anything.")

The term translated "the Sons of God" is, in the Hebrew, בְנֵי־הָאֱלֹהִים, *B'nai HaElohim*, "Sons of Elohim," which is a term consistently used in the Old Testament for angels. It was so understood by the ancient rabbinical sources, by the Septuagint translators in the 3rd century before Christ, and by the early church fathers. Attempts to apply this term to "godly leadership" is without Scriptural foundation.

The "Sons of Seth and daughters of Cain" interpretation strains and obscures the intended grammatical antithesis between the Sons of God and the daughters of Adam. Attempting to impute any other view to the text flies in the face of the earlier centuries of understanding of the Hebrew text among both rabbinical and early church scholarship. The lexicographical antithesis clearly intends to establish a contrast between the "angels" and the women of the Earth.

If the text was intended to contrast the "sons of Seth and the daughters of Cain," why didn't it say so? Seth was not God, and Cain was not Adam. (Why not the "sons of Cain" and the "daughters of Seth?" There is no basis for restricting the text to either subset of Adam's descendants. Further, there exists no mention of daughters of Elohim.)

And how does the "Sethite" interpretation contribute to the ostensible cause for the Flood which is the primary thrust of the text? The entire view is contrived on a series of assumptions without Scriptural support.

The Biblical term "Sons of Elohim," (that is, of the Creator Himself), is confined to the direct creation by the divine hand and not to those born to those of their own order. In Luke's genealogy of Jesus, only Adam is called a "son of God." The entire Biblical drama deals with the tragedy that humankind is a fallen race, with Adam's initial immortality forfeited. Christ uniquely gives them that receive Him the power to become the sons of God. Being born again of the Spirit of God as an entirely new creation, at their resurrection they alone will be clothed with a building of God and in every respect equal to the angels. The very term οἰκητήριον, oiketerion, alluding to the heavenly body with which the believer longs to be clothed, is the precise term used for the heavenly bodies from which the fallen angels had disrobed.

The attempt to apply the term "Sons of Elohim" in a broader sense has no textual basis and obscures the precision of its denotative usage. This proves to be an assumption which is antagonistic to the uniform Biblical usage of the term.

2. THE INFERRED LINES OF SEPARATION

The concept of separate "lines" itself is suspect and contrary to Scripture. National and racial distinctions were plainly the result of the subsequent intervention of God in Genesis 11. There is no intimation that the lines of Seth and Cain kept themselves separate nor were even instructed to. The injunction to remain separate was given much later. Genesis 6:12 confirms that all flesh had corrupted His way upon the earth.

3. THE INFERRED GODLINESS OF SETH

There is no evidence, stated or implied, that the line of Seth was godly. Only one person was translated from the judgment to come (Enoch) and only eight were given the protection of the ark. No one beyond Noah's immediate family was accounted worthy to be saved. In fact, the text implies that these were distinct from all others. (There is no evidence that the wives of Noah's sons were of the line Seth.)

Even so, Gaebelein observes, "The designation "Sons of God" is never applied in the Old Testament to believers," whose sonship is "distinctly a New Testament revelation."

The "Sons of Elohim" saw the daughters of men that they were fair and took them wives of all that they chose. It appears that the women had little say in the matter. The domineering implication hardly suggests a godly approach to the union. Even the mention that they saw that they were attractive seems out of place if only normal biology was involved. (And were the daughters of Seth unattractive?)

It should also be pointed out that the son of Seth was Enosh and there is textual evidence that, rather than a reputation for piety, he seems to have initiated the profaning of the name of God.

If the lines of Seth were so faithful, why did they perish in the flood?

4. THE DAUGHTERS OF CAIN

The "Daughters of Adam" also does not denote a restriction to the descendants of Cain, but rather the whole human race is clearly intended. These daughters were the daughters born to the men with which this very sentence opens:

> "And it came to pass, when men began to multiply on the face of the earth, and daughters were

born unto them, that the sons of God saw the
daughters of men that they were fair; and they
took them wives of all which they chose"
(Genesis 6:1–2).

It is clear from the text that these daughters were not limited
a particular family or subset, but were, indeed, from (all) the
Benoth Adam, "the daughters of Adam." There is no apparent
exclusion of the daughters of Seth. Or were they so without
charms in contrast with the daughters of Cain? All of Adam's
female descendants seem to have been involved. (And what
about the "sons of Adam?" Where do they, using this contrived
dichotomy, fit in?)

Furthermore, the line of Cain was not necessarily known for
its ungodliness. From a study of the naming of Cain's children,
many of which included the name of God, it is not clear that
they were all necessarily unfaithful.

5. THE UNNATURAL OFFSPRING

The most fatal flaw in the specious "Sethite" view is the
emergence of the Nephilim as a result of the unions. (Bending
the translation to "giants" does not resolve the difficulties.) It
is the offspring of these peculiar unions in Genesis 6:4 which
is cited as a primary cause for the Flood.

Procreation by parents of differing religious views do not
produce unnatural offspring. Believers marrying unbelievers
may produce "monsters," but hardly superhuman, or unnatural, children! It was this unnatural procreation and the resulting abnormal creatures that were designated as a principal reason for the judgment of the Flood.

The very absence of any such adulteration of the human
genealogy in Noah's case is also documented in Genesis 6:9:
Noah's family tree was distinctively unblemished. The term
used, תָּמִים, tamiym, is used for physical blemishes.

Why were the offspring uniquely designated "mighty" and "men of reknown?" This description characterizing the children is not accounted for if the fathers were merely men, even if godly.

A further difficulty seems to be that the offspring were only men; no "women of reknown" are mentioned. (Was there a chromosome deficiency among the Sethites? Were there only "X" chromosomes available in this line?)

6. NEW TESTAMENT CONFIRMATIONS

"In the mouths of two or three witnesses every word shall be established." In Biblical matters, it is essential to always compare Scripture with Scripture. The New Testament confirmations in Jude and 2 Peter are impossible to ignore.

> "For if God spared not the angels that sinned, but cast them down to hell [Tartarus], and delivered them into chains of darkness, to be reserved unto judgment; And spared not the old world, but saved Noah the eighth person, a preacher of righteousness, bringing in the flood upon the world of the ungodly" (2 Peter 2:4–5).

Peter's comments even establishes the time of the fall of these angels to the days of the flood of Noah.

Even Peter's vocabulary is provocative. Peter uses the term Tartarus, here translated "hell." This is the only place that this Greek term appears in the Bible. Tartarus is a Greek term for "dark abode of woe;" "the pit of darkness in the unseen world." As used in Homer's *Iliad*, it is ". . . as far beneath hades as the earth is below heaven. . . ." In the Greek mythology, some of the demigods, Chronos and the rebel Titans, were said to have rebelled against their father Uranus and after a prolonged contest they were defeated by Zeus and were condemned into Tartarus.

The Epistle of Jude also alludes to the strange episodes when these "alien" creatures intruded themselves into the human reproductive process:

> "And the angels which kept not their first estate, but left their own habitation, he hath reserved in everlasting chains under darkness unto the judgment of the great day. Even as Sodom and Gomorrah, and the cities about them in like manner, giving themselves over to fornication, and going after strange flesh, are set forth for an example, suffering the vengeance of eternal fire." (Jude 6,7).

The allusions to "going after strange flesh," keeping "not their first estate," having "left their own habitation," and "giving themselves over to fornication," seem to clearly fit the alien intrusions of Genesis 6. (The term for habitation, οἰκητήριον, refers to their heavenly bodies from which they had disrobed.)

These allusions from the New Testament would seem to be fatal to the "Sethite" alternative in interpreting Genesis 6. If the intercourse between the "sons of God" and the "daughters of men" were merely marriage between Sethites and Cainites, it seems impossible to explain these passages, and the reason why some fallen angels are imprisoned and others are free to roam the heavenlies.

7. POST-FLOOD IMPLICATIONS

The strange offspring also continued after the flood: "There were Nephilim in the earth in those days, and also after that. . . ." The "Sethite" view fails to meaningfully address the prevailing conditions "also after that." It offers no insight into the presence of the subsequent "giants" in the land of Canaan.

One of the disturbing aspects of the Old Testament record was God's instructions, upon entering the land of Canaan, to wipe out every man, woman, and child of certain tribes inhabiting the land. This is difficult to justify without the insight of a "gene pool problem" from the remaining Nephilim, Rephaim, et al, which seems. to illuminate the difficulty.

8. PROPHETIC IMPLICATIONS

If one takes an integrated view of the Scripture, then everything in it should "tie together." In this light, then, Who are those beings who are expressly not of the "seed of men" in Daniel 2:43? These strange (non-human?) beings apparently become a major political constituency during the the final empire there described, causing it "to be divided": "partly strong and partly broken."

IN CONCLUSION

It is the author's view that the "Angel View," however disturbing, is the clear, direct presentation of the Biblical text, corroborated by multiple New Testament references, and was so understood by both early Jewish and Christian scholarship; and that the "Sethite View" is a contrivance of convenience from a network of unjustified assumptions antagonistic to the remainder of the Biblical record.

It should also be pointed out that most conservative Bible scholars accept the "angel" view. Among those supporting the "angel" view are: G. H. Pember, M. R. DeHaan, C. H. McIntosh, F. Delitzsch, A. C. Gaebelein, A. W. Pink, Donald Grey Barnhouse, Henry Morris, Merril F. Unger, Arnold Fruchtenbaum, Hal Lindsey, and Chuck Smith, being among the best known.

For those who take the Bible seriously, the arguments supporting the "Angel View" appear compelling. For those who indulge in a willingness to take liberties with the straightforward presentation of the text, no defense can prove final. (And greater dangers than the implications attending these issues await them!)

* * *

For further exploration of this critical topic, see the following:

George Hawkins Pember, *Earth's Earliest Ages,* first published by Hodder and Stoughton in 1875, and presently available by Kregel Publications, Grand Rapids MI, 1975.

John Fleming, *The Fallen Angels and the Heroes of Mythology,* Hodges, Foster, and Figgis, Dublin, 1879.

Henry Morris, *The Genesis Record,* Baker Book House, Grand Rapids MI, 1976.

Merrill F. Unger, *Biblical Demonology,* Scripture Press, Chicago IL, 1952

Clarence Larkin, *Spirit World,* Rev. Clarence Larkin Estate, Philadelphia PA, 1921.

CHECKLIST FOR POTENTIAL CONTACTEES

Based upon the assumption that alien contacts are demonic in nature, the following observations may prove critical. A more complete study of demonology and spiritual hygiene is beyond the scope of this appendix, but the following should prove helpful as a beginning. (It is assumed that the reader is a Christian. If not, see the concluding portions of chapter 14.)

FACTORS WHICH CAN MAKE A PERSON VULNERABLE TO DEMONIC ACTIVITY

1. Some form of idolatry in the family background within the previous four generations.[1] Obvious examples are demonic religions such as Hindu, Buddhist, Native American, Voodoo, Scientology, New Age groups, etc. Also, parlor games such as Ouija boards, *Dungeons and Dragons*, etc. Don't overlook or dismiss more subtle forms of idolatry such as rebellion, arrogance,[2] immorality, impurity, greed,[3] gluttony,[4] et al.

2. Sins of the mind where the person does not retain control over his thoughts,[5] such as drug use,[6] meditation, occultism,[7] hypnosis, uncontrolled anger,[8] etc.

3. Attitudinal issues: excessive guilt and sorrow,[9] pride,[10] lack of sexual self-control, lack of mental peace,[11] disobedience to known truth,[12] secular values,[13] insolence to Christ,[14] breaking marriage vows, casting off early faith, being idle, a busybody, tattler, or malicious talker,[15] arrogance.

4. Volitional participation with demons or the spirit world in a non-Biblical context.[16]

REMEDIAL PREPARATIONS

1. Explicit renunciation of any/all of the above before the Throne of God.[17] There is a "24-hour hotline" available at any time! It is accessible from the privacy of your own will.

2. Ask to receive the benefits of the completed action of Jesus Christ on your behalf.[18]

3. Undertake a specific commitment to the serious study of the Bible as the inerrant Word of God.[19] Make a diligent effort to "put on the whole armor of God."[20]

4. Undertake a daily commitment to spend time with God in prayer.[21]

5. Identify and participate in a fellowship of Christian believers in which the teaching of the (entire) Bible receives the primary priority.[22] Flee any cult groups that do not restrict their allegiance and authority to the Word of God and/or deny the deity of Jesus Christ uniquely.[23]

ACTIONS TO TAKE
UPON AN ENCOUNTER

1. Reject any invitations, deny any requests, and flee any involvement.[24]

2. Take command and plead the Blood of Jesus Christ on your behalf.[25] If you rely on Him, you are in a position of absolute authority.[26] Don't allow yourself to be "bluffed."

3. Seek prayer and counsel from someone who clearly has an adequate *Biblical* background.[27]

4. Do not allow yourself to be hypnotized.

5. It is a warfare. You are a target. The enemy's primary weapon is deception and deceit. Your primary weapon is the Word of God. Your armor is listed in Ephesians 6:10–18. Study these seven elements diligently.

NOTES:

1   Exodus 20:4–6; 34:7; Numbers 14:17–18. Cf. Leviticus 26:40–42; Nehemiah 9:2; Psalm 106:6; Jeremiah 14:20; Daniel 9:4–8.

2   1 Samuel 15:23.

3   Ephesians 5:5.

4   Philippians 3:18–19.

5   2 Corinthians 10:4–5.

6   Revelation 18:23.

7   Isaiah 8:19.

8   Ephesians 4:26–27.

9   2 Corinthians 2:11.

10   1 Timothy 3:6; Proverbs 16:18.

11   Philippians 4:4–9.

12   2 Timothy 2:26.

13   Ephesians 2:1–3; 1 Timothy 3:7.

14   1 Timothy 5:11–14.

15   1 Timothy 3:11; 2 Timothy 3:3; Titus 2:3.

16   1 Corinthians 10:20.

17   "The Christian's Bar of Soap"—1 John 1:9.

18   John 3:16; 5:24.

19   2 Timothy 2:15-16; Psalm 119.

20   Ephesians 6:10–18.

21   Ephesians 6:18; 1 Thessalonians 5:17.

22   Hebrews 10:25.

23   1 John 4:1–4.

24   James 4:7; 1 Peter 5:8–9.

25   Luke 4:35; 9:1; 1 John 4:4.

26   Colossians 1:13.

27   2 Corinthians 12:7–10.

BIBLIOGRAPHY

1 Gallup polls done in 1991 and 1996.

2 George M. Eberhart, *UFOs and the Extraterrestrial Contact Movement: A Bibliography*, 2 vols., Scarecrow Press, London 1986.

3 Release: 96–159. Leaking, in advance, an article which was about to appear in Science, the journal of the American Association for the Advancement of Science, on August 16, 1996. See the briefing package, *The Mysteries of the Planet Mars* for a review.

4 *Scientific American*, October 1996, pp. 20–22.

5 *Science*, November 8, 1996, p. 918.

6 http://www.jpl.nasa.gov

7 "Scientists Consider Moon Ice Theory," *Washington Post*, (AP) December 2, 1996.

8 Brit Elders, *Connecting Link Magazine*, Issue 27, Spring 1995, p. 92. See also the video *Voyagers of the Sixth Sun* produced by Genesis III.

9 *La Prensa*, January 2, 1992.

10 *Voyagers of the Sixth Sun*, produced by Genesis III.

11 Brit Elders, *Connecting Link Magazine*, Issue 27, Spring 1995, p. 92.

12 *Voyagers of the Sixth Sun*, produced by Genesis III.

13 Brit Elders, "UFOs Over Mexico," as it appeared in *Connecting Link*, Issue 27, 1994, p. 94.

14 *Connecting Link Magazine*, Issue 27, Spring 1995, p. 94.

15 *UFO Reality*, Issue 6, February/March 1997, p. 10.

16 *UFO Reality*, Issue 6, February/March 1997, p. 11.

17 *UFO Reality*, Issue 6, February/March 1997, p. 11.

18 Covered extensively in the "X-Files" column of the *Mai'ariv*.

19 *The Plain Dealer Newspaper,* Cleveland, OH, March 31, 1996, section 1f. Copyright 1996 Plain Dealer Publishing Co.

20 *The Jerusalem Post,* February 13, 1997.

21 Daniel Brynberg, *The Jerusalem Report,* March 1996.

22 *USA Today,* June 18, 1997

23 *ibid.*

24 *ibid.,* p. A4.

25 *ibid.*

26 *USA Today,* June 18, 1997

27 One of the mysteries concerning the Phoenix sightings is that it wasn't widely reported until June 18, 1997, when it was on the front page of *USA Today,* and on CNN, NBC, ABC, etc. The authors suspect that this wasn't a UFO, but an test exercise in military holography, a "non-lethal weapons" technology that went deeply classified in 1994.

28 Material for this section is from the "Report on the CSETI Briefings," available at http://www.cseti.org and also from CSETI, P.O. Box 15401, Asheville, NC 28813.

29 This report is available from CSETI, P.O. Box 15401, Asheville, NC 28813.

30 Interviewed on nationwide radio by Art Bell on May 9, 1997.

31 *The Planetary Report,* 13:5, September/October 1993.

32 *Astrophysical Journal,* 415:218, 1993.

33 Personal communication with SETI public relations department on May 28, 1997.

34 Gordon Cooper's letter to the United Nations on July 14, 1978. Published in *Above Top Secret,* Timothy Good, William Morrow Co., New York, NY, 1988, pp. 379–378.

35 "Apollo–14 Astronaut Searches for the Truth," Billy Cox, *Florida Today* staff writer, January 12, 1996.

36 *Above Top Secret,* Timothy Good, William Morrow Co., New York, NY, 1988, p. 384.

37 Maurice Chatelain, *Our Cosmic Ancestors,* Temple Golden Publication, P.O. Box 10501, Sedona, AZ 86336. 1987.

38 Maurice Chatelain, *Our Cosmic Ancestors,* Temple Golden Publication, P.O. Box 10501, Sedona, AZ 86336. 1987.

39 September 18, 1994, at the International Forum on New Science at Fort Collins.

40 An audio track of this intercept has been published in an audio briefing package called "The Return of the Nephilim," available from Koinonia House: (800) 546-8731.

41 *Art Bell Show,* June 11, 1997.

42 I.D.E. Thomas, *The Omega Conspiracy,* Hearthstone Publishing, Oklahoma City, 1986, p. 84.

43 Jacques Vallee, *Passport to Magonia,* Contemporary Books, 1993 ed., p. vii.

44 J. Weldon & Z. Levitt, *UFOs: What on Earth Is Happening?* Harvest House Publishers, 1975, p. 21.

45 *Encyclopædia Britannica,* 1991 ed.

46 Graham Hancock, *The Fingerprints of the Gods,* Crown Trade Paperbacks, 1995, p. 342.

47 See Graham Hancock, *The Fingerprints of the Gods,* Crown Trade publishers, 1995; and Graham Hancock, Robert Bauval, *The Message of the Sphinx,* Crown Publishers, 1996.

48 The "official" position of the Egyptian Antiquities Organization and it director, Zahi Hawass, is that the pyramids and Sphinx were built by Egyptians between 1500 and 3000 B.C.

49 Heinrich Brugsch, *Die Sage von der gelflugten Sonnenscheibe,* 1870. English translation in *The Wars of Gods and Men,* by Zechariah Sitchin, Avon, 1985, p. 27.

50 Metternich Stella, Zechariah Sitchin, *The Wars of Gods and Men,* Avon, p. 43.

51 J. Weldon, Z. Levitt, *UFOs: What on Earth Is Happening?* Harvest House Publishers, 1975.

52 Harold T. Wilkins, *Flying Saucers Uncensored,* New York: Pyramid, 1974, pp. 7, 164; Ralph Blum, *Beyond Earth: Man's Contact with UFOs,* Bantam, New York, NY, 1974, p. 41.

53 J. Weldon, Z. Levitt, *UFOs: What on Earth Is Happening?* Harvest House Publishers, 1975, p. 26.

54 *UFOs: The Hidden Truth,* 1993.

55 Jacques Bergier, *Extraterrestrial Visitations from Prehistoric Times to the Present,* Signet, New York, NY, 1974, p. 89.

56 Aime Michel, *The Truth About Flying Saucers,* Pyramid, New York, NY, 1974, p. 32.

57 Jacques Vallee, *Passport to Magonia,* Henry Regency, Chicago, IL, 1969, pp. 9–10.

58 J. Weldon, Z. Levitt, *UFOs: What on Earth Is Happening?* Harvest House Publishers, 1975, p. 27.

59 Ralph Blum, *Beyond Earth: Man's Contact with UFOs,* Bantam, New York, NY, 1974, p. 44. See also J. Weldon, Z. Levitt, *UFOs: What on Earth Is Happening?* Harvest House Publishers, 1975, p. 28.

60 Jacques Vallee, *Passport to Magonia,* Contemporary Books Publishing, 1993, pp. 4–5.

61 Jacques Vallee, *Passport to Magonia,* Contemporary Books Publishing, 1993, p. 5.

62 The following list is from Jacques Vallee, *Passport to Magonia,* Contemporary Books Publishing, 1993, pp. 6–7.

63 This material is taken from Richard Boylan's *Star Knowledge Conference Report,* available at http://www.execpc.com/ vjentpr/skcrichb.html and also at http://www.execpc.com/ vjentpr/skcanne.html

64 Robert Stanley, *ETs from the Pleiades,* in Unicas, Vol. 4, No. 1, 1995, pp. 26–27.

65 Graham Hancock, *The Fingerprints of the Gods,* Crown Trade publishers, 1995, p. 169.

66 Peter Tompkins, *Mysteries of the Mexican Pyramids,* Thames and Hudson, London, 1987.

67 From the ancient Hindu Sanskrit text of the *Hymns of the Rig-Veda,* as translated by J. Muir. See also Zechariah Sitchin, *The Wars of Gods and Men,* Bear and Co., 1985, p. 68.

68 Zechariah Sitchin, *The Wars of Gods and Men,* Bear and Co., 1985, p. 62.

69 *ibid.* See also the R. Dutt translation of the *Mahabharata, The Epic of Ancient India.*

70 J. Weldon, Z. Levitt, *UFOs: What on Earth Is Happening?* Harvest House, 1975, p. 24.

71 *The American Indian UFO-Starseed Connection,* edited by Timothy Green Beckley, 1992, p. 10.

72 See Eric Van Daniken, *Gods from Outer Space,* Bantam Books, New York, NY, 1972, pp. 161–162.

73 Jim Marrs, *Alien Agenda,* Harper Collins, 1997, p. 55.

74 Zecharia Sitchen, *The 12th Planet,* Avon Paperbacks, 1977, p. vii.

75 We are indebted to the notes from Kent Jeffrey for this summary.

76 Lawrence Fawcett, Barry J. Greenwood, *Clear Intent: The Government Coverup of the UFO Experience,* Prentice-Hall, Inc., Englewood Cliffs, NJ, 1984.

77 A popular video purporting to be an autopsy of one of the aliens seems to have been largely discredited as an elaborate hoax by a number of experts. But, why would someone bother?

78 See Jacques Vallee's books *Confrontations, Revelations, Dimensions,* Ballantine Books statistics on UFO sightings.

79 Edward J. Ruppelt, Jay David, editor, *The Flying Saucer Reader,* New American Library, New York, NY, 1967), pp. 17–25.

80 Jacques Vallee's book *Forbidden Science,* North Atlantic Books, 1992, p. 144.

81 See Jacques Vallee's book *Forbidden Science,* North Atlantic Books, 1992.

82 J. Weldon & Z. Levitt, *UFOs: What on Earth Is Happening?* Harvest House Publishers, p. 9.

83 J. Allen Hynek, *The UFO Experience: A Scientific Inquiry,* Ballantine Books, 1972. ISBN 345-23953-9-150

84 Richard F. Haines, *Project Delta: A Study of Multiple UFO,* L.D.A. Press, Los Altos, CA, 1994. Dr. Haines is a former NASA research scientist specializing in optics and vision. The study included multiple objects, multiple witnesses, some with radar contacts and photographs.

85 See Jacques Vallee's *Messengers of Deception and Dimensions* for a detailed look at such sightings.

86 Physicist James Campbell, *SCP, Journal,* 1977, p. 14.

87 This event was reported on by CNN, Reuters, Associated Press, and numerous other news organizations around the world.

88 Reported worldwide by CNN, Reuters, and Associated Press on December 17, 1996. Available at http://www.cnn.com

89 *ibid.*

90 A copy of this official letter, obtained through the Freedom of Information Act, is included in *UFO: The Government Files,* by Peter Brookesmith, Brown Books, London, 1996. It is also discussed in *Clear Intent: The Government Coverup of the UFO Experience,* by Lawrence Fawcett and Barry J. Greenwood, Prentice-Hall, Inc., Englewood Cliffs NJ, 1984.

91 *Clear Intent: The Government Coverup of the UFO Experience,* by Lawrence Fawcett and Barry J. Greenwood, Prentice-Hall, Inc., Englewood Cliffs NJ, 1984, pp. 215–217.

92 Antonio Huneeus, *UFO Chronicle.* This Privately Published Report can be obtained at P.O. Box 1989, New York, NY 10159. See also http://www.qtm.net/~geibdan/ belgium/ bela.html

93 *ibid.*

94 For an in-depth look at the career, methods, and representative cases Vallee has examined, see his book *Forbidden Science,* North Atlantic Books, 1992.

95 The following case is adapted from Jacques Vallee, *Dimensions,* Ballantine Books, 1988, p. 24.

96 Jacques Vallee, *Dimensions,* Ballantine Books, 1988, p. 81.

97 Brit Elders, "UFOs Over Mexico," as it appeared in *Connecting Link,* Issue 27, 1994, p. 94.

98 Jacques Vallee, *Dimensions,* Ballantine Books, 1988, pp. 231–232.

99 J. Allen Hynek, *Edge of Reality,* 1975, pp. 12–13.

100 J. Allen Hynek interview, *UFO Report magazine,* August 1976, p. 61.

101 John Keel, *Operation Trojan Horse,* 1973, p. 182.

102 Physicist Jacques Lematre, *Flying Saucer Review,* Vol. 15, p. 23.

103 Jacques Vallee, *Dimensions,* Ballantine Books, New York, NY, 1988, pp. 252–253.

104 Cal Tech physicists Kip Thorne and Michael Morris, with Igor Novikov of Moscow State University and others, have published a number of papers in the prestigious *Physical Review* on the physics of time travel and traversable wormholes.

105 For more information see *The Creator Beyond Time* and Space, by the authors of this book (1-800-KHOUSE1).

106 We are indebted to Edwin A. Abbott (1836–1926), a distinguished clergyman, for his entertaining classic, *Flatland*, (1884) for this allegorical approach to dimensionality.

107 A sphere has positive curvature and can contain triangles containing more than 180 degrees. A saddle has negative curvature and can contain triangles containing less than 180 degrees.

108 The Nobel Prize in physics went to Russell Hulse and Joseph Taylor for the study of binary pulsar PSR 1913+16. See Hugh Ross, *Beyond the Cosmos*, NavPress, Colorado Springs, CO, 1996, p. 23.

109 These concepts are explored in Chuck Missler's briefing package *Beyond Perception*, available from Koinonia House (1-800-KHOUSE1).

110 From his study of Genesis 1, the ancient Hebrew sage Nachmonides came to essentially the same conclusion.

111 The size of these curled-up dimensions is called the Planck length, which is 100 billion billion times smaller than the proton, too small to be probed by even our largest atom smasher.

112 Jacques Valle, *Passport to Magonia*, Contemporary Books Publishing, Chicago, IL, 1993, pp.153–154.

113 Roger Highfield, Robert Uhlig, "Atom Smasher Hurls Particle Theory into Chaos," *London Telegraph*, February 20, 1997.

114 C.D.B. Bryan, *Close Encounters of the Fourth Kind*, Alfred Knoph Publishers, 1995, p. 4.

115 John Mack, M.D., *Forward to Secret Life*, David M. Jacobs, Simon & Schuster, Publishing, 1992, p.10.

116 For a brief but detailed description and analysis of this case, see Jacques Vallee's *Dimensions*, Ballantine Books, 1988, pp. 122–124.

117 David M. Jacobs, *Secret Life,* Simon & Schuster, 1992, p. 86.

118 John Mack, *Abduction: Human Encounters with Aliens,* Ballantine Books, 1994, chapter 2.

119 David M. Jacobs, *Secret Life,* p. 306.

120 *Coast to Coast* radio program with Art Bell, June 19, 1997.

121 Jacobs, *Secret Life.*

122 Mack, *Abduction,* chapter 2.

123 C.D.B. Bryan, *Close Encounters of the Fourth Kind,* Alfred Knoph Publishers, 1995, p.142.

124 Mack, *Abduction,* p. 5.

125 Mack, *Abduction,* chapter 2.

126 Carl Sagan, *The Demon-Haunted World,* Random House, 1996, pp. 153–188.

127 Jacques Vallee, *Forbidden Science,* North Atlantic Books, 1992, p. 431.

128 Nicholas P. Spanos, et al., *Close Encounters: An Examination of UFO Experiencers,* Journal of Abnormal Psychology, 1993, Vol. 102, No. 4. pp. 624–632.

129 Poll conducted by Roper in 1991.

130 Bud Hopkins, *Witnessed,* Pocket Books, 1996, p. 4.

131 Budd Hopkins, *Witnessed,* Pocket Books, 1996, pp. 4–5.

132 See http://www.hedweb.com/markp/ufofilm.htm

133 Budd Hopkins, *Intruders,* Ballantine Books, 1987, pp. 286–287.

134 David M. Jacobs, *Secret Life,* p. 305.

135 Budd Hopkins, *Witnessed,* 1996, p. 378.

136 Mack, *Abduction,* pp. 404–405.

137 *ibid.,* p. 414.

138 *ibid.,* p. 416.

139 Jacques Vallee, *Dimensions,* 1988, pp. 143–144.

140 C.D.B. Bryan, *Close Encounters of the Fourth Kind,* Alfred A. Knoph, 1995, p. 4.

141 Michael Denton, *Evolution: A Theory in Crisis,* Adler and Adler, 1986, p. 250.

142 Michael Behe, *Darwin's Black Box,* The Free Press, a division of Simon and Schuster, 1996, p. x.

143 Francis Crick, Leslie Orgel, "Directed Panspermia," *Icarus,* 1973.

144 Francis Crick, *Life Itself—Its Origin and Nature,* Futura, London, 1982.

145 *Nature,* Vol. 294:105, November 12, 1981.

146 *ibid.*

147 Michael Behe, *Darwin's Black Box,* The Free Press, a Division of Simon and Schuster, Inc., 1996, pp. 248–249.

148 For a detailed examination of the question of life's origin, see *The Creator Beyond Time and Space,* chapters 3–4, by Missler and Eastman (1-800-KHOUSE1).

149 *ibid.,* p. 248.

150 Andrei Arkhipov, *Observatory,* December 1996.

151 Michael Denton, *Evolution: A Theory in Crisis,* Adler and Adler, 1986, p.271.

152 Michael Behe, *Darwin's Black Box,* The Free Press, a Division of Simon and Schuster, Inc., 1996, p. 249.

153 Paraphrase, Denton, *Evolution: A Theory in Crisis,* Adler and Adler, 1986, p. 250.

154 The minimum amount of genetic information on the DNA molecule of a single cell of a human being is equivalent to 12 billion letters in the English language. That many letters could fill 1,000 books that are 500 pages thick, with print so small you would need a microscope to read it.

155 Put another way, information is the antithesis, or the rival conjecture, of chance.

156 Available from INTL Raelian Movement Official Web Page, http://www.rael.org as of August 1996.

157 *ibid.*

158 *ibid.*

159 *ibid.*

160 Jeana Lake, *The Extraterrestrial Vision,* Oughten House Publications, 1993, p. 13.

161 See the *Earth Chronicles* series of books by Zecharia Sitchen.

162 Barbara Marciniak, *Earth: Pleiadian Keys to the Living Library,* Bear & Company, 1995, pp. 78–80.

163 Barbara Marciniak, *Bringers of the Dawn: Teachings from the Pleiadians,* Bear & Company, Inc., 1992, p. 25.

164 *ibid.,* p. 6.

165 Brad Steiger, *The Fellowship,* p.170.

166 Barbara Marciniak, *Earth: Pleiadian Keys to the Living Library,* Bear & Company, 1995, p. 86.

167 *ibid.,* p. 90.

168 Janet and Stewart Farrar, *The Witches' Goddess,* Phoenix Publishing, 1987, p.16.

169 See annotated Teacher's Edition, 1991.

170 Judy Pope-Ghostwolf, as stated on *Dreamland,* Art Bell's radio program, May 5, 1996.

171 Acts 1.

172 Matthew 24:30.

173 Timothy Green Beckley, editor, "Channeled by the Ashtar Command," *New World Order,* Inner Light Publications, New Brunswick, NJ, 1990, p. 141.

174 See Matthew 14:33.

175 Timothy Green Beckley, editor, "Channeled by the Ashtar Command," *New World Order,* Inner Light Publications, New Brunswick, NJ, 1990, p. 141.

176 *Shamanism: A Beginner's Guide,* Earthspirit, 1989.

177 See Brad Steiger's book *The Fellowship,* Doubleday, 1988, pp.156–157.

178 David Spangler, *Reflections on the Christ,* Findhorn Publications, Moray, Scotland, 1978, third edition 1981, p. 45, as cited in Alnor, UFOs in the New Age.

179 Brad Steiger, *The Fellowship,* Doubleday, 1988, p. 51.

180 Brad Steiger, *The Fellowship,* p. 62.

181 Timothy Green Beckley, editor, "Channeled by the Ashtar Command," *New World Order,* Inner Light Publications, New Brunswick, NJ, 1990, p. 12.

182 J. Ankerberg, J. Weldon, *The Facts on UfO's and Other Supernatural Phenomena,* Harvest House Publishers, 1992, p. 13.

183 Jaques Vallee, *Messengers of Deception,* Berkeley Press, 1977, pp. 209–210.

184 Art Bell, *The Art of Talk,* Paper Chase Press, New Orleans, LA, 1995, pp. 141–142.

185 *Los Angeles Times,* February 27, 1997.

186 For articles on this and related topics, see the following: "Rapid disintegration of Wordie Ice Shelf in response to atmospheric warming" by D. G. Vaughan and C.S.M. Doake, *Nature,* 1991, Vol. 350 [6316], pp. 328–330; "Recent atmospheric warming and retreat of ice shelves on the Antarctic Peninsula" by D. Vaughan and C. Doake, *Nature,* 1996, Vol. 379, p. 328. (This article shows changes, mostly decreases, in a number of ice shelves on the Antarctic Peninsula); "Rapid Collapse of the Northern Larsen Ice Shelf in Antarctica," *Science,* 1996, Vol. 271, p. 788. (An accompanying comment article, "An Ice Shelf Breakup," by Mark Fahnestock, is on p. 775 of the same issue.)

187 Quinn, T., "Global Burden of the HIV Pandemic," *Lancet,* 1996, Vol. 348, pp. 99–106.

188 Available from the World Health Organization, at http://gpawww.who.ch/aidscase/dec1995/current.htm.

189 World Health Organization, *Weekly Epidemiological Record,* July 5, 1996.

190 Leonard, Horowitz, *Emerging Viruses,* 1996, Tetrahedron, In.

191 *World Watch magazine,* November/December 1995, pp. 10–17.

192 Kay Wheeler, "The Time Is Now," *Connecting Link Magazine,* Issue 23, p. 34.

193 Barbara Marciniak, *Bringers of the Dawn: Teachings from the Pleiadians,* p. 166.

194 *ibid.,* p. 168.

195 Barbara Marciniak, *Earth: Pleiadian Keys to the Living Library*, Bear & Company, 1995, p. 25.

196 In other places in the Bible, "the elect" are the nation of Israel. This is a subtlety that is beyond the scope of this chapter.

197 Ecclesiates 1:9b.

198 Cited in *UFOs in the New Age,* by William Alnor, Baker Books, 1992, and in *I Rode a Flying Saucer,* by George Van Tassel, New Age, Los Angeles, CA, 1952.

199 Tuella, *Project World Evacuation,* Inner Light Publications, 1993 edition.

200 *ibid.,* p. 16.

201 *ibid.,* p. 97.

202 Kay Wheeler, "The Time Is Now," *Connecting Link Magazine,* Issue 23, p. 34.

203 Barbara Marciniak, *Earth: Pleiadian Keys to the Living Library,* Bear & Co., 1995, pp. 220–221.

204 Earlyne Chaney, *Revelation of Things to Come,* Astara, Inc., 1982, p. 23.

205 Barbara Marciniak, *Bringers of the Dawn: Teachings from the Pleiadians,* Bear and Co., 1992, p. 3.

206 *ibid.,* p. 4.

207 *ibid.,* p. 162.

208 *ibid.,* p. 167.

209 Timothy Green Beckley, *Psychic & UFO Revelations in the Last Days,* Inner Light Publications, New Brunswick, NJ, 1989, p. 69.

210 Johanna Michaelson, *Like Lambs to the Slaughter: Your Child and the Occult,* Harvest House, Eugene, OR, 1989, p. 309.

211 *Brookings Institute,* "1960 Report to the 87th Congress," Union Calendar 79, Report 242, for the National Aeronautics and Space Administration. The report can be viewed at http://mmm.simplenet.com/frames/nasa_brookings/nasa.html

212 Yvonne Cole, *Connecting Link Magazine,* Iissue 23, 1994, pp. 12–13.

213 Tuella, *Project World Evacuation,* Inner Light Publications, 1993 edition, p. 16.

214 *ibid.,* pp. 128–129.

215 *ibid.,* p. 129.

216 *ibid.,* p. 118.

217 *ibid.,* p. 119.

218 *ibid.,* p.31.

219 Timothy Green Beckley, *Psychic & UFO Revelations in the Last Days,* Inner Light Publications, New Brunswick, NJ, 1989, p. 68.

220 "Lay not up for yourselves treasures upon earth, where moth and rust doth corrupt, and where thieves break through and steal" (Matthew 6:19 KJV).

221 Both Enoch (Genesis 5:24) and Elijah (2 Kings 2:11) were transported directly to heaven.

222 Henry M. Morris, James C. Witcomb Jr., *The Genesis Flood,* Presbyterian and Reformed Publishing Co., Philadelphia, PA, 1961; Donald W. Patten, *The Biblical Flood and the Ice Epoch, A Study in Scientific History,* Pacific Meridian Publishing Co., Seattle, WA, 1966.

223 Matthew 24:37; Luke 17:26.

224 Cf. Job 1:6; 2:1; 38:7. Jesus implies the same term in Luke 20:36.

225 From 285 to 270 B.C., in Alexandria, 70 eminent scholars translated the Hebrew Scriptures into Greek, which was the international language of that day. Their translation, the Septuagint, is still considered one of the most valuable translations of the Old Testament available.

226 The *Book of Enoch* was esteemed by both rabbinical and Christian authorities from about 200 B.C. through A.D. 200, yet the document was not included in the "inspired" canon. However, Enoch is useful to authenticate lexigraphical usage and accepted beliefs of the period. See R. H. Charles' *The Book of Enoch,* Clarendon Press, Oxford, 1912. Also see James H. Charlesworth's *The Old Testament Pseudepigrapha,* 2 Vols., Doubleday & Co., Garden City, NY, 1985.

227 The term has been transliterated "giants"; however, the Greek root γίγας is a form of γηγενῶν a term meaning "earthborn," a term used of the Titans, or sons of Heaven and Earth, Cœlus and Terra. The appellation of "giants" in the sense of size was coincidental. See Pember, p. 133. Also see Unger, p.48.

228 One of the classic references on this is John Fleming's *The Fallen Angels and the Heroes of Mythology,* Hodges, Foster, and Figgis, Dublin, 1879. See also John Henry Kurtz's *Die Ehen der Söhne Gottes mit den Töchtern der Menschen,* Berlin, 1857.

229 *Titan* in the Greek is equivalent to *Sheitan* in Chaldean, or *Satan* in the Hebrew.

230 It is interesting that the symbol for the European Parliament is Europa, a woman holding a golden cup, riding Zeus portrayed as a beast, over seven hills. See Revelation 17:1–9.

231 On orbit 35, Viking–1 photographed what appears to be a symmetrical face, approximately one mile wide. Some suggest the image was crafted by some ancient civilization.

232 *El Khira* is the Arabic name for the planet Mars.

233 Exodus 12:5, 29:1; Leviticus 1:3; et al. There are more than 60 references, usually referring to the fact that appropriate offerings did not have physical blemishes.

234 Testament of Reuben, Sections 4, 5, *Whiston's Translation, Authentic Records,* Part I, pp. 273, 294.

235 *Liber Jubilaeorum,* translated from the Ethiopic into German by Dillman, *Das Buch der Jubiläen oder die kleine Genesis erläutert und untersucht, u.s.w.,* Rönsch, Leipzig, 1874.

236 *De Gigantibus,* edited by Pfeiffer, 1786, Vol. 2, pp. 358, 388.

237 *Antiquities,* I, 3.1.

238 *Second Apology, Writings of Justin Martyr and Athenagoras,* Transl. Clark's Ante-Nicene Library, Vol. 2, pp. 75–76.

239 *Against Heresies,* 4.36, 4.

240 *Second Apology, Writings of Justin Martyr and Athenagoras,* Trans., Clark's Ante-Nicene Library, Vol. 2, pp. 406–7.

241 *Homilies,* 7.12–15; 8.11–15.

242 *The Instructor* 3.2. *The Clementine Homilies and Apostolical Constitutions,* Trans., Clark's Ante-Nicene Christian Library, Vol. 17, 1870, pp. 142–46.

243 *On the Veiling of Virgins,* 7.

244 *De Velandis Virginibus,* c. 7; *Liber De Idololat.,* c. 9; *De Hab. Muliebri,* c. 2.

245 *Divine Institut.,* lib. Bk. 2, Ch. 15.

246 *The International Standard Bible Encyclopædia,* Wm. B. Eerdmans Publishing Co., Vol. 5, pp. 2835–2836.

247 Homer, *Iliad,* viii 16.

248 Although sometimes translated "preached," the term κηρύσσω, kerusso would be more accurately translated "to proclaim officially after the manner of a herald."

249 Jude is commonly recognized as one of the Lord's brothers. See Matthew 13:55; Mark 6:3; Galatians 1:9; and Jude 1:1.

250 See Jude 6 and 2 Corinthians 5:2, which allude to the heavenly body with which the believer longs to be clothed.

251 See Genesis 18:1–8; 19:3.

252 See Genesis 19:10, 16.

253 See Exodus 12.

254 See 2 Kings 19:35; Isaiah 37:36.

255 See John 20:12; Acts 1:10.

256 See Matthew 22:30; Mark 12:25.

257 See the *Book of Enoch*, chapters 7–9, 64.

258 See Genesis 19:5.

259 See Genesis 14:5; 15:20; Deuteronomy 2:10–12, 22.

260 See Deuteronomy 3:11, 13; Joshua 12:4; 13:12.

261 See Numbers 13:33.

262 See Joshua 6:21; et al. Also see 1 Samuel 15:3.

263 See Joshua 14:15; 15:13; and 21:11.

264 See 1 Samuel 17:4 ff.

265 See 2 Samuel 21:16–22.

266 See Matthew 8:28–34; Mark 5:1–20; and Luke 8:26–39.

267 See Isaiah 26:14. *Rephaim* is often translated "dead" (e.g., in Psalm 88:10; Proverbs 2:18; 9:18; 21:16; Isaiah 14:9; 26:14). Jesus did not become a Nephilim or a Rephaim, nor did he die for them.

268 *Muth,* "death," occurs 125 times in the Old Testament.

269 See Arthur W. Pink's *Gleanings in Genesis,* Moody Bible Institute, Chicago, IL, 1922; Ray C. Stedman's *The Beginnings,* Word Books, Waco, TX, 1978; and Alfred Jones' *Dictionary of Old Testament Proper Names,* Kregel Publications, Grand Rapids, MI, 1990.

270 Methuselah was 187 when he had Lamech, and he lived another 782 years. Lamech had Noah when he was 182 (Genesis 5:25–28). The flood came in Noah's 600th year (Genesis 7:6, 11). So, 600 + 182 = 782nd year of Lamech, the year Methuselah died.

271 This idea is apparently confirmed in 1 Peter 3:18–20.

272 A caveat. Many study aids, such as a conventional lexicon, can prove superficial when dealing with proper nouns. Furthermore, views concerning the meanings of original roots are not free of controversy and other variant readings.

273 Genesis 4:25.

274 Genesis 4:26 is often mistranslated. The classic rendering (*Onkelos,* et al.) is, "Then men began to profane the name of the Lord."

275 Numbers 24:21, 23.

276 Genesis 4:19–25.

277 It is remarkable how many subtle discoveries lie behind the little details of the text. Some of these become immediately obvious with a little study; others are more technical and require special helps. Some of these are described in our briefing package *Beyond Coincidence.* Several are also highlighted in our book *The Creator Beyond Time and Space.*

278 Genesis 3:14, 15.

279 Hebrews 11:5.

280 First Corinthians 10:32 also divides all into three classes.

281 There are examples in particle physics where a positron is understood to be an electron in a time reversal. See *Beyond Time and Space* and *Beyond Perception,* audio briefings with notes, available through Koinonia House.

282 The ancient Hebrew scholar Nachmonides, writing in the 12th century, concluded from his studies of Genesis that the universe has ten dimensions—that four are knowable and six are beyond our knowing. Particle physicists today have also concluded that we live in ten dimensions: three spatial dimensions and time are directly measurable. The remaining six are "curled" in less than 10-33 cm. and are only inferable by indirect means. (See *Beyond Perception,* Koinonia House.)

283 See Isaiah 57:15.

284 See Isaiah 46:10.

285 Examples: *The Sovereignty of Man, The Architecture of Man,* and *From Here to Eternity—The Physics of Immortality,* all available from Koinonia House.

286 See briefing package *The Footprints of the Messiah* from Koinonia House.

287 See Isaiah 11:11.

288 There are an estimated 2,345 references to Jesus' Second Coming, over 320 in the New Testament alone.

289 See Matthew 24–25; Mark 13–14, and Luke 21–22.

290 See Matthew 24:15.

291 See Daniel 9:2; Jeremiah 25:11, 12.

292 For a more complete discussion, refer to our briefing package titled *The Seventy Weeks of Daniel,* which includes two audio cassettes plus extensive notes. Also see the three-volume *Expositional Commentary on Daniel,* available from Koinonia House.

293 See Genesis 29:26–28; Leviticus 25, 26. A sabbath for the land was ordained for every week of years (see Leviticus 25:1–22; 26:33–35; Deuteronomy 15; Exodus 23:10–11). Failure to keep the sabbath of the land was basis for the Jews' 70 years of captivity (see 2 Chronicles 36:19–21).

294 A fascinating conjecture as to the cause of this calendar change is detailed in *Signs in the Heavens,* a briefing package exploring the "long day" of Joshua and the possible orbital antics of the planet Mars.

295 The 3rd, 6th, 8th, 11th, 14th, 17th, and 19th are leap years, where the month Adar II is added. Originally kept secret by the Sanhedrin, the method of calendar intercalation was revealed in the 4th century, when an independent Sanhedrin was threatened, to permit the Diaspora Jews to observe in synchronization. See Arthur Spier's *The Comprehensive Hebrew Calendar,* Feldheim Publishers, Jerusalem, 1986.

296 See Genesis 7:24; 8:3, 4. In Revelation, 42 months = 3 1/2 years = 1,260 days, etc. We are indebted to Sir Robert Anderson's classic, *The Coming Prince,* originally published in 1894, for this insight.

297 See Nehemiah 2:5–8, 17, 18. There were three other decrees, but they were concerned with the rebuilding of the Temple, not the city and the walls. For the decree of Cyrus in 537 B.C., see Ezra 1:2–4. For the decree of Darius, see Ezra 6:1–5, 8, 12. For that of Artaxerxes, in 458 B.C., see Ezra 7:11–26.

298 The English Bible translates *Nagid* as "prince." However, the correct meaning is "king." *Nagid* is first used in reference to King Saul.

299 See John 6:15; 7:30, 44.

300 See Luke 19:29–48. For further reference, see Mattew 21 and Mark 11.

301 Recorded in all four Gospels: Matthew 21:1–9; Mark 11:1–10; Luke 19:29–39; and John 12:12–16.

302 The Hallel Psalm 118. Note verse 26.

303 On this day Passover lambs were presented for acceptability. Four days later, Jesus would be offered as our Passover Lamb.

304 See Luke 3:1. Tiberius was appointed in A.D. 14 + 15th year = A.D. 29. The 4th Passover was on April 6, A.D. 32.

305 See Leviticus 7:20; Psalm 37:9; Proverbs 2:22; and Isaiah 53:7–9.

306 Interval also implied in Daniel 9:26 and Isaiah 61:1, 2. See Luke 4:18–20 and Revelation 12:5, 6. Also see Isaiah 54:7; Hosea 3:4, 5; Amos 9:10, 11; Acts 15:13–18; Micah 5:2, 3; Zechariah 9:9, 10; and Luke 1:31, 32; 21:24.

307 See Luke 19:42, also Romans 11:25.

308 See Matthew 13:34, 35; Ephesians 3:5, 9.

309 Gordon Creighton, *Flying Saucer Review* official position statement, 1996.

310 Jacques Vallee, *Dimensions,* Ballantine Books, 1988, p. 32.

311 Carl Sagan, *Cosmos,* Random House, New York, 1980, p. 4.

312 John Mack, *Abduction,* Ballantine Books, 1994, p. 402.

313 See Genesis 19:1.

314 Refer to the *Book of Enoch*, 15:8–9.

315 This verse is obviously *not* about the king of Tyre. This is a rhetorical device occasionally used by Biblical writers to get to a deeper, "behind the scenes" issue, mainly the tragic career of Satan.

316 See Revelation 12:4.

317 Refer to Jacques Vallee's book *Confrontations,* Ballantine Books, 1990.

318 Dr. Pierre Guerin, *Flying Saucer Review,* Vol. 25, No. 1.

319 John Keel, *Operation Trojan Horse,* Illuminet Press, 1996 edition, p. 192.

320 *ibid.,* p. 266.

321 Stuart Goldman, "They're Here!" (manuscript letter sent to John Weldon on November 29, 1989), as quoted in Ankerberg & J. Weldon's *The Facts on UFOs and Other Supernatural Phenomena,* Harvest House Publishers, 1992, p. 26.

322 Whitley Strieber, *Transformation,* Avon Books, 1988, p. 36.

323 *ibid.,* p.190.

324 Jacques Vallee, *Confrontations,* Ballantine Books, 1990, p. 159.

325 John Mack, *Abduction,* Ballantine Books, 1994, p. 413.

326 *ibid.,* p. 411.

327 J. Ankerberg, J. Weldon, *The Facts on UFOs and Other Supernatural Phenomena,* Harvest House Publishers, 1992, p. 13.

328 *ibid.,* p. 27.

329 Lynn E. Catoe, "UFOs and Related Subjects": USGPO, 1969; prepared under AFOSR Project Order 67-0002 and 68-0003.

330 *London Times,* February 28, 1997.

331 See Matthew 23–24; Mark 13; and Luke 21.

332 Hal Lindsey, *The Rapture,* Bantam Books, 1983, pp. 148–149.

333 Essentially, chapters 6–9 of Revelation are a detailing of the strange events which will occur during the 70th week prophesied in Daniel 9. (These events will also be discussed in chapter 14.)

334 See Luke 21:24.

335 See Daniel 2:37, 38; 7:4.

336 Daniel 2:39; 7:5.

337 This would be further detailed, remarkably, in Daniel 8. Also see Daniel 7:6.

338 See Chuck Missler's *Expositional Commentary on Daniel,* available through Koinonia House.

339 See Daniel 2:40 ff; 7:7, 8.

340 Daniel 2:40, 41. Most commentators equate the ten toes of Daniel 2 with the ten horns of Daniel 7:7, 8, 20, 24, and Revelation 12:3, 13:1, 17:3, 7, 12, 16.

341 For a Biblical perspective of the current developments in Europe, see our briefing package titled *Iron Mixed with Clay.*

342 Most commentators equate the ten toes with the ten kings as well as the ten horns and ten heads in Daniel 7:7, 8, 20, 24 ff; Revelation 12:3; 13:1; 17:3, 7, 9 10; et al.

343 See Daniel 2:44, 45. Also refer to Daniel 7:9, 13, 14; and Revelation 13; et al.

344 *Mire,* in the Hebrew, means "dust" or "dirt" to be swept away.

345 The word *Rephaim* (giants) is translated "dead" in Psalm 88:10; Proverbs 2:18; 9:18; 21:16; and Isaiah 14:9; 26:14.

346 *Encyclopædia Britannica,* 1992 edition.

347 Refer to Augustine's classic, *City of God,* 15, chapter 23.

348 The English translation of selected portions is provided by Jacques Vallee in *Passport to Magonia,* Contemporary Books, 1993 edition, pp. 127–129.

349 R. P. le Brun, *Histiore des Superstitions* (Paris:1750), IV, 398, as cited in Vallee's *Passport to Magonia,* 1993 edition, p. 127.

350 Alexander Hislop, *The Two Babylons,* Loizeaux Brothers, 1916, 1943, 1959.

351 If Nimrod were a Nephilim, then his father, Cush, would have had to consort with a fallen angel in the form of a succubus (the female form).

352 George King, D.D., *The Day the Gods Came,* The Aetherius Society, 1965, p. 68.

353 *ibid,* p. 69.

354 Carefully study 2 Thessalonians 2. For a more complete discussion, refer to our *Expositional Commentary on Thessalonians* or briefing package *From Here to Eternity.*

355 See Daniel 2 and 8.

356 See Revelation 13.

357 See 2 Thessalonians 2:4.

358 See Revelation 16.

359 In his concern for world peace, he made similar remarks several times, e.g., on December 4, 1985, in Maryland; and on May 5, 1988, in Chicago.

360 Jacques Vallee, *Messengers of Deception,* And/Or Press, 1979, p. 20.

361 See Richard Boylan's Open letter, available on the internet: http://www.users.cts.com/sd/d/density4/brethren/aviary.htm

362 See Zechariah 11:17.

363 Psalm 2 appears to be a "staff meeting" among the Trinity. Carefully analyze the three speakers involved.

364 Jacques Vallee, *Dimensions: A Casebook of Alien Contact,* Ballantine Books, 1989 edition, quote from foreword by Whitely Strieber.

365 Jacques Vallee, *Dimensions: A Casebook of Alien Contact,* Ballantine Books, 1989 edition, p. 192.

366 See Genesis 3:14, 15.

367 *ibid.*

368 See Genesis 12, 15, et al.

369 See Genesis 12, 20. For reference to the famine, see Genesis 50.

370 See Exodus 1:15–20.

371 See Exodus 14.

372 See Genesis 12:6. "The Canaanite was already then in the land."

373 See 2 Samuel 7.

374 See 2 Chronicles 21.

375 See 2 Chronicles 22.

376 See Isaiah 36, 38.

377 See Jeremiah 22:30.

378 Also of profound significance are the legal specifications adapted in the case of the daughters of Zelophehad (Numbers 27:1–11; 36:2–11; Joshua 17:4). Every detail of the Torah, "The Law," ultimately focuses on the Messiah.

379 See Esther 3:8, 9 ff.

380 See Matthew 1.

381 See Matthew 2.

382 See Luke 4:24–30.

383 See Mark 4:35–41; Luke 8:22-25. Remember, these were experienced fisherman who knew those waters well, and they feared for their lives.

384 See Luke 24:39.

385 Hugh Ross, *Beyond the Cosmos,* NavPress, Colorado Springs, CO, 1996.

386 Lambert Dolphin, "What holds the Universe together?" *Personal Update,* January 1997.

387 See John 8:59.

388 See John 10.

389 John Keel, *Operation Trojan Horse,* Illuminet Press, 1996 edition, p. 266.

390 See also Deuteronomy 13:5, Jeremiah 14:14–15, and Zechariah 13:3.

391 See 1 Corinthians 10:4; Psalm 118:22; Isaiah 28:16; Zechariah 3:8, 9; Matthew 21:42; Luke 20:17, 18; Acts 4:11; Romans 9:33; Ephesians 2:20; and 1 Peter 2:4–8.

392 See Jude 14, 15; Revelation 19:11–16.

393 See Acts 4:12; Philippians 2:10.

394 See Matthew 24:24.

395 See Romans 10:9, 10.

396 Chuck Missler, P.O. Box D, Coeur d'Alene, ID 83816.

Certificate

$20.00 Value

This certificate entitles the holder to a full year's subscription to *Personal*UPDATE, Chuck Missler's monthly newsletter highlighting the Biblical relevance of current events, new discoveries, etc. (new subscribers only).

_____
NAME

_____
ADDRESS

_____
CITY   STATE   ZIP

Mail information to:
Koinonia House, P.O. Box D
Coeur d'Alene, ID 83816–0347